TENDING
BRIGID'S
FLAME

ABOUT THE AUTHOR

Lunaea Weatherstone is a priestess, writer, teacher, and tarot counselor who has been serving the woman-spirit community for thirty years. In 2013, she was named by *SageWoman* magazine as one of the Wisdom Keepers of the Goddess Spirituality movement and among those who contributed to its blossoming in the 1970s and 1980s. As Grove Mother for the Sisterhood of the Silver Branch, Lunaea offers year-long programs in goddess spirituality. Lunaea lives with her feline companion in Portland, Oregon, where she gets almost enough rain to satisfy her Celtic soul. Visit her at www.lunaea.com and www.thegoddesspath.org.

TENDING BRIGID'S FLAME

AWAKEN TO THE CELTIC GODDESS
OF HEARTH, TEMPLE, AND FORGE

LUNAEA WEATHERSTONE

Llewellyn Publications
Woodbury, Minnesota

FIRST EDITION
Seventh Printing, 2020

Cover art: iStockphoto.com/40422502/©Chunhai Cao
            iStockphoto.com/1818768/©2create
            Shutterstock/187562690/©3drenderings
            Shutterstock/76704451/©earthvector
            Shutterstock/150972005/©enterlinedesign
Cover design: Kevin R. Brown
Interior illustrations: Wen Hsu
"Imbolc" ©2004 Lisa Thiel used by permission.

Llewellyn is a registered trademark of Llewellyn Worldwide Ltd.

Library of Congress Cataloging-in-Publication Data
Weatherstone, Lunaea.
  Tending Brigid's flame : awaken to the Celtic goddess of hearth,
temple, and forge / by Lunaea Weatherstone. — First Edition.
      pages cm
  Includes bibliographical references and index.
  ISBN 978-0-7387-4089-8
  1. Women—Religious life. 2. Brigit (Celtic deity) 3. Spiritual life.
I. Title.
  BL625.7.W427 2015
  299'.1612114—dc23
                          2015026998

Llewellyn Worldwide Ltd. does not participate in, endorse, or have any authority or responsibility concerning private business transactions between our authors and the public.
  All mail addressed to the author is forwarded but the publisher cannot, unless specifically instructed by the author, give out an address or phone number.
  Any Internet references contained in this work are current at publication time, but the publisher cannot guarantee that a specific location will continue to be maintained. Please refer to the publisher's website for links to authors' websites and other sources.

Llewellyn Publications
A Division of Llewellyn Worldwide Ltd.
2143 Wooddale Drive
Woodbury, MN 55125-2989
www.llewellyn.com

Printed in the United States of America

OTHER BOOKS BY LUNAEA WEATHERSTONE

Mystical Cats Tarot

(Llewellyn, 2014)

The Victorian Fairy Tarot

(Llewellyn, 2013)

Dedicated to the late Patricia Monaghan,
for her generous encouragement in the early days of this book
and for years of friendship and inspiration.

CONTENTS

ACKNOWLEDGMENTS

Thanks to Joanna Powell Colbert and Ellen Lorenzi-Prince for encouragement like a breath blowing embers into flame.

Thanks to Elysia Gallo of Llewellyn Worldwide for helping make my dream come true.

Thanks to editor Andrea Neff. Virgo authors are the *worst*, and I felt safe and well cared for in your hands.

Thanks to Kim Diane of Ord Brighideach, Kathy Jones of the Glastonbury Goddess Temple, and especially Mael Brigde of Daughters of the Flame for connections, resources, and support.

Thanks to Domi O'Brien for translation help. Any errors in the Irish are mine, not hers!

Grateful blessings to the nineteen wisewomen who so generously added their voices to honor Brigid: Wendy Alford, Jenny Beale, Sharon Blackie, Joanna Powell Colbert, Jen Delyth, Pat Fish, Selena Fox, Mara Freeman, Erynn Rowan Laurie, Ellen Lorenzi-Prince, Mael Brigde, Margie McArthur, Mickie Mueller, Domi O'Brien, Rebecca Reeder, Susan Smith, Ruth Temple, Lisa Thiel, and Marvelle Thompson.

Slán abhaile, Dennise Brown; I will make good use of what you bequeathed me.

Finally, thanks to Mickie, Dan, and Pj for kitchen-testing the beer. *Sláinte!*

INVOKING BRIGID

A match flares to life, and a woman's voice speaks:

In Brigid's name, I light my flame…

Alone at her kitchen table, she tenderly applies match to candle,
and the twilight-darkening room is illuminated in a golden glow.

Brigid is my protector, Brigid is my maker of song…

Lifting a cup in a ritual gesture,
she sips pure sweet milk in grateful communion.

Brigid is my sword and my shield, Brigid is my guide…

Who is this Brigid so lovingly invoked? To her devotees worldwide, she
is goddess, saint, muse, and spirit companion. Brigid crosses the borders
of theology, appealing to those who worship in both grove and church,
circle and convent. She brings with her the traditions of the past, evolv-
ing naturally into the living faith of the present and beyond.

The rekindling of interest in Celtic spirituality in recent years has
its roots in many sources: widening acceptance for diversity of beliefs,
increased respect for earth-centered traditions, and a longing for connection with ancestral ways. Celtic spirituality is very much an earthly
path, connected to the daily and seasonal cycles of time, as well as the
timelessness of poetry, creativity, and magic. The supernatural and the
mystical have never been lost. The Celtic tradition honors many deities,
both local spirits of a particular place and those who bless a wider realm

of universal understanding. Of these holy ones, Brigid shines brightest. Her influence is invoked to bless all aspects of life, from midwifery to metalcraft.

I am a priestess and flamekeeper vowed to Brigid. The purpose of this book is to present her as a fiery force in the world today, specifically as an inspiration in the lives of women. Modern devotion to Brigid is a combination of tradition and revision, and that's as it should be, though perhaps it's more accurate to say "add-vision" rather than "revision." I encourage you—and Brigid encourages you!—to add your own lore to the store of knowledge about this goddess who encompasses so much. New aspects of the divine will always be revealed, and faith will always evolve to stay alive and relevant.

I offer ways to weave a daily relationship with Brigid, to bring her into your home, your work, your creativity, and your soul. Some of these are traditional and some are intuitive, drawn from my own experience of knowing Brigid and listening for her guidance. What we know about Brigid isn't written in stone—or rather, it isn't written *just* in stone. It is written in stone, water, and wind. It is written in flame.

MY JOURNEY TO BRIGID

My thoughts, my words,
My deeds, my desires,
My will, my wonder:
I offer all in gratefulness.[1]

Having a close relationship with the Goddess is a deeply personal and subjective thing. She comes to you in the form that speaks to your heart. She shows you how your life is meant to unfold. This book is about finding out who Brigid is for *you*, so it seems right to begin with who Brigid is for me.

As a teacher of goddess-centered spirituality, I've often watched women search in a conscious way to find a matron goddess. The God-

----

1. Adapted from verse 42 of Alexander Carmichael, ed., *Carmina Gadelica*, a collection of folk prayers and incantations.

dess, it is said, has 10,000 names, and all her myriad aspects can be bewildering. The idea of having one particular aspect of the Great Goddess who walks beside you on your path is empowering and mystical. For some women, the call is immediate and clear: a goddess's name is spoken and a deep echo of that name resounds within the soul. For others, different goddesses step forward at different stages of the woman's life. Artemis leads a young woman warrior into righteous activism. Yemaya sings lullabies in harmony with a new mother. Cerridwen brings wisdom and vision to the transformations of maturity. Inanna stands at the gate of the underworld when the time comes to drop the veils and release the earthly.

When I first became aware of the Goddess in the early 1980s, she came to me as the moon—an ever-changing goddess, light and dark and light again. This resonated with my own restless nature, and the concept of the Triple Goddess, when I learned of her, made sense too. She is Maiden, Mother, and Crone, all in one and separate, and it's a mystery that can't be comprehended in any rational way. I like mystery, in the deepest sense of that word. Mystery is the foundation of faith for me—to accept that some things just can't be analyzed or defended logically and yet are profoundly true. The vastness of the sacred feminine, going back so many thousands of years, filled me with awe. Holding a small replica of the Goddess of Willendorf in my hands, I felt a shiver of recognition.

Having awakened to the Great Goddess of 10,000 Names, I naturally wanted to know some of those names better. Like many women, my first knowledge of goddesses came in childhood with the Greek and Roman myths. Looking at them through adult eyes, it was as if faint pencil sketches suddenly sprang into richly detailed paintings. In particular, Persephone spoke to me. I felt a strong affinity with the pull between her upperworld and underworld aspects. As I grew older, I understood better how Persephone's descent each year isn't a punishment or a sacrifice. In the underworld, she is queen. She has a purpose that calls forth her skills and her power. She comes into her own. She offers divine service.

One difference between devotee and priestess is the offering of service. To offer my life in service to the Goddess, however she wished to use it, was the vow I wanted to take as priestess. But like someone who wants a long engagement before the wedding, I waited many years before taking that vow. I heard a whispering around the edges of my consciousness, felt gentle tugs at my sleeve. Some piece was missing, though, something that would snap it all into focus for me.

In the early 1990s, my path came to a crossroads, with significant changes in several realms. To get some clarity, I had a diloggún reading with Yoruba priestess Luisah Teish. Sitting in my living room, her gaze direct and discerning, she said that I was a daughter of Oshun, the ori-sha of love, beauty, and delights. The oracle declared that I was called to commit myself to the path of priestess, and that Oshun would wel-come me into her tradition if I wished. But the first step was to consult my ancestors. Their approval and blessing would be needed if I were to proceed down this path. I was tempted—and terrified. The idea of a strong religious community, of living teachers in a living tradition, was something that had called to me since childhood. Teish and I parted with the understanding that I could get in touch with her if I got the nod from my ancestors.

And here is where Brigid enters the story. I asked my ancestors, and they said without hesitation that I needed to study and follow my own ancestral spiritual heritage, and not go haring off in such a wild pursuit of something sparkly in the distance. (They know me well.) So, I asked, what is that heritage then? You're already following it, was the reply. You just don't know its roots. Paganism, Wicca, earth-based worship, magic, divination, the yearning for mystery that had been pulling my soul-boat along all these years—these were all found in Celtic spiritual traditions. And the Goddess? She was there too, and in such powerful aspects that to merely say her names was a chant of awesome power: Áine, Danu, Cailleach Bheur, Ériu, Banba, Macha, the Mórrígan, Epona, Dea Matronae, Arianrhod, Rhiannon, Cerridwen.

Brigid.

There she was, the Triple Goddess of my earliest love for the sacred feminine. A goddess who changed in aspect, who had her finger in so many pies that even my restless nature could never be bored. A goddess who blessed, comforted, strengthened, fed, inspired. A goddess who was present in the most homespun tasks and in the eternal mysteries of transformation. A goddess of words, by which I earned my living. A fire goddess. A water goddess. An earth goddess. It was as if she had always been there, but I just hadn't seen her.

Now it felt like the most natural thing in the world to take vows for life as her priestess. She whispered a new priestess name that means "oak of Brigid." She guided me to get oak leaf and Celtic spiral tattoos, permanently marking me with her symbols. She inspired me to work with metal in creating goddess rosaries. She told me to create a sisterhood of priestesses who were all in sacred service, each in their own way.

In other words, she told me to get busy—because Brigid is all about *doing*, not just *being*, though the *being* is vital as well. When the time came, she told me to get busy writing this book. And here we are.

ABOUT THIS BOOK

Among her many attributes, Brigid is a goddess of poetry. In the ancient Celtic sense, this wordcraft encompasses history, lore, ancestral memory, charms, and prayers. Poetry is the path of creative imagination, moving from thought to thought as if following a line of Celtic knotwork, in and under and through and back to the beginning again. This is the path I follow in these pages.

Chapter 1, "The Source of the Flame," introduces the goddess Brigid and her people, the Celts, and tells the tale of Saint Brigid, which may surprise you a bit.

In the next three chapters, you'll come to know Brigid through three aspects of her sacred flame:

- **Hearth: The Welcoming Flame** opens the door to receive Brigid into your home, to protect and make sacred all the activities of everyday life. Food magic, hospitality, and house-blessing are some of the ways Brigid keeps your home fires burning.
- **Temple: The Devotional Flame** explores Brigid's allies, seasons, symbols, and sacred places. You'll meet Brigid's sister goddesses, both Celtic and worldwide, and learn about the timeless custom of

flamekeeping and other ways you can offer your devotion to Brigid within the temple of your heart.

- **Forge: The Transforming Flame** shares ways in which Brigid transforms and inspires through craft and creativity, healing of body and spirit, the power of words, and tempering your skills into personal excellence.

The final chapter, "Tending Your Flame," brings it all together and celebrates your connection with Brigid and her place in your world.

I've invited nineteen wisewomen to add their thoughts about Brigid—nineteen for the priestesses who each tended Brigid's flame in one-day shifts. On the twentieth day, the Goddess tended the flame herself.

It is my hope that you will know Brigid not only as a goddess to be worshiped but as an *anam cara*, a soul friend. Brigid stands in this world, and the Otherworld, and between the worlds, and in all aspects of life, wherever she is made welcome. Let us begin to welcome her now.

CHAPTER ONE

THE SOURCE OF THE FLAME

Before the moon was born, before the sun,
Before all the worlds were born,
I was as I am now.

BRIGID THE GODDESS

The ancient goddess Brigid is enshrouded in veils of conjecture. Modern writing about Brigid draws from older writing—up to a point. The further back you go, the less there is. The Celts didn't write down their religious beliefs, and they didn't freely share them with cultures that did record such things, such as the Romans. Celts believed that important tales should only be told to good people, to the initiated, and to those who understood their context. We mostly know about the deities of pre-Christian Celts through descriptions written by their conquerors or by monks in a much later age, and we can add some speculation based on archaeological finds and sacred sites. Many customs and legends associated with Brigid have made their way through in the form of folklore. We also can guess and intuit the powers of the goddess Brigid by looking at which attributes were preserved when the goddess was called a saint. Piecing it all together, a vision of Brigid begins to shine through the veils.

You may know her as Brigid, Brigit, Brighid, Brighidh, Brigindo, Bride, Bridey, Brigantia, Brid, or Bridget. Pronunciations vary according to local dialect, and you'll see various sources firmly telling you that she

should be called "Breej" or "Breed" or "Breet" or "Bree-id" or "Brigg-it." I
simply say "Bridge-id." Some say her name comes from the Old Irish *brig*,
"power," or the Welsh *bri*, "renown." Others say it comes from *breo-saigit*,
"fiery arrow," or *breo-aigit*, "fiery power." Still others say that her name
just means "high one" or "exalted one," and that "Brigid" may have been
used as a general term for "goddess." As all the name variations attest, her
worship was widespread, encompassing not only Ireland, Scotland, and
Britain, but also much of Europe.

Knowing Brigid begins with knowing the people who worshiped
her from ancient times. Celtic history, mythology, culture, archaeology,
spirituality, and so many more topics on all things Celtica fill shelf upon
shelf in most libraries. I offer just a wee bit of their tale to set the scene
and provide a context for what follows.

The Celts

The Celts (pronounced "Kelts") as a particular society are said to have
originated in central Europe around 1200 BCE. They were tribal people
rather than a centralized empire, and they probably didn't call themselves
Celts at all, but that's the name that stuck, courtesy of the Greeks, who
called them the Keltoi. For more than a thousand years, the Celts spread
throughout Europe, leaving their mark and memory wherever their journeys took them. Moving ever westward, the Celts eventually crossed the
water into Britain.

Through the Bronze and Iron Ages, the Celts became masters of
the metal arts, and rich archaeological finds of these pieces have given
many clues as to the nature of Celtic culture and religion. But much remains a mystery—or at least a subject of passionate debate. When very
early history isn't recorded in words but only in symbols, those symbols
are always subject to interpretation. To paraphrase the old joke, if you
read three books on the Celts, you're going to get six opinions. In the
words of classical archaeologist Paul Jacobsthal (writing about Celtic
art, though to me it applies to the culture as a whole), it is "elaborate
and clever; full of paradoxes, restless, puzzlingly ambiguous; rational
and irrational; dark and uncanny." [2]

....

2. Paul Jacobsthal, *Early Celtic Art*.

What we think of now as Celtic culture is a potent distillation of what was retained over centuries of tribal movement. Everywhere they went, the Celts found their goddesses and gods in the land itself. Each individual tribe had their own deities: "I swear by the gods my people swear by." The result was a complicated and chaotic religion, largely lost over time and much debated. More than four hundred names of Celtic goddesses and gods have been recorded. A multitude of earth goddesses were known, each with her own well, her own grove, her own hill. Because the Celtic tribes were always on the move—whether warring on others or being exiled themselves—ultimately these local deities didn't serve as well as a portable deity who was ever-present, and some "superstars" in the Celtic pantheon had wider influence. We know who had predominance by looking at whose stories survived once the tribes settled permanently. And one of those was Brigid.

Romans and Christians and Celts (Oh My!)

Very few facts about Brigid were recorded by early chroniclers. The Celts didn't go in much for pantheons with complicated familial relationships, as the Romans did. Generally speaking, Celtic goddesses were associated with the specific place the tribe inhabited, the earth, and fertility, while gods were associated with the tribe itself, the sky, and war. Julius Caesar associated the Celtic deities with Roman ones, and he said that the goddess the Celts called Brigid was in fact Minerva, the goddess of all arts and industry, crafts, poetry, learning, and wisdom. (Minerva's Greek counterpart is Athena.) It was recorded that Brigid's father was the Dagda (the "good god"). A ninth-century Irish glossary briefly referred to Brigid as a "matron of *filidhecht*," the lore that includes poetry and learning, divination and prophecy.[3]

And that's about it. Little else was written, or if it was written, it was lost.

Christianity was present in Britain as early as the first century CE, probably brought there by Roman traders and artists along with tales of their own gods and goddesses. In Ireland, monasteries and hermitages

....

3. Stokes, *Cormac's Glossary*.

were well established by 400 CE. In 432, Patrick arrived, with the assignment to establish an organized Catholic Church in Ireland, which he quite successfully did. (More about him later.)

The Irish Church became renowned for scholarship and the preservation of history and literature. It was much more independent from Rome than the European branches. Communication was slow and unreliable, and what communication there was tended to be, shall we say, argumentative. The Irish clergy had their own ideas about how things should be done and saw no reason why they should take orders from higher-ups they had never even met. Because of this, old pagan observances were kept alive, and some deities were simply rebranded as saints. The Celts had been adaptive all along. For instance, when they arrived in Britain, they absorbed the even more ancient culture of the megalithic people, those who loved the great stones. When the Christians came, they adapted again, keeping their old beliefs while adding the new religion's ideas. Even today, Celtic Christianity is earth-centered, heroic, otherworldly. The magic was never lost.

The downside is that, because the old and the new were blended together, Celtic history was largely overlaid with Christian interpretation. Lore and mythology recorded by monks and nuns were inevitably put through their own filters, no matter how much integrity they had about preserving the truth. It's likely they just left some things unwritten, rather than compromise their beliefs by seeming to approve of questionable elements of the older culture. Some of the information we have has to be put back through those filters to see the underlying essence. And this is where our beloved goddess Brigid comes back into the tale—a tale that survives because of Saint Brigid.

THE FLAME ENDURES: BRIGID THE SAINT

Why include a saint in a book largely intended for Pagan readers? To put it plainly, it's because the saint and the goddess are one and the same. She never left. No other Western goddess has an unbroken history of worship. No other goddess has been clung to so passionately by her devotees, no matter what other canons of faith they accepted. To write a book about Brigid without including her saint aspect would be denying half her powers:

- The power of endurance
- The power of practical love
- The power of bridging differences

As a Pagan, there was a time when I assumed that the goddess Brigid had simply been co-opted and whitewashed by the Church into something more manageable, less powerful. I see it somewhat differently now.

Travel back through time and imagine yourself as a Celtic woman in the mid-fifth century or so. Yours is a warrior society, and violent conflicts frequently end in brutal death. Women are often captured as slaves and their children raised as slaves. You are proud of your heritage, but life is hard, so hard. A new religion makes its way through the land, a gentle faith that promises peace. The new faith has a holy trinity, a concept familiar and dear to Celtic hearts, whose deities often appear in threes. It espouses hospitality, charity, care for the humble and downtrodden, and freedom from slavery. These are all things that your goddess Brigid has always meant to those who love her. What mother wouldn't welcome the chance to spare her children a lifetime of war, exchanging it perhaps for a lifetime of learning? And if this means that the new religion wants to call your goddess a saint, does that really matter so much? She is still Brigid.

I can easily understand this from a Pagan perspective, because the cauldron of modern Goddess spirituality is also a melting pot. We love Demeter and Isis and Sarasvati and Pele and Changing Woman and Kuan Yin. Many of us also love Mary. It's not a stretch for me to believe that the nuns in Saint Brigid's monastery and the countrywomen tending their cattle, and all the thousands upon thousands of people since, loved the same qualities in their saint that I love in my goddess. As Celtic scholar Proinsias Mac Cana writes:

Paradoxically, it is in the person of her Christian namesake St. Brighid that the pagan goddess survives best. For if the historical element in the legend of St. Brighid is slight, the mythological element is correspondingly extensive, and it is clear beyond question that the saint has usurped the role of the goddess and much of her mythological tradition … It must be accepted, therefore, that no clear distinction can be made between the goddess and the saint and that in all probability Brighid's great monastery of Kildare was formerly a pagan sanctuary.…Brighid became St. Brighid and her cult continued uninterrupted. [4]

"Continued uninterrupted"—how wonderful that is! Envision a perpetual flame dedicated to the Goddess, tended faithfully by women. When the new religion came, the holy women built a monastery on their sacred site, and the flame continued to burn there uninterrupted, tended now by nuns. As late as the twelfth century—*six hundred years* after Saint Brigid's death—the flame still burned. It may have burned until the sixteenth century, when the monasteries were suppressed. In 1993, the perpetual flame was relit, and it burns to this day.

Brigidine Sister Mary Minehan has said, "There are no historical facts about [Saint] Brigid at all but an amalgamation of folklore, myth, and legend—which is in our collective memory and which we must not dismiss." [5] I love that idea that what we carry within our collective memory is a deep truth, no matter what facts may or may not have been recorded. This is at the heart of Paganism, too—folklore wisdom handed down not just from person to person but from lifetime to lifetime. The stories of the lives of saints reveal more about the hearts and minds of the people who tell them than about actual fact. The people loved the goddess Brigid so much that they would not let her go. Much in the same way that some other saints are venerated for having the qualities of Jesus, Saint Brigid was venerated for having the qualities of, well, Brigid. Saint Brigid was and remains a very goddess-y saint. Let me tell you her tale, and see if you will love her as much as I do.

....

4. Mac Cana, *Celtic Mythology.*
5. Interview with Sr. Mary Minehan by Melissa Thompson, February 19, 1999, www.tallgirlshorts.net / marymary / sistermary.html.

A Sun Among the Stars of Heaven

Saint Brigid was marked for mystical greatness from her birth—and indeed, before her birth. A "wizard" (druid) prophesied over her pregnant mother: "Marvelous will be the child that is in her womb. Her like will not be seen on earth, radiant, who will shine like a sun among the stars of heaven." [6] The daughter of an Irish chieftain named Dubthach and a slave woman named Broicsech, Brigid was born around the year 450 CE. Her birth came at sunrise as her mother stepped over the threshold, one of the magical between-places that have such power in Celtic lore. She was neither in the house nor outside it, both in the world and not in the world. Broicsech was returning from having milked the cows, and the newborn Brigid was bathed in *lemlacht*, new milk still warm from the cow, which was thought to have magical powers.

As an infant, Brigid refused all nourishment until she was given the milk of a white cow with red ears—a faery cow, in other words. Another legend from her infancy says that her mother went out to tend the cattle while Brigid was sleeping and was called back in haste by a neighbor screaming that the cottage was on fire. Broicsech saw her house all ablaze but rushed in anyway, and there was Brigid sleeping peacefully in her cradle, in a house that was not burning at all. The radiance of the sleeping child had made the cottage appear to be in flames. A wee fire goddess, to be sure!

Brigid grew in skills and virtues—"She tended the sheep, she satisfied the birds, she fed the poor." Though born to a slave, Brigid was given her freedom as a maiden ("when boldness, strength, and size came to Brigit"), perhaps because her habit of giving away her father's goods to the poor made her less than popular at home. She wandered for a time, and on her travels her miraculous feats became intentional, rather than the early miracles of fire that signified her supernatural nature—she turned well water into beer, for example, and magically increased foods such as bacon and butter.

....

6. All the quotes in this section on Saint Brigid, unless otherwise noted, are from Stokes, *Lives of Saints, from the Book of Lismore.*

Brigid's mother was still bound in servitude, having been sold as a dairywoman to another master. A more powerful and confident Brigid was now determined to free her. She found Broicsech ill and exhausted from the ceaseless labor demanded of those who worked in bondage. Brigid tended to her sick mother and "began setting the dairy to rights." I love this description, imagining Brigid pushing up her sleeves and putting things in order the way she thought they should be done.

The lord of this house was a druid, and he asked about the new woman who had taken charge of his dairy. Could it be that he had heard of Brigid's magical feats and wanted to test her skills? He and his wife went down to the dairy, taking with them a hamper that was eighteen hands high. Brigid welcomed them with good cheer, washing their feet and giving them food in the Celtic tradition of hospitality. The druid's wife then asked Brigid to show them how much butter she had made. There were only one and a half churnings left in the dairy, and the wife mocked her, saying sarcastically, "*This* quantity of butter is good to fill a large hamper!"

With a knowing smile, Brigid went back into the dairy kitchen and sang a chant asking to be blessed with abundance. She emerged with another churning of butter, and then another, and another. Again and again she came forth, singing all the while. She filled the huge hamper with butter, and indeed, "if [all] the hampers which the men of Munster possessed had been given to her, she would have filled them all." The druid and his wife marveled at this wondrous feat and offered Brigid their kine (cattle) as a tribute. But she refused them, saying, "Take thou the kine, and give me my mother's freedom." Both were given to her— and not surprisingly, Brigid gave the cattle away to the poor.

Brigid of Kildare

Brigid refused all suitors and sought a life of service to the wider world. Becoming a nun in that day (and maybe today, too!) can be seen as an act of independence, even defiance. To follow the call of a sacred vocation was fairly revolutionary in a land where women were expected to stay at home and have children. Brigid chose not to marry, to remain celibate, a virgin. From our modern perspective, this may seem like a weak choice—to remain forever a maiden, sheltered and naïve. On the contrary, Brigid's decision to have a career in the church was an act of courageous self-determination. She was setting herself up to follow her inner guidance.

Brigid and eight other women journeyed to a certain Bishop Mél to take their vows as nuns. Mél plays a part in many of Brigid's legends, acting as advocate and champion. He recognized her holiness immediately, not least because as he moved to place the veil upon her, "a fiery pillar rose from her head to the roof-ridge of the church." Mél declared that rather than merely consecrating Brigid as a nun, he must ordain her as bishop. When another priest protested, Mél said, "No power have I in this matter. That dignity was given by God unto Brigit, beyond every other woman."

After taking their vows, Brigid and her sisters formed a monastery on the sacred site of Kildare, with Brigid as abbess. (More about Kildare on page 105.) No husband or father was going to control or limit her— and that included the Holy Father in Rome. As I mentioned earlier, the Irish Church at that time wasn't as constricting as the European Church, and communication with the Vatican was sporadic (and often ignored). Unlike monasteries in other countries, Brigid's at Kildare had both nuns and monks, and although the men had a male bishop overseeing them, Brigid was abbess over them all. Men as well as women looked to her for leadership and spiritual guidance, though only women were allowed to tend the perpetual flame, honoring the tradition that predated Christianity.

From the place of authority and grounded power that Brigid found in her own monastery, her miracles and magical workings on behalf of the needy began to pour forth. Unlike other saints whose miracles were meant to make a statement of faith or an example of martyrdom, most of Brigid's miracles were practical, homely acts of magic. She mended broken vessels by breathing upon them. She turned stone into salt, water into beer. She enchanted cows to give more milk than was possible, "a lake of milk" on at least one occasion. Over and over, the stories of Brigid tell how she increased food to feed far more people than the original quantity could have fed, providing "bread and butter and onions and lots of courses." Making sure the people did not go hungry was a passionate cause for Brigid, and if a precious domestic animal died or was stolen, Brigid would magically restore it to the grateful family.

Her power as healer came into its fullness too. Brigid healed lepers, sometimes with her touch and on one occasion with her own blood. She also insisted that others care for the lepers in practical ways and not shun them. Once a woman visited Brigid with a gift of a basket of apples, which Brigid proceeded to give away to the lepers. When the woman protested that the apples weren't meant for such untouchables, "it was an annoyance to Brigid," who then cursed the woman so that all of her apple trees would be barren ever afterward.

As her influence grew, Brigid began to use her power on behalf of slaves and others in captivity—a cause dear to her no doubt because her own mother had been a slave. She magically transported political prisoners and prisoners of war back to their homes. One such prisoner merely called out in despair, "O Brigid, carry me home!" and found himself at his own cottage door.

Known by now as *Muire na nGael*, Mary of the Gael, Brigid was an advocate for all who suffered and could not speak for or defend themselves. When one of her nuns became pregnant, Brigid refused to censure or punish her. Her seventh-century biographer Cogitosus says, "Brigid, exercising with the most strength of her ineffable faith, blessed her, caused the fetus to disappear without coming to birth and without pain"—hence, Saint Brigid is the matron saint of Ireland's pro-choice movement today.[7] She was said to confer blessings of victory in righteous battle, sometimes appearing as an apparition in the sky above the battlefield. Over and over in her legends, she offers healing and protection, healing and protection: "For this was her desire: to satisfy the poor, to expel every hardship, to spare every miserable man."

In her youth, Brigid had given her father's bejeweled sword to a starving family, incurring his wrath but remaining true to her principles, which never wavered during her lifetime. Though she was often given costly treasure as a tribute, she gave away so much to the poor that her

....

7. Cogitosus, *Vita Sanctae Brigidae*, circa 650.

nuns used to hide some of it to make sure there was enough left to take care of their own needs too: "Little good have we from thy compassion to everyone, and we ourselves in need of food and raiment!" (They didn't get away with this, by the way. Brigid always knew where the cache was stowed.)

Brigid and Patrick

While most nuns in cloistered convents tended to the needs of those in their immediate communities, Brigid traveled widely and met with other religious leaders, including Saint Patrick. So, what about this Patrick? Is he a villain, the one who destroyed the beautiful pagan faith and replaced it with oppressive Christianity? Some say the story of him driving the snakes from Ireland is a reference to the druids or to the pagan Celts with their snakelike tattoos, since there never *were* any snakes in Ireland. It's important to remember that the tales of Patrick were written hundreds of years after his death by people who definitely had an ax to grind and an agenda to push. One thing that stays with me is that the conversion of Ireland to Catholicism was largely peaceful. This certainly wasn't the case in the rest of Christendom, then or since. Something about Patrick and his mission appealed to the people—and these were strong, fiercely independent people, not sheep waiting for a shepherd. Most simply added the new religion to the ancient beliefs they held so deeply. Saint Patrick is well-beloved to this day, and there are few saints who are still so widely invoked and celebrated in any part of the Christian world. He and Saint Brigid appear together in many stories, and religious medals with Patrick on one side often have Brigid on the other.

Reading between the lines of the pious and reverential "Lives of the Saints" tales, the relationship between Brigid and Patrick has a certain sibling sassiness that is endearing. They treat each other as equals and as comrades with a common purpose. When Patrick spoke to the people, Brigid as usual magically increased the available food to feed the crowd that had gathered. "When Patrick had finished the preaching, the food was brought to Brigit that she might divide it. And she blessed it; and the two peoples of God, Brigit's congregation and Patrick's congregation, were satisfied."

Note that Brigid has her own congregation, which is not subordinate to Patrick's. Throughout their mutual tales we get a sense of strong female power, dedicated and determined.

Both saints are associated with the elements—Brigid with fire and water, Patrick with wind and rock. Mystic power flows strongly in them both, and the tales show their respect for each other's wisdom and autonomy. During one of Patrick's sermons, a thunderous storm arose over his head. Afterward, the crowd turned to Brigid to ask what it meant. "Ask Patrick," she said. Patrick replied, "You and I know equally well. Reveal this mystery to them." On another occasion, Brigid fell asleep while Patrick was preaching. When he finished speaking, he woke her and complained that she hadn't been listening, to which she replied that she'd had a vision in her sleep. Patrick listened with interest to her dream vision:

> I beheld four ploughs in the southeast, which ploughed the whole island; and before the sowing was finished, the harvest was ripened, and clear well-springs and shining streams came out of the furrows. White garments were on the sowers and ploughmen. I beheld four other ploughs in the north, which ploughed the island athwart, and turned the harvest again, and the oats which they had sown grew up at once, and were ripe, and black streams came out of the furrows, and there were black garments on the sowers and on the ploughmen.

Patrick's interpretation of her vision reveals his point of view as a missionary. He says that the four ploughs in the southeast are the two of them, working together to bring the four gospels to the people, and what they sow is faith, belief, and piety. Even before their teachings are complete ("before the sowing was finished"), the work has taken hold. And then, "the four ploughs which thou beheldest in the north are the false teachers and the liars who will overturn the teaching which we are sowing."

It's not recorded how Brigid responded to this interpretation. I'll offer another one. The striking imagery of the clear shining streams and the black streams, the white garments and the black garments, speak to

me of the light and dark times of the year, which were such an important part of the Celtic cosmology, as we'll see later. The fact that Brigid
dreamt that both ploughings brought forth grain could symbolize the
fruitfulness of the dark time as well as the light. The harvest is turned
over in the fields, the seed turned back into the soil and the darkness.
The southeast, a place of sunrise and warmth, is balanced by the north,
a place of darkness and cold. The four ploughs could be the four directions, each plough moving out from the sacred center, dividing the land
just as the four holy days of Imbolc, Beltane, Lughnasadh, and Samhain
divide and mark the year. Brigid is an earth goddess, and her saintly
counterpart is also profoundly connected to the earth and its seasons.

Because the histories of both saints were written so long after their
lives, nothing factual about them can be accepted as absolute. Some
scholars say it's unlikely that Patrick and Brigid knew each other, because of the varying dates given for their births and deaths. In my view,
whether they ever met isn't the point. The stories that are told about
them reveal the reverence in which Brigid was held, so great that it was
important to include her in Patrick's legends, which certainly stand
on their own without such additions. Patrick's presence in the tales of
Brigid gives extra validation to her power too, but he isn't there to prop
her up or condescendingly approve; he's a colleague.

From Goddess to Saint to Goddess

At the end of his biography of her, Cogitosus sums up Saint Brigid's character in a list of virtues: she was "modest, gentle, humble, sage, harmoni-
ous, innocent, prayerful, patient, firm, forgiving, loving." Based on the
tales he told of her, he could easily have added that Brigid was powerful,
courageous, generous, passionate, righteous, and brilliant. She was, in the
true sense of the word, awesome.

It's a mistake to pooh-pooh Saint Brigid as if she were a Brigid im-
poster, a pale substitute for the great goddess who preceded her. I was
predisposed to dislike her, but the more I learned, the more she appealed to me. She is praised for her kindness and sweetness, but she's
feisty too. There is a fierceness about her. She is a woman with a temper
and little tolerance for fools. She stands up for herself as well as for the

downtrodden. She talks back. She has a sense of humor. (Her most famous prayer includes her wish to provide a lake of beer for Jesus, and I just know that was said with a twinkle in her eye.) It's easy to love a saint who knows how hard it can be to find enough food to feed a family, who will summon up a cart full of bacon with a wave of her hand. This is not a forbidding holy father, lord, or savior. This is a sister.

The big question is: Was there ever really a living, human Saint Brigid? My feeling is that, yes, there probably was. Someone, after all, founded that monastery. The perpetual flame was burning when Brigid came to Kildare, and she kept that fire alive. Those who followed in her footsteps—and under her instruction—kept it burning for centuries.

Earlier I said that when I came to know the goddess Brigid, it was like she had always been there. Brigid *has* always been there—first as goddess, then as saint, and, when the world was ready, as goddess again. Through all the changes of the rolling world, her worship has never ceased.

CHAPTER TWO

HEARTH:
THE WELCOMING FLAME

Walls against the wind,
Roof against the rain,
Hearth to hold the fire,
And Brigid encompassing all.

Come close and be blessed at the hearth of Brigid. Here you will find nourishment of body and nurturance of spirit. Brigid encompasses, encircles, and protects with unceasing care. Just as the hearthfire is the heart of the home, Brigid is at the heart of daily life. From that glowing and comforting center of warmth, she will always welcome you home.

CÉAD MÍLE FÁILTE:
A HUNDRED THOUSAND WELCOMES

Both the yearning to wander and the yearning for home have always run deep within the Celtic soul. You can hear it in Celtic music that pulls at the heartstrings, a lonely melancholy that has no earthly cure, perhaps because it springs from the depths of ancestral longing. For a wanderer, the blessed return to the hearth is symbolized by the welcoming open door, light streaming forth.

The Door and the Threshold

The between-places, where you are neither in one place nor in the other, are special places of magic in Celtic spirituality. The threshold is such a place, marking the crossing-over between your home and the outside world. The door is the seal of this between-place, which you open and close at will. Making this everyday motion a conscious act of protection is merely a matter of shifting your awareness—and invoking Brigid. The doors of your home are symbolic of the threshold between this world and the Otherworld, between the seen and the unseen, between what is inside and what is outside, literally and metaphorically. Each time you pass over the threshold of a door, you are in that liminal between-place where magic happens.

Brigid is the guardian of the home, and the threshold is one of her power places. Saint Brigid, as you may recall, was born on the threshold of her mother's cottage. The symbolism of this is twofold (at least!)—Brigid was born between the worlds as both human and goddess, and she was born between the domestic concerns of the home, which she would always bless, and the worldly concerns that would involve her in later life.

Doors that lead to and from the outside world are protective and enclosing. They are the gateways between what is your home and what is not your home. They keep out what is harmful and keep in what is beneficial and precious. Just as your parents would tell you to close the door so you didn't let all the heat out, doors preserve the love and contentment that dwell in a house, while allowing loved ones to safely come and go. It is the nature of a doorway to act as a sort of force field, a place where what is on one side of the opening and what is on the other side meet and yet stay separate. It is a holy place, and the little rituals you perform at your front door are the beginning of asking Brigid to be present in every part of your domestic life.

Making your doorway a sanctified between-place can be as simple as touching an amulet or a blessing object, such as the Jewish tradition of the mezuzah, a small box mounted to the door frame containing a Torah verse that reminds the reader to love and serve God. Touching the mezuzah is an acknowledgment of these instructions and a tacit promise to respect them. You can adapt this custom to your devotions to Brigid by using symbols that represent her, such as a Brigid's cross or a triskele (see page 59). Put a small dish of water at the doorway or a holy-water font that hangs on the wall (these can easily be found online and are available with Celtic designs). Dip a finger into the water and anoint yourself in the name of Brigid, goddess of the sacred wells. Touch your forehead with the water to awaken to spiritual awareness, touch your heart to expand the love you feel for your home and its inhabitants, and finally, anoint your hands to do Brigid's work in the world with gratefulness. You can bless your guests in this way as they enter or invite them to bless themselves.

Another way to awaken your sense of the sacred is to ring a bell when you come in the front door. The use of bells has a venerable tradition in many cultures, ringing for protection, consecration, and celebration. Mundane uses for bells have the same common root: to get your attention. Bells summon children back to class, alert a shopkeeper to your presence, signal that the cookies are done, and remind you to put on your seatbelt. Each bell in your life says, "Stop what you're doing for a moment and do something else." And so it is with the threshold bell. It says that you are now entering a sanctuary, and your attention is required to honor that. On my front porch, I have a wheel of bells that chime delicately when the wheel is turned. Standing at the doorway until the last echo of the bells is gone roots me in understanding that my home is a blessing and I am honoring it with gratitude. Other sound-makers can speak to you in different ways—for instance, a door harp, with balls that bounce on small harp strings as the door is opened, sounds a delicate reminder that Brigid, goddess of the bard's harp, is present in your home.

The Going Out and the Coming In

Here is a simple ritual to bless your threshold and all who pass through it.

Open your door and stand just inside it. Place your hands on either side of the door frame. Close your eyes.

Feel the empty between-place where you stand. Sense the liminal power that is contained within the frame of the portal. You are at the transition between *here* and *there*.

Feel the solidity of your home behind you. Feel the expansiveness of the world in front of you.

With your hands still on the door frame, imagine a golden light that emanates from the center of your chest. The light spreads outward until the entire between-place of the open door is glowing.

Feel the energy of the living light, the flame of Brigid that burns in your heart.

Offer this prayer:

The light of Brigid be about me
On my going out and on my coming in.
May she walk before me on every road.
May she stand behind me at every challenge.
May she hold the map of my journey
And bring me safely home at journey's end.

When you are ready, open your eyes and gratefully close the door.

Sacred Hospitality

The Celtic tradition of sacred hospitality goes back many thousands of years. Perhaps it originated because the wandering tribal people remembered the welcome they received at some hearthfires and the rebuffs they suffered at others, and resolved that in their own halls there would always be a welcome for the stranger. Aristotle and Posidonius both wrote about the Celts' strict rules of hospitality, especially to strangers. A householder was bound to offer food and drink even before finding out a visitor's business. By Saint Brigid's time, the custom of hospitality was deeply ingrained in the Celtic spirit. Brigid's monastery at Kildare was a haven and sanctuary, a refuge that welcomed the sick, the poor, and fugitives from injustice.

Most of us don't live with the open-door policy that was practiced by our Celtic ancestors. Too many of us have gone too far the other way, perhaps, and don't even know our closest neighbors. But hospitality extends beyond mere socializing. Brigid invites you to examine your heart and see how welcoming you are, beyond practical and literal hospitality. To welcome others into your home as Brigid herself would welcome them means to have an open heart as well as an open door. The guest is sacred, a gift, a blessing. Saint Brigid was said to welcome every guest as if she or he were Jesus. We can welcome each guest as if she or he were Brigid.

While most casual comings and goings don't really allow for formal blessings, make a point of centering yourself and consciously changing your internal attitude to one of true welcome when a guest arrives. As they cross the threshold, they will feel how you have imbued that between-space with magic. Beyond décor and architecture, people can really feel when a home is a sanctuary. It comes from those who live there and the spirit of sacred hospitality they honor.

In traditional Irish homes, when a guest arrived they were immediately shown to the hearthside and given the best seat there. Food and drink were offered before anything else was discussed, and a lapse in this was cause for shame. This tradition surely had spiritual connotations along with the practical ones. The goddess (or the saint) was present at the hearthfire, and the guest was invited to draw close to her presence and be blessed.

This practice is part of what you can do today—drawing guests in with true warmth and placing them at the heart of your home, wherever you feel that to be. Continue your welcome with nourishment offered in the spirit of Brigid, who never wants to see anyone hunger or thirst. Don't ask if your guests want anything—we are all far too likely to say, "No, thank you." Just give the offering and know it will be received at the spirit level, whether or not your guests actually eat or drink what you offer.

The spirit of sacred hospitality has to start with you. Do *you* feel that your home is a sanctuary? Do you feel the presence of Brigid there, warming and sustaining, strengthening and protecting? Part of the work of creating a home is internal and part is external. The externals have to do with removing irritations, such as clutter and noise, and adding things that please your senses. The internals are about moving past all of that, paradoxically, and loving your home exactly as it is. Being grateful for shelter is fundamental to worshiping Brigid.

Make Yourself at Home

Here are two good ways to feel at home in your home. The first is to have other people come visit, for an hour or a week or however long you enjoy having company. In parts of rural Ireland, an old custom continues of the *cuaird*, the "circuit." On a designated night of the week, friends in the village have open house after dinner. It's very informal—no invitations are necessary, no RSVP. You might receive visitors or you might choose to go visiting yourself. The lights in the windows let the visitors know whose houses are filled with friends that night. Once there, the informality continues—there are no elaborate refreshments, no planned activity, no agenda or expectations. The friends tell stories of their week or old stories from the past; a musician might be asked to bring out his fiddle. The community's connectedness is woven more closely by this intimacy, as everyone is family.

Some of us had this kind of hangout scene when we were younger, but nowadays it is far more likely that we meet friends outside the home, when we meet with them at all, and it is an event, not a regular occurrence. In those rural Irish homes, there is often a spare chair that lives just inside the front door, symbolizing the welcome that any guest will meet if they wish to drop in and pull up the chair to the hearthfire. You might put such a chair by your own door to remind you of what a blessing it is to share your home warmth with others. Welcoming others into your home pleases Brigid no end, and you will feel that increase in happiness within the walls of your shelter.

The second good way to be at home in your home is to leave it for a time. Whether you're coming home at the end of the workday or returning after a journey of many weeks, Brigid embraces you with a loving welcome as you cross the threshold. When you attune yourself to her welcome, it will continue to warm you. From that place of contentment, your gratitude for having such a welcoming home will grow—and the gratitude will enhance the contentment.

AN ELEMENTAL HOMECOMING

Ask Brigid to help you feel at home in your home by creating an encircling knotwork of elemental blessing, using the Celtic triad of earth, sea, and sky. It combines the practical with the spiritual, as always with our dear Brigid.

Earth: Begin with the element of earth. Your home provides refuge from the stress of the outside world, and earth is present when you feel safe enough to relax. Like our ancestors retreating to their stone cottages, you should feel protected and secure in your home sanctuary. From this place of security, your spirit can comfortably ground itself in the bedrock of your well-being. Do an assessment of your home and see if you detect any ways in which you don't feel safe or sheltered, perhaps at an unconscious level until now. For example, in one place where I lived, the front of the house was uncurtained glass, and the living room was partially visible to anyone walking by. The neighborhood was safe, and I felt no danger, so I only gave it a passing thought now and then in the five years I lived there. But when I moved to a place where I could draw the curtains and completely enclose myself, I immediately felt relief from the accumulated stress of being in the open all those years. Take care of any such vulnerabilities in your own home, and seal them with this prayer:

May Brigid's blessings of earth be on this place:
Stability of mountain,
Rootedness of tree,
Abundance of grain,
Be with us this day and every day.

Sea: Next, invoke the element of water in your home. What does your spirit thirst for? Your home sanctuary should be an ever-renewing wellspring in which your heart can be restored to wholeness. If your emotional waters feel stagnant, call upon Brigid of the holy wells to help those waters run clear again. Most homes contain beloved mementos of dear ones and special times. Look around and see if there are also things that trigger a *negative* emotional response from you—

a photograph of someone with whom you have unresolved issues, for example. While you will continue to heal past hurts with Brigid's help, there is no reason to live with reminders every day. Put such objects gently away, with respect for their teachings. Replace them with things that tap into the boundless sea of joy, and affirm them with this prayer:

May Brigid's blessings of sea be on this place:
Connection of currents,
Patience of tides,
Wisdom of depths,
Be with us this day and every day.

Sky: Air is the element of thought, ideas, and inspiration. Most homes have way too much air, metaphorically speaking. Books and magazines, music, games, television, smartphones, computers and tablets—all of these contribute to a cacophony of mind-numbing and soul-battering noise. If you want the wise voice of Brigid to be heard, you need to turn down the constant jabber of modern life, and home is one place where you have control of this. Pay attention to what you choose to let through the air filters of your mind. Ask yourself: Does this enhance my spirit? Does this excite my mind in a positive way? In your home sanctuary, you need both healthy mental stimulation and peace of mind. The element of sky gives your spirit wings to fly. As often as possible in every day, make some space in which to listen to the silence, and welcome it with this prayer:

May Brigid's blessings of sky be on this place,
Inspiration of wind,
Beauty of cloud,
Vision of stars,
Be with us this day and every day.

THE PLACE OF GATHERING

The traditional Irish home had its hearth at the exact center of the house. The room with the hearth was simply known as "the room," and all other places in the home were referred to as above the room, behind the room, and so on. Every day began with gathering at the hearth for the morning meal, and every day ended with stories, music, and prayer at the hearthside. The fire there was tended all day long and smoored at night to preserve its embers—to start a fire from scratch takes more effort, not to mention the cold that creeps in when a fire has gone completely out. Keeping the fire alight was a matter of life and death, and without it the family could freeze or starve. No wonder their most beloved home guardian was she who sustained that fire and was present in its dancing light.

If you have a fireplace in your home, you already know about the magic of this timeless place of gathering. Gazing into the fire, feeding it, watching as it flares up and dies down, marveling at the mesmerizing sparkle of the embers—it is truly a blessing that should never be taken for granted. The spirit of all our ancestors lives on in that fire. I'm amused (and a bit appalled) at the current trend of putting a giant television right above the hearth, for what could ever compete with the enchantment of living flames?

I've lived in houses where a woodstove was the only source of heat, and it's true that the romance of the flame is tested a bit when it has to be kept going for bodily warmth or to heat water. Our ancestors weren't sentimental about the work that a hearthfire requires, both in tending the fire itself and in the gathering of fuel. While we can pick up a bundle of firewood at the grocery store, the cutting of wood was an ongoing task for those earlier people. And not just wood—in Ireland to this day, peat is cut from the bog turf and dried as fuel, a backbreaking job in the days before machines.

Though the hearthfire was a practical concern, our ancestors still looked on it in spiritual and magical terms. Precisely because it was such a vital part of every day, blessing and honoring the fire became second nature. There were prayers for stirring up the fire, for putting the fire to bed, for adding fuel and cutting fuel. One such prayer invokes "Brigid of the peat-heap," acknowledging her gift of (and help with) this most beloved of fragrant fire fuels. An old Irish text specifies which woods are good for burning and which are not, describing each tree as having particular magical purposes. Here is a bit of it:

> *Burn not the precious apple tree of spreading and low-sweeping bough…*
> *The noble willow burn not, a tree sacred to poems…*
> *The graceful tree with the berries, the wizards' tree, the rowan burn.*[8]

But what about those of us who don't have functional fireplaces? What then is the heart-center of the home? If you are a flamekeeper, you keep a devotional fire, but that serves a different purpose (which we'll talk about later). The hearthfire is the gathering place, the settling place, where comfort is found and company is shared. As strange as it may sound, one such place in many homes is the coffee table. Cozy seating around a low central table where food and drink may be shared functions much as the hearth did in olden days. We may call it the living room now or the family room, but it is essentially "the room." Make a place for fire on this central table, perhaps changing it with the seasons. This isn't an altar, any more than the functional hearth of old was an altar, so you don't need to be formal about it. Just invite Brigid to your gathering place. I have a round marble coffee table that was my mother's, and in the center I have three pillar candles on a tray, with tiny river rocks surrounding them in the summer, acorns in autumn, and glittering branches in winter. In the spring, beginning at Imbolc, the candles stand on their own, pure and simple. When I light the candles in the evening, their living light brings Brigid's peace to my gathering place.

The Roof and the Floor and All Between

In traditional Celtic folk customs, charms and superstitions are woven all through each day's activities. With many little ways to incur bad luck, both in the house and outside, it's no surprise that prayers for protection abound. My feeling about superstitions is they are closely akin to magical intuition—if you feel that something should be done in a certain way to align it with the correct functioning of the cosmos, then that is the correct way for you. Of course, if such beliefs become debili-

....
8. O'Grady, *Silva Gadelica.*

tating or fearful rather than enriching your life with enchantment, you need to get back into balance.

Protective prayers form a kind of force field against anything unwelcome. Many Celtic prayers use the image of encompassing and encircling, much the same as casting a magic circle in Wiccan and Pagan practices. A traditional Celtic charm for protection involves walking three times sunwise (clockwise) around the object to be protected while carrying "a burning brand"—a candle will do nicely. Begin and end in the south. This charm invokes Brigid both in the use of flame and in the powerful number three (see page 57). You can perform this simple protective blessing on anything, from people to possessions to pets, and expand it to include your whole house. If you can walk around your dwelling outside, do so, but if that's not possible, just walk around each room three times in turn or, depending on your home's layout, walk through the rooms in a loop three times. As you perform this charm, envision the flame making a trail of protective fire that encircles your dwelling with the protective power of Brigid.

> I call for the encircling of Brigid:
> Protect the house and all within,
> Protect the house from beam to wall,
> Protect the house and the household all,
> The roof and the floor and all between.[9]

Brigid's Cross

Brigid's cross is her most well-known symbol, appearing in jewelry, artwork, and sculpture as well as the traditional rush weavings. Although it has been absorbed into devotions to Saint Brigid, this equal-armed cross has origins that go back far before Christianity. A 1952 Irish Catholic journal stated that "although they are called 'crosses,' it will be seen that several of the types have no elements of a cross at all and it is likely they represent a pagan custom Christianised by association with a saint." [10] Brigid's cross stands for the sun-wheel, a symbol of the light returning

....

9. Adapted from traditional prayers.

10. Lucas, "St. Brigid in Tradition and Art."

at Imbolc and the eternal cycle of the seasons. When it is hung in the home, it protects from fire, keeping that powerful element in balance and under the care of fire-goddess Brigid. It also symbolizes the four directions of before, behind, above, and below, placing the maker at the center of the sacred space as she weaves her protective charm. The symbolism of being centered in your spiritual life is affirmed—as Brigidine Sister Mary Minehan says, "When you're making a Brigid's cross, unless you keep the center together, the whole thing falls apart." [11]

The crosses are made on Imbolc night to greet Brigid as she passes each home, but they can be made anytime as a meditation on the intricate weavings of Brigid's presence in your life. They are traditionally made of rushes. The symbolism for this may be drawn from the custom of laying rushes down in a birthing chamber. Rushes are therefore associated with Brigid as midwife and as the one who brings forth the birthing of spring. The rushes gathered for Brigid are pulled, not cut (another birthing metaphor, perhaps). Since rushes may not be convenient for you to gather, the instructions that follow are for crosses made of sparkly pipe cleaners (sometimes called tinsel stems, available at craft stores). Because they stay right where you want them when bent, pipe cleaners are a good choice for beginners. I also like pipe cleaners because they are made of wire, invoking Brigid as a goddess of metalcraft. Other shapes of "crosses," such as one with three arms instead of four, can also be made. Do a web search to find instructions.

You will need:
36 pipe cleaners or more
String or wire
Scissors

Making a Brigid's cross is easy to do, once you understand the central idea that you are folding each new "arm" over the ones that went before. In the following diagrams, the darker arm is always the active one. To begin, choose one pipe cleaner as the "anchor stem."

....
11. Interview with Sr. Mary Minehan by Melissa Thompson.

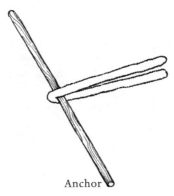

Anchor

Step 1: Bend or fold the first arm around the anchor stem at the center of the anchor.

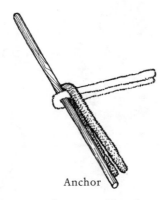

Anchor

Step 2: Take another pipe cleaner and bend it over the first arm, keeping it as close as possible to the anchor stem.

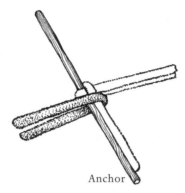

Step 3: Take another pipe cleaner and bend it over the arm you just added.

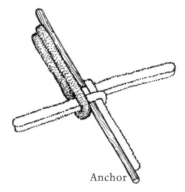

Step 4: Take another pipe cleaner and bend it over the last one.

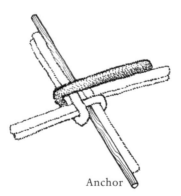

Step 5: Add another pipe cleaner over the last one and alongside the first one, tucked as closely to it as possible.

As you can see, you are working your way around clockwise/ sunwise. Once you get the rhythm down, the process can be trance-inducing. It can also be done merrily, singing or chanting as you weave your energy into each cross. Continue adding new arms as shown here.

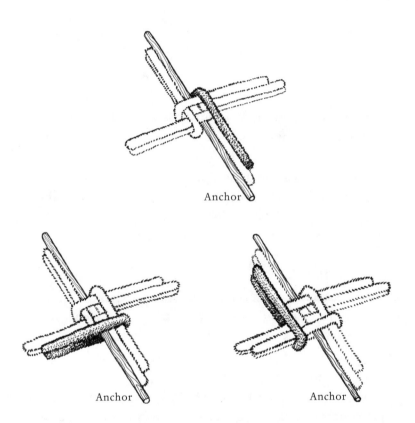

Anchor

Anchor   Anchor

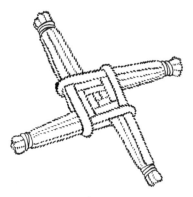

Step 6: Stop when you feel your cross is complete. You may want to use twenty pipe cleaners—nineteen for the priestesses of Brigid who tended her flame and one for the Goddess herself. When you are done weaving, use string, ribbon, or wire to bind the ends (I just use another pipe cleaner), then trim them evenly. Hang the cross high in the house, above a door or from the eaves, and let it spin a protective blessing on your home and household.

Blessing the Herd

Domestic animals have always been under Brigid's protection. From ancient days, the Celts were dependent on sheep, pigs, and cows for survival, and Brigid was invoked to "be on the herd" and keep them well. Most of us don't keep such large animals these days, but our herd is just as precious to us—and to Brigid.

If you have a fireplace in your home, it's the perfect place to make a small shrine to welcome Brigid as protector of cats and dogs, who so love the heat of the hearth. Use your creativity here—perhaps a Celtic-knotwork picture frame with a photo of your furry friends, or a Brigid's cross tied with paw-print ribbons. If you don't have an actual hearth, you can place protective symbols of Brigid near your animals' food dishes or even on the food dishes themselves. Small pottery bowls with Celtic designs can be blessed to hold your cat's food. Dogs are a little harder on dishes than most cats are, but you can draw symbols of

Brigid's protection (such as a triskele) or write prayers on the outside of any sturdy dish using a permanent marker.

Bless your animals' sleeping areas too, whether it is an actual pet bed or just a favorite snoozing spot. Because our animals spend so much time sleeping, imbuing that spot with extra blessing energy will reinforce the protection every time they return there. Your animal has already made it their sanctuary, and a blessing invoking Brigid's presence affirms that. Make the encircling by moving three times around the spot with a flame (if you can't walk all the way around, simply move the flame itself over the spot three times), while saying this prayer:

> May the encompassing of Brigid protect you,
> May the encircling of Brigid keep you,
> May the soft hand of Brigid soothe you,
> May the eye of Brigid be ever on you,
> To guard you and to cherish you,
> For today, forever, for eternity.

Small, inexpensive Saint Brigid medals are easily found and can be added to a collar. There are many different designs. The one I like best for pet protection shows Brigid standing before a grove of trees with a contented cow at her feet. This medal usually has Patrick on the reverse, but if you're persistent, you may find her on her own. Triskeles and other Celtic knotwork or spiral designs can be added to conventional pet tags and collars. Tiny Brigid's cross charms are also widely available and could be added to a collar, though the pointed edges may annoy your cat more than the rounded medals. The important thing with any such charm is the intention you place on it. Find the symbol that speaks of protection to you. Ask Brigid to be present there, and she will be.

The following traditional blessing can be read over your animal companions to soothe and calm them in stressful times and to invoke Brigid's healing when they are ill. Brigid may not have specifically mentioned your type of pet, but it surely falls under her care just the same.

The charm placed of Brigid
About her cows, about her kine,
About her horses, about her goats,
About her sheep, about her lambs:
To keep them from eye, to keep them from omen,
To keep them from spell, south and north,
To keep them from venom, east and west,
To keep them from envy and from wiles of the wicked,
To keep them from hound and from each other's horns,
From the birds of the high moors and from the beasts of the hills,
To keep them from wolf, from ravaging dog,
To keep them from fox, from the swiftest of pursuers.[12]

WELCOMING THE WEE FOLK

Brigid is a faery goddess. She is one of the Tuatha Dé Danann, the tribe of the goddess Danu who became the Sidhe, the faery folk. Some say that, in fact, Brigid *is* Danu, and that all of those with fae blood are her descendants. This is easy for me to believe—for all her practicality, Brigid is imbued with enchantment.

Celtic faery lore is vast, describing hundreds of types of faeries and otherworldly creatures and myriad tales of human encounters with them, both benevolent and malevolent. There are faeries who dwell in palaces deep within hollow hills, faeries who inhabit places in nature, and faeries who wander, sometimes posing a threat to travelers caught unawares. And then there are the domestic faeries, who cohabit with humans—sometimes by invitation and sometimes in a state of wary truce. These fae spirits are under Brigid's keeping, as protectress of the home and all who dwell there, mortal and immortal, seen and unseen.

Much of Irish faery lore deals with troublesome faeries, and many of the charms for dealing with faeries are to ward them off. "But why would I do that?" you might ask. "I *love* faeries!" I can only reply that the Irish have perhaps the longest and most intimate connection with the fae, and they advise cautious respect. Such matters are not mere su-

....
12. Adapted from *Carmina Gadelica*, 368.

perstition in the Celtic culture. Faeries are as real as any other folk who cross your threshold. They do not live by human rules of proper behavior, and it's wise to stay in their good graces. Ask Brigid to introduce you to some fae friends and to instruct you in the correct ways to honor and welcome them to your hearth.

One of the most delightful of the Irish wee folk is the Bean-Tighe, the faery housekeeper. The term *bean-a-tighe* means woman of the house, and her otherworldly counterpart helps the mortal *bean-a-tighe* by completing any chores that remain undone at the end of the day. Not every household is lucky enough to have one, but you can increase the likelihood of attracting a Bean-Tighe by leaving some strawberries and cream by the door on a summer's evening. This small, round faery woman with her feather broom will come in and assess the situation to see if she is needed—she is especially likely to help spinsters and crones. If you feel the presence of a Bean-Tighe, be sure to thank her in your devotions. A tiny dish of milk placed by the hearth (and a ripe berry when they are in season) will also be appreciated.

Although the Bean-Tighe is always happy to offer assistance, not every faery is so obliging, and asking for faery help around the house can backfire, as in this tale:

One night after her husband and the rest of the household had gone to bed, a *bean-a-tighe* still sat at her spinning wheel, for she had fallen behind in her woolworking. She sighed and said, "Oh, that someone would come from land or sea, from far or near, to help me with this work!" No sooner had she spoken than there was a knock at the door, and a strange little woman all in green entered and without a word sat down at the spinning wheel. At once there was another knock, and another weird woman came in and began to card the unspun wool. Yet another knock, and another fae woman entered and began to weave the wool. The *bean-a-tighe* was grateful at first, but then another faery entered, and another, and another, until the room was filled with faeries all making a frightful din with their work.

The *bean-a-tighe* knew she must feed them all, out of courtesy for the guest, but no matter how hard she worked to keep the food coming, it was never enough for the faeries, whose appetites kept pace with their labors. The room was filling with spun wool and newmade cloth, more than could ever be used in a year or many years. The *bean-a-tighe* thanked the faeries and begged them to stop, but to no avail. She tried to wake her husband and household, but they were sleeping like stones and could not be moved. In desperation she ran from the house and shouted, "The faery hill is in red flames of fire! Dúnbhuilg is burning!" All the faery women rushed out to see, and as they went they cried:

> *My cheese and butter kegs,*
> *My sons and daughters,*
> *My oatmeal chests,*
> *My comb and wool-cards, thread and distaff,*
> *Cow and fetter, harrows and hoard,*
> *And all the ground bursting,*
> *My hammers and anvil!*
> *Dúnbhuilg is on fire, and if Dúnbhuilg is burnt,*
> *My pleasant occupations and merriments are gone!*

As they fled toward the faery hill, the *bean-a-tighe* ran back inside, bolted the door, and turned everything the faeries had touched upside down to break the spell. When the faeries saw that their home wasn't in danger, they returned and demanded admittance, but their enchantment had been undone. None of the items they had touched would answer their commands, except one little loaf of bread, which eagerly leaped up and made for the door when the faeries spoke to it. But the *bean-a-tighe* was too quick for it and popped it into the bread box, saying, "I made you for the service of the living, not the undying!" The faeries gave up and dispersed with the morning mists.[13]

I love this tale not only for its "sorcerer's apprentice" whimsy, but also because its faeries and humans hold common things as valuable that are under Brigid's care: the children, the cows and their dairy products, the sheep and their wool, the bounty of the land, the tools of metalwork— and most of all, the "pleasant occupations and merriments" of home. Here are a few ways to include the wee folk in your own occupations and merriments:

- When you are at home, play music that was inspired by the faeries. The music of the seventeenth-century Irish harper Turlough O'Carolan is said to actually *be* faery music. The poet Yeats wrote, "Carolan, the last of the Irish bards, slept on a rath [faery hill], and ever after the faery tunes ran in his head." [14] O'Carolan surely knew and was inspired by Brigid—his father was a blacksmith, and even as a child Turlough had an exceptional gift for poetry. His beautiful harp melodies are widely available on CD and online.

- Offerings of any dairy products are always appreciated by the fae, and indeed, if you have a cow (or goat or sheep), the faeries may help themselves directly from the source. Because the fae are so fond of silver, I offer creamy gifts to them in a small silver bowl—it's actually the bottom part of a silver tea strainer set. Find a wee dish that can hold your own offerings and place it by the hearth, at the back door, or near the kitchen stove. It doesn't have to be silver; any material will do other than iron (or iron alloys) or rowan wood. Faeries tend to go a bit crazy for butter; if its theft is a problem in your home, put a pin in the butter and the faeries will leave it alone.

- If you are considering building a new house, make sure that your proposed site hasn't already been claimed by faeries. Lay out a line of small stones aligned with the moonrise, and if the stones are

....

13. Story retold by author and verse taken whole from Campbell, *Waifs and Strays of Celtic Tradition*.

14. Yeats, *Fairy and Folk Tales of the Irish Peasantry*.

undisturbed when you check them in the morning, the faeries have approved your plan. If the stones are in disarray, it's best to find another location, or be prepared to appease your new fae neighbors with gifts for a long time to come! [15]

- As beings who pass between the worlds, faeries love the liminal energies of between-places such as thresholds. If you are already asking for Brigid's blessing at your doorway, add a welcome for her wee folk. Another place where faeries may linger is the garden gate. Leave offerings for the fae there—they particularly like to dance on the top of gateposts. Weave a garland of flowers, grasses, or berry sprays, and crown the gatepost to decorate their dancing space. [16]

By invoking and attending to the faery presence in your home, you will tune into magic that is always there for the taking. Invite their good company in your home, offer shelter and sustenance, and always remember, these are not cute or foolish children. These are immortals, of the tribe of Danu, and they know more about us than we will ever know about them. Speak respectfully of the wee folk, thank them for their help, and look for signs of their comings and goings. You are affirming that you have *faery-faith*, a belief in something beyond what can be fully explained by logic. Envision this faith as a rush of flying golden sparks rising from the steady flame that is Brigid. Follow its faery flight and see where it leads you.

SHRINE AND ALTAR

Your connection to Brigid takes place everywhere, in every moment of every day. But creating (and maintaining) places of worship at home is a particularly powerful and grounding way to stay in touch with her. It's good to have places of your own where you can always return to your sacred center.

I differentiate between shrines and altars. A shrine is a bit more casual. Shrines hold images representing the deity or saint to whom they are dedicated, and devotees leave offerings, light candles, burn incense,

---

15. Evans, *Irish Folk Ways*.
16. Ibid.

and so on. Shrines can be approached by all respectful visitors, whether it's a public shrine or a private home shrine. A shrine dedicated to Brigid is a reminder of her presence in your house. You might have artwork depicting her, crystals and stones that are associated with her energy, a small vessel of water or tabletop fountain to represent her sacred wells, and a flame of some kind. Flowers and other seasonal offerings speak of Brigid's presence throughout the Wheel of the Year.

An altar may hold similar items, but generally speaking, an altar is a place where devotions and rituals are performed, and where you know you can communicate with Brigid because the connection is always active there. It's your hotline to the Goddess. There's something especially powerful about a place in your home where you *only* interact with the Divine. An altar has no other purpose.

For me, one of the hallmarks of an altar is that I am careful what I put on it. At my house, there is a table by the front door that has seasonal items, along with goddess images, cards from friends, and small objects that appeal to me for their beauty and symbolism. I light candles there to welcome guests. But I don't consider it an altar. Why? Because I also toss my keys and purse and mail there. I don't keep the space's energy charged with magical intention, and I am casual about what I add to it. Sometimes, for special occasions, I do turn that table into a temporary altar. But in general, it is simply a table that has some spiritual objects on it, and I make that distinction.

Although I create sacred space throughout my house, I have one altar that functions solely as a place for focused spiritual practice, with no other use. When I come to this altar, no matter what else is going on in my chaotic world, I feel my spirit quieting. Any space that is maintained solely for spiritual pursuits is going to hold that energy, and you can step into it and be surrounded by its power and comfort.

If you already have an altar or shrine to Brigid, at least once a year (Imbolc is a good time) take everything off of it, and clean and bless the space. As you add objects back, touch and bless each one with your full attention. Don't just slap those same old candleholders on the table—honor them, love them, really look at them. Remember where you got them, and what they mean to you, their associations and their symbolism. Do this for each item. Don't add anything automatically or because it's always been there. Sacred items have energy and a life of their own. Ask them—and ask Brigid—if they still belong on your altar, and if so, ask why. Listen for the answer.

If you feel the energy has become stagnant or dull at your altar, try something new—different symbols and objects, more ornate or more simple than you usually use. I have found that the most profoundly powerful altar can be a bare wooden surface and a single candle. In that utter simplicity, nothing will distract you from whatever Brigid wants you to hear.

Altars are very personal, and no one can tell you what you should or should not have on them—except right now, when I'm going to tell you. The one thing I believe every woman should have on her altar is a mirror. We have no problem saying to other women, "You are Goddess," but far too many of us have trouble saying it to ourselves, and we need the practice. Brigid loves you unconditionally, and she will heal any wounds you may have in your own self-image. Make it part of your devotions to gaze into your own eyes. That light shining in their depths is Brigid's flame.

BRIGID IN THE GARDEN

Making sacred space outdoors invites all of nature to join you in your worship. Obviously, one of the best ways to welcome Brigid into your garden is to include some of the plants traditionally associated with her (see page 101). But let your creativity bloom! Perhaps a section of your garden could contain flowers in the colors of fire and with flame-shaped blossoms. Celosia, for example, has flower heads that rise to a point like flames; its name comes from the Greek for "burned." Or try the stunning flame lily—its six flame-shaped petals rise from their base in colors that move from gold to red and seem to flicker upon the breeze. Pay homage to Brigid with a garden aglow with flower-fire!

Water is essential for your garden's well-being, and it is evocative of Brigid's presence as lady of the holy wells. Fountains and ponds are wonderful additions to your garden, but simple birdbaths and bowls invoke her too. You can find ceramic or cast-cement birdbaths that have Celtic designs—listen to your intuition for what feels right for your own garden devotions. Place your chosen vessel in a place where you can sit beside it and gaze into the waters. Shining stones or glass pebbles in the depths enhance the sparkle of sunlight on the surface. In Celtic spirituality, a symbolic well (or hill, or stone, or tree) connects energetically to holy sites—your simple bowl of water becomes one with Brigid's wells at Kildare and Liscannor and everywhere else where her sacred waters run. Here you can ask for healing and offer your prayers for the healing of others. Your blessings are added to the collective blessings offered at sacred sites around the world.

Brigid is a goddess of light and music, and she would love some light-catchers and wind chimes in your outdoor space. Bring in whatever garden elements summon the sacred to your mind and spirit. I have a statue in the center of my garden that the sculptor intended to be Mary, but for me the flowing mantle, the hands outstretched in blessing, and the peaceful gaze all speak of Brigid. Whether you are making sacred space indoors or out, remember to expand your horizons to find sacred items from other faiths and cultures that also work for Brigid. It's a way of forging bridges of understanding, even if no one knows it but you.

A lovely way to use your outdoor space for devotions is with prayer stones, set out in a pattern so you can walk from one to the next. These could be flat stepping stones or larger upright stones. At Solas Bhríde in Kildare, the Brigidine Sisters have created a pilgrimage walk with five such stones. At each of the stones an aspect of Brigid is honored and prayers are offered.

- The first stone: Brigid of the land, Brigid the earth-woman
- The second stone: Brigid the peacemaker
- The third stone: Brigid the hearth-woman, Brigid of hospitality
- The fourth stone: Brigid the healer
- The fifth stone: Brigid the champion of the poor

The Solas Bhríde walk culminates at Brigid's Well. Create your own walk that leads to a place of contemplation in your garden or a circular walk that can be done repeatedly, such as three stones walked three times.

In addition to creating sacred places for Brigid in and around your home, brainstorm on a larger scale too. You can honor Brigid by contributing to (and participating in) tree planting, community gardens, and the preservation of sacred places and archaeological sites.

Gairdín Bhríde: *Brigit's Garden*

JENNY BEALE

Jenny Beale is the founder and director
of Brigit's Garden in the West of Ireland.

———

I had a dream to make a meditation garden in Connemara, one that drew on the wonderful old Celtic wisdom but blended it with contemporary design to make a place that speaks to us in the twenty-first century. The vision was to create a very special and beautiful garden, where people could find peace and tranquility and reconnect with nature. Celtic spirituality and the Brigit tradition are rich in stories and symbolism that connect us to the natural world. For instance, the Celtic seasonal festivals of Samhain, Imbolc, Bealtaine, and Lughnasa not only mark the start of each season and reflect the agricultural year but also symbolise the cycle of life. This cycle can be a powerful tool for reflection as well as a way of finding a deeper level of connection with nature.

I was introduced to Brigit at wonderful weekends celebrating the festival of Brigit in the west of Ireland in the mid-1990s, where women from all walks of life who were into Brigit as saint or goddess came together to share ritual, music, and song, to celebrate and explore the relevance of the Brigit tradition today.

They were rich and inspiring experiences—and once the idea of the garden came to me, it had to be Brigit's Garden.

The Imbolc Garden is all about the stories and symbols of Brigit, but for me personally my favourite parts of the garden are wild areas with old hazel trees and mossy boulders which have a sense of ancient presence and the deep spirit of nature. We always celebrate Brigit's Eve with ritual, making Brigit's crosses and putting out the *Brat Bhríde*, and we also have a family afternoon when people can make crosses and enjoy traditional music. In 2014 we had our first international Brigit gathering with participants from North America and Scandinavia as well as all over Ireland. It was a wonderful and magical weekend. At that weekend we had a keynote address from Brigit scholar Mary Condren, author of *The Serpent and the Goddess: Women, Religion, and Power in Celtic Ireland*, who gave a fascinating talk about how Brigit is present in different forms in each of the Celtic festivals. So in that sense we are celebrating her at Bealtaine, Lughnasa, and Samhain also.

It is very important to me that Brigit's Garden is a not-for-profit project and a recognized charity. It is a resource for the community and a place for everyone, from the very young to the elderly, women and men, and people from all over the world. I hope that everyone who comes experiences some sense of connection—connection with nature, with the Celtic spirit, and with the people who work here and provide the hospitality. We aim to give everyone who comes here a warm personal welcome, and the garden itself is a very welcoming, relaxing place.

The experience of turning the vision of the garden into an actual place was a long and humbling journey, full of what I came to call "Brigit's luck." It was as if the project had a flow of its own, and my job was to tune into it and facilitate what needed to be done. If I imposed too much of my own agenda, things didn't work out so well. If I went with the flow, there were lots of synchronicities, from getting three adjoining pieces

of land with an old ring fort in the middle, to sourcing standing stones and finding the right designer, or getting unexpected
financial help when it was needed. It's still the same today, as Brigit's Garden continues to develop and change. If we keep Brigit
at the centre of what we do, things always work out.

For more about Jenny, see the Contributors appendix.

Brigid in the Kitchen

Brigid, bless the things I create
And the things I did not create:
Honey from the hive,
Milk from the cow,
Salt from the sea.

Providing abundant food has always been one of Brigid's primary concerns. We can see this in the tales of Saint Brigid's food miracles, but it
goes back much further: buried offerings of milk and butter vessels have
been found in the bogs of Ireland and Scotland. We can't know for sure
what these offerings meant to the people who buried them, but their
very presence indicates a connection between the earthly body and the
otherworldly realm—and the goddess who brings the milk and butter.

Remind yourself of Brigid's presence in your kitchen by making a
shrine for her there. Having a shrine in your kitchen may strike you as
too casual or even disrespectful, as the kitchen is often the place where
we display our most lighthearted décor. But remember that Brigid
doesn't demand solemnity in her worship, only love. She is a goddess
who rolls up her sleeves and sets things to rights, and she is a goddess
who loves laughter, music, and feasting. Traditional Celtic faith is practiced in every part of daily life, and nothing is more sacred than food.
Every activity connected to food was blessed and prayed over, from
sowing to reaping to baking to eating. Brigid will get along just fine
with your collection of ceramic pigs.

One of my favorite books is Rumer Godden's *The Kitchen Madonna*, which tells of the creation of a kitchen shrine for a homesick cook. The house just wasn't home to her until the kitchen had a "good place" where the sacred feminine was honored. Where in your own kitchen could you make a good place to honor Brigid? It doesn't take much space to accomplish this—all you need is a reminder that your activities there are worshipful and that what you put into the food you prepare is what you will get out of it. A simple icon (see page 154 for some ideas), a plaque with a favorite prayer, a small shelf where a candle can be lit, a windowsill with a light-catcher that has a Celtic design, a prayer card to Saint Brigid—use your creativity to honor Brigid in the kitchen. Be sure to keep the shrine active by making additions and offerings there from time to time, and set a regular time (perhaps once a month or on the Celtic holidays) to thoroughly clean it.

Your Kitchen Hearth

When our ancestors worshiped Brigid as goddess of the hearth, they only had one hearth in mind. The fire at the center of the home provided physical warmth and social warmth—and, of course, it also cooked their food. Today, whether or not you have a fireplace in your home, you do have a hearth where Brigid is present every day: your stove. It doesn't matter whether your stove is gas or electric—Brigid's warming fire is present in both. This simple ceremony affirms that.

1. Prepare by cleaning your stove until you feel satisfied. I say this because you may or may not wish to completely clean your oven and broiler, but you need to feel good about that decision. Doing any kind of ritual is all about the energy you put into it, and if you are doubting yourself or feeling squirrelly about having done a less thorough job than Brigid wants, you should just wait until a day when you can give it your all.

2. When the stove is clean, place your hands on the stovetop and invite Brigid to bless it:

    Brigid of the hearth flame, Brigid of brightness,
    Brigid of the hearth flame, Brigid of warmth:

Be on this cook place, be on the food,
Be on the spoon that stirs it and on the one who stirs,
This day and every day, this night and every night.

3. Taking your hands off the stove now, light each burner, starting with the lower left and going sunwise (clockwise), then turn on the oven. Keep each unit on low—you're going to be here for a little while and you don't want to bake.

4. Stand before the stove and close your eyes, feeling the heat, letting it warm you just as a hearthfire would. Envision Brigid's fiery presence encompassing you and the heart of your kitchen.

5. Now imagine a stove from a hundred years ago and the women who cooked there. Visualize the lighting of that stove, the work of making food. Then go back another hundred years, and visualize the stove or hearth where food was cooked, the heat, the flame, the pots, the labor, the food gratefully received at the end of a long working day.

6. Keep making jumps back in time, as far as Brigid inspires you to go. At each point in time, see the sacredness of preparing food, the holiness of receiving it.

7. When you've reached what feels like a stopping place in your visualizing, see that oldest cooking place clearly, and envision Brigid there. She has always been present. She is present still. With your eyes still closed, hold your hands up before you, palms toward the heat of your stove, and feel the connection over the ages with all the women who have stood before their stoves and hearths and felt Brigid's presence.

8. Linger as long as you wish. Then turn off the oven and the burners in the same order, beginning with the lower left and moving sunwise (you are not closing down the energy or dispersing it, as you would if you moved in the opposite direction). From now on, whenever you turn on a burner or the oven, envision Brigid as the source of the heat, the fire coming from her hands and heart to yours as you feed yourself and your loved ones.

Any household task can be made more meaningful by thinking back to how our foremothers performed the same task. Brigid's domestic worship has never been interrupted, and this kind of visioning will always invoke her presence in your home.

Brigid's Pantry

There are many foods associated with Brigid, among them blackberries, honey, salmon and other fish, hazelnuts, oatmeal, bacon, beer, and dairy products. Books often say that such-and-such is sacred to Brigid, but they don't often say *why*. Some connections are obvious, such as milk and butter for she who protects the cattle. There are dozens of food-related tales of Saint Brigid, such as the time she wished for honey and magical bees suddenly appeared to fulfill her wish. (They appeared under the floorboards, by the way, so it's also a cautionary tale about being specific with your wishes.) But in many cases we need to use our intuition to discern why a food is Brigid's. Oats, for example, are symbolic of fertility in many traditions, but Brigid really isn't a fertility goddess as such—at least, not for humans! What she is, though, is a goddess of *nourishment*. She ensures that her people have good food and plenty of it, and therefore she blesses the humble pot of porridge simmering over her hearthfire.

Enjoying her favorite foods is another way of welcoming Brigid into your home. Here are a few you may want to try.

A Bit o' Blessed Butter

One of my earliest memories is my kindergarten teacher showing the class how to make butter from scratch. My memory is that it was the very first day of school, and if so, I salute that teacher for handing a lot of strange five-year-olds baby-food jars filled with cream. In any case, what I do remember clearly is the taste of that butter. My mother was a margarine girl, so this was probably my first experience of the real thing. Spread on a saltine cracker, the fresh new butter was the best thing I had ever eaten. Brigid was undoubtedly smiling on me.

Brigid is the provider of all dairy products, but butter may just be her favorite. Remember how Saint Brigid did that trick with the magical never-ending butter when her domestic powers were doubted? In the traditional Celtic household, the *bean-a-tighe* (woman of the house) was always in charge of butter-making, an important domestic art. When a bride entered her new home for the first time, her mother-in-law presented her with the fire tongs, as mistress of the hearth, and the churn-dash, as mistress of the butter. Brigid, mistress of both, was present in these gifts.

Fire and butter-making seem an unlikely pairing, but charms to help the churning included keeping the tongs in the fire and not taking any fire or ashes out of the house until the butter was successfully finished. The churn itself was protected from faery enchantment by a pattern of iron nails or a branch of rowan bound around it. Yet sometimes no matter how diligently she churned, the *bean-a-tighe* just could not make the butter come, perhaps because the disgruntled house faeries had not been given their share. Then Brigid was called upon in a charm repeated while churning:

> *Come, thou Brigid, goddess calm,*
> *Hasten the butter on the cream,*
> *Thou who bless my hearth and home,*
> *From humble floor to high roof beam:*
> *Come, ye rich lumps, come!*
> *Thou who put light in moon and sun,*
> *Thou who put fish in stream and sea,*
> *Thou who put food in flock and herd,*
> *Send sweet butter now to me!* [17]

Making fresh butter offers you two opportunities to honor Brigid: in the making and in the eating. Small hand-cranked or electric butter churns are available for sale if you want to make this a regular ritual, and you can also easily make butter using a mixer or food processor (search online for instructions). But you can make a small batch using nothing more than a jar, a strainer, and strong wrists.

....
17. Adapted from *Carmina Gadelica*.

You will need:
1 cup heavy cream, preferably organic
Salt (optional, add when the butter-making is finished)
A lidded jar (2-cup capacity or larger)
A fine colander or strainer

Pour the cream into the jar and let it stand until it reaches room temperature (don't rush; this could take 2–4 hours). When you are ready to begin, invoke Brigid to bless your task, then shake the jar. And shake it. And shake some more! The process time can vary; butter comes when it is ready, as any *bean-a-tighe* could tell you. Be sure to chant the charm, and promise to give your house faeries some when you're done.

The cream will go through stages of thickening and then separating into butter and buttermilk. When you see a thinner liquid start to pull away from the solids, carefully pour it off, using the strainer to catch any of the rich lumps you've been chanting for. Shake again until the butter has fully come and you don't see any more change happening. Pour off all remaining buttermilk and transfer your butter to a bowl. Gently add ice-cold water to wash the butter, and strain it again. Do this two or three times until the buttermilk is all washed away and the water runs clear. (You can skip this step if you're going to eat it right away.) One cup of cream yields half a cup of butter. Gaze proudly upon your creamy creation, and give thanks to Brigid for all her delicious gifts!

Anraith Prátaí do Bríd: Potato Soup for Brigid

The ancient Celts didn't have the potato—it was introduced in Ireland from the New World around the sixteenth century. But once established there, it became the primary foodstuff for country folk. It grew prolifically even in poor soil, and a small potato patch could feed a family enough to survive on. So dependent were they on potatoes for survival that when the Great Blight in 1845–52 wiped out most of the potato crops in Ireland, more than a million people died of starvation and disease, and several million desperately emigrated to America and other places. Surely their prayers to Brigid wrung her heart during those terrible times.

In our own time, many of us are blessed with an abundance of food and need not fear starvation. But this simple soup, made with some of Brigid's favorite ingredients, reminds us of how little we really need to be content and comfortable. It's a great soup to include in a soup supper, where friends each bring a different soup, thus multiplying the blessings of sustenance, hospitality, and love. Brigid would definitely approve.

You will need:

4 tablespoons butter

3 large leeks, washed and sliced, white part only (a little green is fine)

3 or 4 medium Yukon Gold potatoes, peeled and cubed

1 quart chicken broth (water or vegetable broth can be used instead)

½ cup half-and-half

6 slices lean bacon, cooked until crisp and crumbled (optional)

Fresh chives, finely chopped or snipped

Salt and pepper

1. Melt the butter in a soup pot over medium-low heat. Add the leeks and cook until they start to soften. Keep an eye on them and stir often. You don't want the leeks or the butter to brown.

2. Add the potatoes and the broth or water. Turn the heat up and bring to a simmer. Cook until the potatoes are soft and start to fall apart.

3. Using a potato masher or just a fork, mash some of the potatoes to thicken the soup. If you prefer it completely smooth, you can puree the whole thing. I like some lovely potato lumps in mine.

4. Add the half-and-half. Half a cup is just a suggestion—add it until the soup is the consistency you want. Add the bacon (if desired) and chives. Simmer until the soup is hot again, then season with salt and pepper to taste.

This soup is similar in spirit to colcannon, a popular Irish dish eaten at Samhain, which is made with mashed potatoes, cabbage or kale, leeks or scallions, milk and butter, and sometimes bacon. Because Brigid is a practical goddess, she wants you to adapt this humble country soup to suit what you have on hand. If you don't have Yukon Gold potatoes, use regular potatoes and increase the butter a bit to make the flavor richer. If you don't have leeks, use onions or scallions. If you don't have half-and-half, use cream or milk—you get the idea. Receive the simple gifts of the land with gratitude and use them with love.

BRIDEY'S BRAMBLY CRUMBLE

This is a sweet summertime treat with a relaxed attitude and flexible measurements. It uses three foods sacred to Brigid: oats, butter, and blackberries. Blackberry, with its brambles and its rampant growth, symbolizes the tenacity and endurance of Brigid—she who held the hearts of the people through centuries of changes with her strong sweetness intact.[18]

You will need:
Blackberries
White sugar (optional)
Flour (can be omitted for a gluten-free crumble)
Cinnamon (optional)
Old-fashioned rolled oats
Brown sugar
Butter, softened
A shallow baking dish and a mixing bowl

You'll notice I haven't given specific measurements for the ingredients. This is a true *bean-a-tighe* recipe, making use of what's at hand and using the common sense Brigid gave you. Here are the steps:

1. Preheat your oven to 350°F.
2. Pick over your blackberries for bits of leaf or anything else you don't want in your dessert. *Do not wash the berries!* Washing makes berries mushy and waterlogged.

---

18. An interesting Irish legend about blackberries is that you should not eat any that were picked after Samhain because the Púca—a shapeshifting faery—despoils them as he passes. There aren't many berries left by then, so it may be moot, but I thought I should warn you nonetheless!

3. Put your berries in the baking dish. The amount of berries you have will determine what size baking dish you need. What you want is a layer of berries about 2 inches deep.

4. Sprinkle a bit of white sugar over your blackberries and about a tablespoon of flour. Add a dash or two of cinnamon if you wish. Gently mix with your hands. You can skip this step if your berries are sweet enough for you and if you don't want to use flour.

5. In the bowl, mix a measure of oats with half a measure of sugar and a quarter measure of flour. For example: 1 cup oats + ½ cup brown sugar + ¼ cup flour. Don't feel you need to get out the measuring cups for this—the recipe is very forgiving, and you can approximate everything and always end up with deliciousness.

6. Using your hands, gradually add softened butter to this mixture until the dry ingredients feel well incorporated. Again, the amount will vary, but if you use 1 cup of oats, it will be about 1 stick (½ cup) of butter. More butter is always good! Distribute the crumble topping over the berries.

7. Bake for about 30 minutes, until the berries are bubbling and the topping is golden. Baking time will vary depending on how big your dish is, so keep an eye on it.

8. Let the finished crumble rest for at least 20 minutes. The blackberry filling will thicken slightly during this time and make it all the more delectable. You can use the time to whip some cream to accompany it!

Brigid's Brew

Brigid is associated with beer through her clan, the Tuatha Dé Danann, among whose gifts to humankind was ale of such sublime quality that to drink it was to achieve immortality. Saint Brigid's tales overflow with ale—literally—as she transformed well water and her own bathwater into beer, and on at least one occasion magically created enough for seventeen churches' celebrations out of ingredients that should barely have made one household's ration. She was also known for withholding beer from those whose greed and selfishness displeased her. She would change water into beer for the poor, and beer into plain water for the high and mighty who refused to care for them.

This hot brew for Brigid honors her as goddess of the hearth. The stout takes on a smooth, burnt-caramel flavor.

You will need:
Guinness stout or some other stout/porter you enjoy (look for seasonal treats like pumpkin stout)
A sturdy mug that can tolerate a very hot beverage
A fireplace with a good fire going
A clean iron poker

1. Pour your stout into the mug, leaving an inch or more at the top. Place the mug on a plate or pan in case of overflow.

2. Heat the tip of the poker in the heart of the fire until it is red-hot, then plunge it into the stout.

3. Iron + Fire + Beer = Brigid! Add an Irish drinking song to make the magic complete.

————

Make an effort to cook something every day, no matter how busy you are. This is the most basic fire magic, ancient and powerful. The act of preparing and consuming food invokes fire twice: once when you cook it and again when your body transforms it into energy. Many people eat their meals away from home most of the time or grab something on the run. Even making a cup of tea or a piece of toast affirms your power to control and move energy in a fiery way, and it honors Brigid as the source of that power. This creative energy ignites other dim corners of your spirit as well.

THIS DAY AND EVERY DAY

Celtic prayers and blessings often include the phrase "this day and every day, this night and every night." I love this way of expanding the sacred present moment into all the moments to come. All the activities and experiences of the day, all the mysteries and magic of the night, are under the care of Brigid. This is a truth that is never-changing. What changes is our perception, which wavers and flickers like a flame in the wind.

Living a spiritual and magical life comes down to two simple and profound elements: attention and intention. If you pour yourself a cup of coffee while reading your email and drink it without really tasting it, it will still warm you and give you a lift. If you take a moment to appreciate the beauty of the cup, the scent of the coffee, the pattern of the waft of steam arising from the surface, and the sensation of the liquid as it moves down your throat and becomes part of your body, you are moving in the direction of devotion. Whether you say the words or not, you are making your prayer: *Thank you, Brigid, for the blessings of pure water and fire to heat it and the knowledge of your presence. Thank you, Goddess, for this quiet moment.*

Now add intention to your attention. Your mundane intention is probably to wake up a bit through the judicious use of caffeine, but you can add a higher intention. Invoke Brigid's presence as you drink your brew and ask that it awaken your creativity, inspire you with eloquence, or help you focus on the day's tasks ahead. You can do this with any and all undertakings of an average (or exceptional!) day. Ask Brigid to help you sanctify tasks that can be humdrum at best and tedious at worst. As an example, let's clean your house!

Brigid's Broom: Mindful Housecleaning

Begin by focusing your attention and intention as you gather your cleaning tools. The broom, the feather duster, the sponge, the vacuum cleaner—your intention flows from your heart and mind, through your arms and hands, through the tool, and into your home, making it sacred space where Brigid dwells. Engage your senses. Do you like the scent of your cleansers? Are you comfortable with their impact on the environment? What about the color of your sponges? What can that symbolize for you—the rosy pink of happiness, the green of healing, the white of purification? Dedicate your intention to make your cleaning activities purposeful on a spiritual level as well as a practical level.

When you put your full attention and intention on the tasks of cleaning and washing, you are charging those acts with your devotion.

The Celtic belief in everyday magic can be powerfully present within the walls of your home. Like the act of "programming" a crystal or empowering a ceremonial tool, you can charge the armchair to hold you close with love, the plate to bless your food with healing, the rug to energize you as you walk upon it. This may sound a bit Disney-esque, but why not? If it makes your life richer to believe your teapot loves you back, do it!

Begin at your front door. Wash the woodwork, polish the doorknobs, sweep the threshold. Renew and refresh any blessing and welcoming items you may have here at the passage from one realm to the next. Wash all the doors in the house in the same focused way. Meditate as you do so on the sacred nature of doors and thresholds, and Brigid's powers there: opening, enclosing, welcoming, protecting.

Now move to your windows. In cleaning them, give thanks for vision, for clarity, for perspective, for freedom. Give thanks for the view from the window, whatever it is. Think of those who are imprisoned and have no view, and remember that Brigid comforts the oppressed. Find something to love, some lesson, in each picture framed within each of your windows.

As you continue to move through your rooms—tidying, organizing, discarding, preserving—hold the intention that you are claiming every element of your home as sacred. Not just the candles and the icons but also the cutting board and the computer screen. What miracles of nourishment and connection are wrought through these tools! Feel the warm embrace of Brigid's cloak in cotton sheets just out of the dryer, crackling with fiery sparks of energy and folded with blessed intent. Those sheets will foster deep dreaming.

Can you see how this is sacred work? What a blessing to have a home to clean! What bliss, what incredible luck to have a bed to make cozy and welcoming, a kitchen that can get messy with the glorious chaos of preparing a feast. This is Brigid working through you to brighten every task with joy and with gratitude for your prosperity.

THIS NIGHT AND EVERY NIGHT

Every Celt knows that nighttime is when spirits and supernatural beings are abroad. This world and the Otherworld occupy the same space, and we coexist peacefully with these (mostly) unseen ones as long as we maintain a respectful awareness of the proper rules of conduct. Country Celts stayed inside at night, or if they did go out, they didn't go alone. In our modern world, we think we have conquered the night, but its mysteries and powers remain fully intact. We are not so far removed from our ancestors, after all.

The ancient Celts invoked Brigid's protection against demons. Today when we speak of demons we are usually talking about the ones on the inside—demons of doubt, guilt, fear. We invoke Brigid for all manner of protection, but sometimes we just need her to dispel our demons. Worries about money, health, aging, and other basic survival issues can create an overall feeling of being ill at ease. Or your fear may not be even that defined, but just an underlying anxiousness. Women in particular are very good at taking an emotion and finding many reasons why it's valid—there's always *something* to worry about! It can be hard to see a way toward solutions when fear has you in its grip, and the darkness can bring a sense of vulnerability to those demons.

Shutting out the night from any dangerous intrusion falls under Brigid's purview. Many traditional prayers and charms deal specifically with the night hours, and blessings for protection abound.

Be the encompassing of Brigid around me
From every spectre, from every evil,
From every shade that is coming harmfully
In darkness, in power to hurt.
Be the encompassing of the strength of Brigid
Shielding me from every harm,
Be keeping me from everything ruinous
Coming destructively toward me this night.[19]

....
19. Adapted from *Carmina Gadelica*.

The otherworldly beings are often named in detail, as if avoiding any loophole that might let some bold ghoulie or ghostie or long-leggedy beastie slip in. If you want to be specific, here are some you want to avoid on the road at night and definitely do not want wandering through your home uninvited:

> *Be the encompassing of Brigid around me*
> *From every firbolg and Formorian,*
> *From all ballybogs and buachailleens,*
> *From howlers and the Hag of the Dribble,*
> *From púca and from Fin Bheara,*
> *King of the Faery Dead.*

A simple ritual of night shielding is to turn off the lights, light a candle, and carry it from window to window, seeing the flame in the dark mirror of the glass. This is Brigid's protection shining bright. Now that what's supposed to be inside is in and what's supposed to stay outside is out, it's bedtime!

Smooring the Fire

In olden times, when the fire at the center of a home was essential for cooking as well as life-sustaining warmth, the hearth would be banked with coals and covered over with fine ash before the household went to bed. This ensured that it would smolder through the night and not need to be restarted from nothing in the morning. A quick stirring of last night's coals would provide a start for the peat or kindling of the new day's fire. This act of putting the hearth to bed is called *smooring*.

Most of us don't depend on fire for cooking or heat on a daily basis, but smooring serves a ceremonial function. It invokes Brigid's blessing on your home and those who dwell within, entrusting their well-being and sustenance to her care. Performing a smooring at the end of the day connects you to all your foremothers at their hearthfires. It can be part of your bedtime devotions or an offering of gratefulness after the evening meal as you turn off the oven and stove and finish cooking for the day. Here is a traditional prayer:

> *I will smoor the hearth*
> *As Brigid herself would smoor.*
> *In the name of Brigid:*
> *Be on the hearth,*
> *Be on the herd,*
> *Be on the household all.*[20]

As I recite this prayer, I reach out to feel the presence of Brigid, to connect with the words and understand what it means to smoor "as Brigid herself would smoor"—with love, with intention, with strength. With the words "be on the hearth," I spread my arms wide as I envision her blessing flowing around my home in a protective encircling, Brigid wrapping her cloak around my house and all that is within. The "herd" is just one small cat, but he receives Brigid's blessing all the same, and then I extend that blessing to all animals, especially the neighborhood feral cats. I live alone, so the "household all" is me and any friends I welcome into my home. When the prayer is complete, my inner hearth of devotion has been banked and protected against the darkness and the cold. Smooring affirms that the eternal fire endures even when tangible flames are extinguished.

....

20. Adapted from *Carmina Gadelica*, 323.

CHAPTER THREE

TEMPLE:
THE DEVOTIONAL FLAME

Threefold wisdom of Brigid's oak:
Leaf-wisdom of change, ever releasing,
Branch-wisdom of growth, ever reaching,
Root-wisdom of endurance, ever deepening.

The path you follow is well worn. Back through the mists of time, a thousand years, a thousand more, the voices of women can be heard raised in chants to Brigid. Follow the sound down to the center, the heart of spiritual power. Here is where the flame of devotion is tended, whether it burns in an oak grove, a stone circle, a monastery, a village square, or upon a simple home altar. This is the place of lore, where the devotee comes to learn more about her goddess. Come, enter the temple. Brigid awaits you.

BRIGID AND THE POWER OF THREE

Three is a sacred number that appears everywhere in Celtic lore. The world is made up of earth, sea, and sky. In epic tales, people are often described with three names that signify three characteristics that make up the whole person: *Fionn, confounder of giants; Fionn of the bright spear; Fionn the quick-witted.* Celtic deities often appear in threes, and invocations and prayers are chanted in a rhythm of three. Breaking out of the rigid structure of dualism, three moves you into the realm of free choice: this thing, that thing, or another thing. In the Celtic view, doing things in threes intensifies an action and completes a cycle or a set. Three is the number of ultimate empowerment.

The Triple Brigid

Like many other Celtic deities, Brigid is known by three aspects, and there are several ways of looking at this. (Celtic spirituality is never simple!) Early observers of the Celts said they worshiped three goddess sisters, each named Brigid. One was associated with healing, one with smithcraft, and one with poetry. These are attributes we associate with Brigid today, though we may not always see her as three individual sisters.

It is a Mystery, in the sacred sense of the word, to comprehend a goddess as having three aspects. Brigid is a triune goddess—one as well as three—just as we are one person made of body, mind, and spirit.

> *Three folds in my garment, yet only one garment I wear,*
> *Three leaves in a shamrock, yet only one shamrock I bear,*
> *Frost, ice, and snow, these three are only pure water,*
> *Three women in Brigid, yet only one goddess is there.*[21]

The modern Pagan concept of the Triple Goddess as Maiden–Mother–Crone may not have been known to the ancient Celts. Their triple deities were more likely to have equality of stature and roles, such as three mothers or three sisters. Nevertheless, Brigid as Triple Goddess can be associated with her traditional attributes as goddess of poetry, healing, and smithcraft:

- Brigid as Maiden is the poet's muse, the flash of inspiration, the "glimmering girl," as the poet Yeats says—she who is forever sought but never contained or commanded.

- Brigid as Mother is mistress of healing lore and the loving touch, the nurturing goddess who draws you close to the hearthfire and asks what ails you.

....

21. Adapted from traditional Irish verse, author unknown.

- Brigid as Crone hammers the soul's metal into shape with un-flinching strength and a sense of time passing, drawing you ever closer to the raging fires of transformation and rebirth.

Even Saint Brigid can be seen as three-in-one. She is the Maiden who chose her own vocation, defying convention to embrace independence and her true calling. She is the Mother who fed the hungry, healed the suffering, and guided her nun daughters (and monk sons) toward their own fulfillment through sacred service. And she is the Crone who talked back to power, stood her ground against injustice, and trusted her own wisdom for guidance.

The Three who are over me,
The Three who are below me,
The Three who are above me here,
The Three who are above me yonder;
The Three who are in the earth,
The Three who are in the air,
The Three who are in the heavens,
The Three who are in the great pouring sea.[22]

Triskele and Triquetra

Two symbols of the number three are especially significant in Celtic spirituality. Both of these symbols are particularly evocative of Brigid.

The triskele comes in many variations, but always with three spirals around a connecting center. This is the number three as the activator,

....
22. *Carmina Gadelica*, 245.

the initiator of energy. The three spirals rotate together, linked by their common center, and yet each has its individual movement too, spiraling outward and inward, inward and outward. This is Brigid as the triune goddess with her three realms of influence: poetry, healing, and smithcraft. Each is active on its own while blessing and sustaining the whole. Everything is in motion, changing, growing, experiencing the cycles of life.

Tracing the triskele with your finger is a meditation similar to working with a tabletop labyrinth.

1. Print out a full-page version of the pattern (which can be easily found online) or draw one yourself.

2. Laying it on a table before you, start at the center and trace upward around the top spiral to its center, then out again.

3. Move down to the left spiral. Trace into its center and out again.

4. Go to the spiral on the right and do the same thing, and then back to the center and upward, repeating the whole pattern.

Feel the rhythm of Brigid's great spiral dance with your whole being. Listen for her wisdom as you move along her cosmic paths.

The triquetra is a triple knot design, sometimes with a circle linked through the knots. It is also called the trinity knot and has been adopted as a symbol of Celtic Christianity as well as Celtic-based Paganism. The triquetra symbolizes Brigid as three-in-one, and I also see this knot as representing the triple flame: hearth, temple, and forge. The design still implies movement, like the triskele, but there is stability here too. The serene strength of the triquetra symbolizes the eternal quality of Brigid's perpetual fire. Through all the changes the centuries have wrought, her flame could not be extinguished—and never will be.

"Dryad: Spirit of the Oak" by Jen Delyth

Intertwining Connection of All Things
JEN DELYTH

Artist Jen Delyth creates paintings and illustrations that explore the language of myth and symbol inspired by Celtic folklore and the spirit within nature.

———

Celtic knotwork art uses a two-dimensional form to talk about a three-dimensional experience. The spirit is what moves within the lines; the energy is created among them. Although we will never truly know what the ancient artists intended, it seems to me that the language of Celtic design patterning, the eternal interlace and spiraling motifs, express the intertwining connection of all things. The key patterns represent our human journey from birth to death and round again. The triple spiral patterns represent the energy and rhythm of life, as do the interlace designs moving to the center and out again, with no beginning and no end. For me it is this creativity and rhythm, the power of the symbols beneath the work, that is most important.

I am an artist and I'm married to a poet, and Brighid is our patron. I love that she is both midwife and mistress of the forge. I see her as a guardian of the fire of inspiration. The womb is the foundry of new life, forged from the elements with fire—sexual fire, the fire of love, and of our life blood, which I visualize as a green fire of life. This esoteric fire is also the source of inspiration of the poets and artists, the musicians. We channel the creative energies through our process to birth and forge our work.

The Celtic tradition expresses a wealth of wisdom and understanding of the natural world of plants and animals, and also the inner world of active imagination and our psyche. Our ancestors' world was not the wounded, complicated world we now live in. That is not to say that the world of the ancients was a simple paradise. It was often a difficult struggle to survive, and there was much war and bloodshed, as today. We are people of the twenty-first century—I am not advocating a return to the past—but with all our sophistication, we have often created a tangled and disintegrated relationship with ourselves and our environment. Working with the patterns, sacred images, and myths of the ancient Celts renews my connection between the past and the present, the inside and outside, the seen and the unseen—life in all its mystery and interconnectedness, expressed through art and story.

For more about Jen, see the Contributors appendix.

BRIGID'S SISTERS

One of the wonderful things about practicing a Goddess-based spirituality is that she doesn't demand monogamy—or, I should say, monotheism. Ours is not a jealous deity but an embracing one, with 10,000 aspects of powerful female divinity. Exploring these aspects allows you to connect to your own cultural roots as well as those that speak to you for reasons that remain a mystery—perhaps a past life, or perhaps just a need your soul has on its journey in this lifetime. The many goddesses provide doorways to understanding yourself, the world, and the cosmos.

Just as women support each other as sisters, Brigid too has sisters among the goddesses—some by traditional associations and some by affinities of purpose. Invoking them in your vision journeys, rituals, and devotional practice can lead to new revelations about Brigid herself and about your connection with her.

Brigid's Celtic Kin

The Celtic pantheon is rich with powerful aspects of the Goddess. Some of them seem to overlap, and there is confusion in some of their personas, names, and associations. Others, like Brigid, stand unique and unmistakable in their attributes. Other than her triple aspect, there doesn't seem to be much traditional connection between the lore of Brigid and that of any other Celtic goddess, except that they were all Tuatha Dé Danann, children of the goddess Danu. But then again, few Celtic myths have *any* of the deities interacting much (unlike, say, Greek myths). That is simply not the focus of their legends or the way of their telling. Nevertheless, I feel sure that these goddesses know each other, support each other, and share power. They are part of Brigid's world.

THE MÓRRÍGAN

The Mórrígan is a battle goddess, fierce and uncompromising, whose emblem is the night-black crow of death. But she is also a fertility goddess and a goddess of passionate sexuality. On Samhain, the Dagda (Brigid's father) and the Mórrígan lay together in a ritual coupling that ensured the protection of the land and its people. As some sources say that Brigid was born in the seventh month, perhaps she is the fruit of this union, and the Mórrígan is her mother. Not everyone agrees with this (remember those six opinions?), but it makes sense to me. A fire goddess could be conceived at a fire festival from two such fiery deities, and if she was born at the end of the seventh month, that could make her birthday on Lughnasadh, another fire festival (July 31; Celtic holidays begin at sunset).

Another clue that the Mórrígan is Brigid's mother is the legend that the newborn Saint Brigid refused all milk but that of a red-eared white cow. The Mórrígan kept a herd of such faery cattle and shapeshifted into one herself from time to time. Perhaps the story of the infant saint originated with the story of the infant goddess being nursed by her divine mother in the shape of an otherworldly cow. The Mórrígan is also connected with bards and the power of sound and words; in particular, she is the inspirer of war cries and battle songs—all attributes of Brigid. Did the young goddess learn to love poetry at her mother's knee?

The Mórrígan (whose name means "phantom queen") is a triple goddess, like Brigid. In her case, the triad is made up of three distinct goddesses: the Mórrígan, Badb, and Nemhain, all war goddesses. Going with the idea of the Mórrígan as Brigid's mother, let's get to know her aunts.

Badb and Nemhain

Badb (her name means "scald crow") is the most fearsome of the three. A shapeshifter like her sisters, she appears most frequently as a shrieking crow over the battlefield but is also seen as a bear, a wolf, a cow, or a deathly hag who foretells the warriors' doom. Sometimes she wanders along the edges of the battle, ragged robes trailing, her long grey hair blowing in the wind, screaming her prophecies. Or she can be found at the side of a stream, washing bloody linen and weapons in the clear water until it runs red—those who encounter her there are the next to die. This is Badb in her guise as the Washer at the Ford, an aspect of the Bean-Sidhe (Banshee).

Nemhain is the embodiment of her name: "battle frenzy." Appearing (like her sisters) as a huge crow or raven, her harsh cries incite warriors to panic, resulting in chaos, confusion, and widespread death. Little else is known of her. Unlike the Mórrígan, who is known to take sides in a war—though she sometimes changes her mind later—Nemhain is possessed of simple bloodlust, flying among the warriors and indiscriminately urging them to slaughter.

Since Brigid is such a peace-loving goddess, how could these furies be related to her? Perhaps it is that very difference that provides the answer—great destruction must be balanced by great creation. But Brigid herself knows war. Her sword and shield have seen battle, and she is invoked (as goddess and as saint) for victory in righteous causes. She may not be bloodthirsty like some of her kin, but she does not flee from the good fight.

Now, like almost everything in Celtic mythology, there are arguments about who is who and what is what. Some sources say that "the Mórrígan" is a title rather than a name of an individual goddess, and that it encompasses three goddesses: Badb, Nemhain, and Macha. Others say that Macha is separate, and the triad is made up of the Mórrígan, Badb, and Nemhain. Some say that the Bean-Sidhe is the Mórrígan, others say that she is Badb, and still others maintain that she is a unique entity with no other associations. Brigid has a connection with the Bean-Sidhe through the practice of keening (see page 213). As always, the intricate knotwork of Celtic lore provides endless opportunities for exploration and conjecture. What matters is how the Goddess speaks to *you* and how she influences your life today.

Ériu, Fódla, and Banba

Another triad of sister goddesses, these three embody the spirit of the land of Ireland itself. When the first human settlers arrived in Ireland, they battled with the Tuatha Dé Danann, who had ruled for thousands of years. The Tuatha, wise and full of foresight, saw that their destiny lay along other paths, and chose to yield the middle-world to humans and remove themselves into otherworldly realms, becoming known as the *Sidhe*—the faery folk. The humans' leader, Amairgin, then met with the three goddesses of the land, Ériu, Fódla, and Banba, each of whom demanded that he name the land after her in exchange for her continued blessing of prosperity and happiness. Amairgin chose to swear to Ériu, whose magnificent presence at the very center of Ireland could not be denied. He promised that forever after the land would be called after her, and so it is: Éire is the Irish name for Ireland.

Ériu has an obvious association with Brigid in that she is an embodiment of the sacred land itself and a protector of its welfare. But what of Fódla and Banba? They too are guardians of the land, still invoked as poetic names for the spirit of Ireland. Little is known of Fódla's lore, but Banba shares some additional symbols with Brigid—the hazelnut of wisdom, the salmon of knowledge, and the pig of prosperity.

Sul

When the Romans conquered the British Isles, one of the sacred sites they came upon was a shrine dedicated to the goddess Sul at a natural hot springs in what is now the city of Bath in southwest England. They built a temple and then a magnificent bath complex there, *Aquae Sulis*, which became hugely popular among people seeking healing in the miraculous steaming waters. The Romans equated Sul with Minerva, whom they also equated with Brigid. The connection seems clear. Both Sul and Brigid were known to have schools of priestesses who tended a perpetual flame, Brigid's at Kildare and Sul's at the hot springs. Both are associated with the sun and with the magical combination of fire and water that brings healing. Both are goddesses who have endured over millennia, through invasions and conquerors and new religions. The timeless waters continue to flow at Bath, and the name of Sul is still spoken there, every day.

Bóand

This Irish goddess, named for the otherworldly white cow, has much in common with Brigid. The River Boyne, named for her, was formed when Bóand lifted the stone that covered a forbidden well and released its waters. The well water was said to confer wisdom on any who drank from it, and now the water rushed through the countryside rather than being contained. How many such tales of women's rebellion against restriction have we heard over the millennia? From Eve onward, the feminine soul has thirsted for free-flowing knowledge. Bóand and Brigid both offer inspiration as well as wisdom—drinking from the Boyne in June is said to confer the gifts of seership and poetry.

Bóand is the goddess of Newgrange, *Brú na Bóinne* (palace of Bóand), a sacred site that some have also associated with Brigid in an ancient pre-Celtic aspect. The triple spirals and snake motifs on the walls of Newgrange, and its association with the mystery of light reborn in the depths of darkness, all speak of Brigid as well as Bóand. A familial connection is made through Brigid's father, the Dagda, with whom Bóand bore a son, Aengus Óg. This half-brother of Brigid was the Tuatha Dé Danann's god of poetry, and he was always accompanied by four white swans, Brigid's bird.

DEAE MATRES

Little is known of this Triple Goddess, yet the Deae Matres (Divine Mothers) or Matronae must surely be included among Brigid's kin. Hundreds of sculptures of these three mother goddesses have been found throughout the Celtic world, though they are most associated with Britain. The three sacred figures hold baskets or cornucopias with fruit or flowers, and other items that might be bread or votive offerings, and sometimes one of them holds a child. Their faces are strong and serene, their feet are firmly planted, and there is a sense of equality among them, even when one is standing while the other two sit. We can only speculate what the Matronae meant to those who worshiped them—reverence for motherhood, gratefulness for the abundance of the earth, respect for ancestral foremothers. Because the Celts considered the number three to amplify the energy and meaning of a symbol, the Matronae are the power of the Goddess times three.

SHEELA NA GIG

This fascinating goddess is depicted as a squat, often grinning, naked female figure holding open her vagina with her hands. Her carved image appears on churches and other buildings in Ireland and England, sometimes tucked away in a secret spot and sometimes boldly over the door. The origin of these sculptures isn't known and is (as ever) the source of much argument. Because some of the Sheelas are made of materials different from the buildings themselves, some scholars think they were brought there by devotees of the Goddess and placed as protest or as additional protection, bringing the old ways into the new. Sometimes the Sheela figures have full breasts and seem to be an image of fertility. Other versions are skeletal, with aged breasts and a lined or tattooed face. Her eyes are often huge, exaggerated, as is her yoni. Sheela na Gig is confrontational, demanding attention, commanding acknowledgment. Does she want to tell us about life, or death, or both?

I include Sheela na Gig among Brigid's Celtic kin for a couple of reasons. First, like Brigid, she is a connection between ancient beliefs and Christianity. Someone who loved her placed her image on the brick-and-mortar body of the Church itself, and there she remains. There are more than 150 known Sheela carvings, each declaring that the great mystery of the sacred feminine survives despite centuries of patriarchy. Brigid and Sheela also share the imagery of the threshold, the gates of birth and rebirth. The open vagina of the Sheela na Gig is spread wide not as an incitement to lust, but as a symbol of life passing through. Brigid is the midwife catching that new life as it emerges.

The Cailleach

Perhaps the oldest of the goddesses we think of as Celtic, the Cailleach was already present when the first Celts arrived in the Western Isles, and indeed may have been known for more than seven thousand years before the Celts came. Like Brigid, the Cailleach has several names (among them Cailleach Bheur, Black Annis, Bronach, Cally Berry, Carlin, and Caillech Bhear), attesting to her widespread influence, and her roles vary from region to region. She is known as the goddess of the abundant harvest, or as a protector of wild creatures (with her companion, a monstrous cat), or as a shapeshifting woman who bestows blessings of sovereignty on rightful kings.

But her most powerful role is as the great hag of winter, who tucks the natural world in for its long sleep until Brigid wakes it in the spring. She and Brigid are the seasons' tag team—the Cailleach carries a black staff that she bangs upon the earth, freezing it; at the turn of the year, she hands the staff over to Brigid, and in her warming hands it becomes a white branch budding with new life. The Cailleach then turns to stone, awaiting the turning of the Wheel of the Year when she will again take up her duties.

For people who lived close to the land and depended on it for life itself, the coming of winter was fraught with dread. The frightful appearance of the Cailleach, with her blue skin, her single piercing eye, and her red teeth, expressed just how terrible those frozen months could be. The Celtic deities aren't always pretty—indeed, pretty is pretty rare. As Thomas Cahill writes, "It would be an understatement to assert that the Irish gods were not the friendliest of figures. Actually, there are few idols that we have retrieved from barrow or bog that would not give a child nightmares and an adult the willies." [23] But although the Cailleach was feared, the fear was threaded through with respect. None of her myths tell of her harming humans or acting upon them with wrath. The Cailleach is awful—awe-full—and she is a necessary part of the cycle of life and death. Without the harshness of the Cailleach's winter, would we feel so much joy at the coming of Brigid's spring?

Sisters Across the Seas

Envision a gathering of goddesses, a conclave of powerful female divinity, called together by Brigid for the benefit of humanity. The realms of her concern are represented, each goddess adding her gifts in her own particular way. Let's move from table to table and visit with a few of them.

GODDESSES OF FLAME

Her name almost synonymous with "hearth" in the Pagan community, *Hestia* is honored as the center and spirit of the home. This Greek goddess was not depicted in statuary, as were other members of her

---

23. Cahill, *How the Irish Saved Civilization.*

pantheon, for she was in the flame itself. The first offering at any feast was given to her, and when a new home was built, fire from the city's central Hestian altar was brought to bless it. Though she is often associated with Hestia, *Vesta* is not merely her Roman equivalent. Though she too blesses hearth and home, she has ceremonial associations that are all her own. Her priestesses, the Vestals, tended her temple with its sacred fire, performed rites in her honor, and mediated disputes to keep the peace. In the home, Vesta was honored with daily offerings at the hearth. When you gaze into a hearth flame in Siberia, you are in the presence of *Poza-Mama*. Like Brigid, she attends to the practical aspects of fire, keeping life-giving warmth alive through the brutal Siberian winters.

Goddesses of Poetry and Learning

As the mother of memory, the Greek goddess *Mnemosyne* knows well the value of oral tradition, so precious to Brigid. Her nine daughters are the *Muses*, goddesses of history, comedy, tragedy, music, astronomy, dance, and three flavors of poetry: sacred, love, and epic. These gifts are combined in the Hindu goddess *Sarasvati*, who blesses all the arts and sciences. There is a lively discussion happening here at our goddess conclave between Sarasvati, the Sumerian *Nisaba*, and the Egyptian *Seshat*—each of whom is credited with the invention of writing. Great minds think alike! Nisaba is known for advancing literacy and sharing astrology and other oracular teachings. She has that in common with Seshat as well, along with knowledge of architecture and the most auspicious alignment for buildings and cities.

Goddesses of Healing and Midwifery

The Hindu goddess *Ganga* is embodied in the river that bears her name, the Ganges. To bathe in her holy waters is to receive soul healing. Even after death, Ganga continues to bless those whose ashes are offered to her. She is matched in divine power by the Persian goddess *Anahita*, another deity of sacred waters. Anahita is the protector of her people, blessing them with fertility and health; in particular she looks after pregnant and nursing mothers. *Ix Chel*, the Mayan medicine goddess, is another guardian of birthing mothers, but she also blesses crones in menopause and beyond. The Roman goddess *Lucina* is a goddess of light (as her name makes clear). Because the first time we see the light is when we are born, Lucina is present at every birth and assists the laboring mother to bring the child forth to greet her. Whether as Juno Lucina, Santa Lucia, or Saint Lucy, she is invoked by candle flame, like her friend Brigid.

GODDESSES OF SPRING

Brigid sets the greening of spring in motion at Imbolc, and the Germanic goddess *Eostre* and her Roman sister *Maia* take it from there. Like Brigid, both are fire goddesses, turning up the heat as spring moves toward summer. Eostre's association with rebirth is marked by the use of her name for the Christian springtime festival of renewal, Easter. Maia gives her name to the month of May, when winter is well and truly banished and the world celebrates the warming days. The Slavic goddess *Erce* is also busy in the spring, adding a libation of new milk to the freshly plowed furrows to feed the earth so that she may give forth food for her children—evoking Brigid's miraculous rivers of milk. And then there is *Persephone*, the Greek goddess whose return from the underworld signals the return of the fertile months. Her deepening time is the winter, when she rules as Queen of the Dead. Emerging when Brigid increases the light at winter's end, Persephone then moves among the living with compassion and joy.

GODDESSES OF CRAFT

The Germanic goddess *Perchta* has much in common with Brigid. She ensures the fertility of the fields and the well-being of cattle in particular, and she blesses sheep and those who work with their wool. She is exacting in her standards and can be stern with sloppy spinning or weaving work. Like Brigid, she encourages excellence. Greek *Athena* and her Roman sister *Minerva* are also matrons of spinning, weaving, and all domestic crafts. They know that these are the basis of civilization itself, and are not trivial "women's work." Another who honors women's work in the world is *Mokoš*, a Slavic goddess who protects sheep and oversees the production of woolen goods. Like Brigid, she also guards women in labor and their newborn babes. Yet another weaving goddess, Egyptian *Neith*, weaves the patterns of life and death on her own loom, and bestows her blessings on all domestic arts that are practiced in her name.

GODDESSES OF NOURISHMENT

These goddesses are the special guests of Saint Brigid, whose particular pleasure is ensuring that there is more than enough food for all. First is *Dame Habondia*, a Germanic goddess revered by Witches and praised for providing endless abundance in all aspects of life. The Indian goddess *Anapurna*, whose name means "food-giver," offers nourishing sips all around from her sacred ladle of sustenance. The Roman goddesses of peace and plenty, *Concordia* and *Copia*, came together to our gathering, dispensing endless blessings from their cornucopias, supplying all present with whatever their heart most desires (chocolate flows freely). Finally, Brigid welcomes *Nuestra Señora de Guadalupe*, nurturing protector of Mexico (her oldest friends call her *Tonantzin*), from whose loving bounty the needy are cared for and the hungry are fed.

Brigid and Mary

Mary can be controversial in the Goddess-spirit community. Some Pagans, especially those who have been wounded by patriarchal religion, don't consider Mary to be among the goddesses or hold her in reverence as an exemplar of feminine divinity. My own feeling about Mary is that she is one of the most powerful aspects of the Goddess. As with Brigid and Saint Brigid, qualities of ancient goddesses were overlaid on the human woman Mary and became part of her legend. Like countless primal goddesses of creation, Mary gives birth by parthenogenesis, impregnated by spirit alone. Like Isis and Asherah, she is Queen of Heaven. And like Brigid, she is companion, advocate, and protector of the people.

In the early days of Christianity, Mary played a fairly small role in the religion. But beginning in about the fifth century, Mary inspired a passion in her devotees that echoes the passion people have always felt for the sacred feminine. The Goddess always comes through in a form that is most recognizable and accessible to the culture, and Mary is the latest aspect of the timeless Great Mother. To this day, more churches are named for Notre Dame, Our Lady, than are named for her son.

Over the years, I've observed how various goddesses come forward in popularity, which seems to depend upon the world's need at the time. A few years ago, for example, Kuan Yin was seen everywhere in women's spirituality, offering an outpouring of mercy and benevolence that was sorely needed. I don't think it's a coincidence that the powerful re-awakening of interest in the Goddess happened around the time of the election of Pope John Paul II, a pope with a strong and vocal devotion to Mary, to whom he dedicated his life and his work. Sacred feminine energy was swirling around the planet then and continues to do so— Mary in her sphere of influence and the Goddess in hers, working together, bridging faiths.

Mary and Brigid seem to me to be the closest and most loving of sister goddesses. Their iconography is similar, both cloaked in a mantle that symbolizes their encompassing protection. They both are invoked for help in all realms of earthly and spiritual need, from a good birth to a good death. Saint Brigid is known as "Mary of the Gael," a title given not just for her loving care and compassion but for her influence and her power. She is also known as the "midwife of Mary" and the "foster mother of Christ" (see pages 208 and 216 for more on these roles). Many traditional Celtic prayers invoke both Mary and Brigid:

> Incantation of Bride of the locks of gold,
> Incantation of the beauteous Mary Virgin,
> Incantation of the Virtue of all virtues.[24]

One of my favorite tales about Mary and Brigid is told by Lady Gregory in her *Book of Saints and Wonders*. Mary was bothered by crowds that followed her everywhere (yes, even the divine are bothered by fans and paparazzi), and coming upon Brigid, she asked her for help. Brigid said, "I will show them a greater wonder." She held up a harrow

....

24. *Carmina Gadelica*, 149.

(a farming tool like a large rake with many pins) and caused each pin to burn like a candle. The crowd was dazzled and Mary was able to go on her way. When she later asked Brigid how she would like to be rewarded for this kindness, Brigid said, "Put my day before your own day," and so it is that Saint Brigid's day is February 1 (Imbolc) while Mary's day is February 2 (Candlemas).

Celtic charms and spells often call upon the powers of both Mary and Brigid to work together on behalf of the supplicant, such as this spell against the evil eye:

> *The spell the great white Mary sent*
> *To Bride the lovely fair,*
> *For sea, for land, for water, and for withering glance,*
> *For teeth of wolf, for testicle of wolf.*
> *Whoso laid on thee the eye,*
> *May it oppress himself,*
> *May it oppress his house,*
> *May it oppress his flocks.*
> *Let me subdue the eye,*
> *Let me avert the eye,*
> *The three complete tongues of fullness,*
> *In the arteries of the heart,*
> *In the vitals of the navel.*[25]

No meek and mild maidens these! Mary and Brigid were (and are) seen as towering figures of protection and righteous justice, and yet their sweetness and comforting love link them as well. The invoking titles for Mary in Celtic prayers can easily be shared with Brigid: *vessel of peace, fountain of healing, well-spring of grace, shield of every dwelling, comforter of the world.* If you haven't gotten to know Mary, or if you have a notion of her as being submissive or irrelevant to modern feminist spirituality, invite her to join you and Brigid in your devotions. The combined strength of these two divinities is formidable indeed.

---

25. *Carmina Gadelica,* 152.

BRIGID BETWEEN THE WORLDS

From ancient times, the Celts have been wanderers, a tribal people whose curiosity and inner sense of destiny kept them moving from place to place. Blessings for travelers abound, such as the well-known "May the road rise up to meet you and the wind be at your back..." Brigid herself is a wanderer, moving over the land to bring the spring, going from home to home to bestow blessings, visiting holy wells to bring healing. But it is not just in this middle world that she wanders— Brigid travels between the worlds, tending to our needs from the depths of the underworld, where her chthonic creatures dwell, where her sacred waters spring from the earth's heart. She moves in the Other-world, inspiring the poet, the seer, the visionary, the music maker. She draws forth the magic of the worlds unseen and makes them manifest through art and craft and song. Brigid is a presence in our dreams, moving through the cluttered mindscape and setting things to rights, showing us in symbol and metaphor how to better our lives in the waking world.

Seek Brigid in the between-places—the edge of sea, lake, or river, the place where meadow meets forest—and at the "thin times" of day, dawn and dusk, when the passage is easy between the worlds. For all her practicality, Brigid is part of a culture that moves in all the worlds with ease and for whom the possibility of magic is a given. Celtic lore is filled with tales of ghosts, mystical encounters, and shapeshifting creatures. Faeries of all kinds roam the Celtic lands freely, for belief in them has never faltered.

Between the day and the night, between the known and the unknown, a glimmer of faery fire can be seen. It is carried in Brigid's hand, sheltered from the wind. Walk with her now through the gloaming. In the place between light and dark, you must move slowly, attentively. Everything has meaning if you choose to see it. Brigid has seen all the sorrows of the world and all its joys. In the place between the two, things just *are*, neither good nor bad, but all accepting. When you reach this place inside yourself, you are open and receptive to Brigid's wise guidance.

BRIGID'S EARTHLY JOURNEY:
SEASONS AND FESTIVALS

Our knowledge of Celtic seasonal celebrations comes from the first-century Coligny calendar. Two major festivals are shown on this calendar, Beltane and Lughnasadh. Other historical sources filled in the other two significant festivals, Imbolc and Samhain, and these four are the well-known Pagan holidays celebrated today. Imbolc begins the season of spring, Beltane is the first day of summer, Lughnasadh welcomes the autumn, and Samhain opens the door into winter. In the common calendar, the beginnings of seasons are usually noted at the solstices and equinoxes (that is, June 21 being called the first day of summer), but by the Celtic calendar, these are actually the middle of the seasons, not the beginning. Logically, this makes perfect sense. If seasons are measured by the length of days, the arc of summer reaches its zenith on the longest day (summer solstice) and then declines. The winter's nadir is reached on the shortest day (winter solstice), and then the days grow longer from that point. We see remnants of this when the terms *midsummer* and *midwinter* are used poetically for the summer and winter solstices.

In the Celtic reckoning of time, each new day starts at sunset, so the dates for the four holidays are:

Imbolc: Sunset on January 31 to sunset on February 1

Beltane: Sunset on April 30 to sunset on May 1

Lughnasadh: Sunset on July 31 to sunset on August 1

Samhain: Sunset on October 31 to sunset on November 1

Brigid's new year begins at Imbolc, and we begin there too.

Imbolc

Many people only think of Brigid at Imbolc, though of course she is present throughout the year. It's rather like your birthday—you are loved year-round, but on your birthday it's *all* about you. Imbolc is the day that's all about Brigid.

Imbolc (or Oimelc) is the point on the Celtic Wheel of the Year where the passing of winter is marked, even though there may still be wintry weather ahead. In the Celtic calendar, the seasons are delineated by changes in light, and by Imbolc the lengthening days are definitely noticeable—an oft-repeated saying is "From Brigid's festival onwards the days get longer and the nights shorter." For our rural ancestors whose lives depended on crops and the birth of animals, any sign of the return of spring must have been eagerly sought. Though the earth is still frozen, the light affirms that life is awakening.

The source of the increasing light and heat is Brigid. On Imbolc, she moves across the land, bringing the promise of renewal and the return of joy. The name Imbolc means "in the belly," and Oimelc means "ewe's milk." The fertility of sheep and the abundance of their life-sustaining milk are at the root of this holy day. The dangerous part of winter, when sheep might die, when lambs might freeze, has passed. The tribe has survived.

The many customs of Imbolc speak to how beloved Brigid is and how warmly she is welcomed. Offerings of milk, butter, bread, and beer sustain her on her journeying. (You can partake of these too, as a ceremonial communion with the Goddess.) Brigid's crosses are made, their sun-wheel shape symbolizing the increasing strength of the light (see page 25). For the first time all winter, the hearthfire is completely extinguished, the hearth is swept, and the fire is rekindled as an invocation of Brigid and an expression of trust in her care. An alternate custom is to smooth the ashes in the fireplace and in the morning look for signs that Brigid has been there.

Another custom evokes the tradition of sacred hospitality and invites Brigid to come and take her rest within the shelter of the home. A symbolic bed is lovingly prepared for her in a basket, and a doll dressed in pure white is made and tucked in for the night. Prayers and lullabies are offered to this *Brídeóg*, or "Bridey doll," giving back to the Goddess all the tenderness and care that she bestows throughout the year. A variation of this custom is to dress a sheaf of oats from the last harvest and place it in the bed with a wand-shaped branch, symbolizing the God. The divine couple will join together in a union that ensures the fruitful abundance of the coming seasons.

A Family Imbolc
MARGIE MCARTHUR

Margie McArthur has been a student of metaphysics, mysteries, and magic for nearly fifty years and a priestess of the Old Religion for almost forty of those years. She is an Archdruidess of the Druid Clan of Dana of the Fellowship of Isis.

_____

When our kids were little, we described Brigid to them as an important goddess to many people of Celtic descent, including our family. We brought Brigid into our children's lives primarily at Imbolc, a feast that we've come to call simply "Brigid." Each year when the children were young we had a big celebration that involved as many themes of the festival as possible. We lit a special candle for Brigid and said a special prayer to her. We read stories about her—among our favorites were "The Coming of Angus and Bride" from Donald Mackenzie's *Wonder Tales from Scottish Myth and Legend*[26] and "The Earth-Shapers" from Ella Young's *Celtic Wonder Tales*.[27] The children did the Brigid play that's included in the Imbolc chapter of my book *WiccaCraft for Families*. We had a feast, which always included foods associated with the celebrations of Brigid—milk, honey, and oats in the form of bannocks. As the children got older, we added other things. We made a Bridey doll and a bed for her, and we designated a piece of cloth to be a "brat" and set it out to be blessed by Brigid as she passed by at night.

One of my favorite memories is of a Brigid weekend in the late 1980s. We were living in the Santa Cruz mountains in California, having moved there a few years earlier from the Los Angeles area. A couple of friends from our old magical group came to visit us for Imbolc and brought their children. So the house was full of children—eight of them—ranging in age from

....

26. Mackenzie, *Wonder Tales from Scottish Myth and Legend*.

27. Young, *Celtic Wonder Tales*.

two and a half to thirteen, six of whom were boys. We set up a candle-making station on the dining room table, and all of us quietly circled the table, taking turns dipping weighted wicks into the pot of heated beeswax that sat within a larger pot of hot water on the camp stove, while one of the moms read aloud a wonderful story about Brigid. The kids were enchanted by the sight of their candles growing thicker with each dip. When the candles were done, we decorated them. I had purchased a bag of beeswax strips of many colors, and the kids had fun wrapping the strips around the still warm candles, or cutting the strips into different shapes (stars, diamonds, etc.) and gently pressing them into the candles. In the evening we finished off the day with a special ceremonial dinner, and after that, the Brigid play.

Here is something I wrote many years ago for our family Brigid ceremony:

> *Blessed Brigid, Flame of Delight in the many worlds,*
> *May the fires of your sacred hearth be rekindled.*
> *May they burn brightly, their flames bridging the many worlds,*
> *Bringing the star-power of the heavens down to enliven*
> *The stars that live deep within the heart of Mother Earth.*
> *Grant us the gift of your brightness and warmth:*
> *The fire that is inspiration.*
> *Let us draw sustenance from your Well of Deep Peace*
> *That nourishes all of life.*
> *Enfold us in your mantle of protection and healing.*
> *Guide us as we heal, and in our creative endeavors.*
> *Grant us the inspiration that enables*
> *The creation of true beauty and harmony.*
> *Blessed One, Fair One,*
> *This do we ask of you,*
> *As we offer you the inextinguishable light*
> *Of our love and homage.*

For more about Margie, see the Contributors appendix.

Cloak and Candles

When I first began exploring the Pagan holidays in the early 1980s, it was not as common to refer to Imbolc as such, but rather to use the name Candlemas, which is the Christian holy day of purification and candle blessing. You'll still see that name used from time to time, and the concept of honoring the sacred flame is part of both holidays. Each Imbolc, I bless eight pairs of altar candles for the coming turn of the Wheel. Some years I simply buy the candles, and other years I set aside the time to make them myself, and you may enjoy doing this too. The simplest to make is a rolled-beeswax candle. The beeswax comes in sheets of many colors, and you simply roll it up around a length of cotton wick. If you cut the rectangular sheets diagonally and stack two different colors of the wax triangles and then roll them from the wide side down to the point, you'll end up with a two-color spiral candle.

Whether you make or buy your candles, give some thought to what colors (and scents, if you like scented candles) will be appropriate for the coming celebrations of spring equinox, Beltane, summer solstice, Lughnasadh, autumn equinox, Samhain, winter solstice, and Imbolc again. For extra sparkling energy, you can roll your candles in very fine glitter—this can pop a bit when you burn them, so be attentive. Envision the energy of the growing light, and ask Brigid to bless and charge each candle. Wrap them and label them for their intended use, and store in a quiet place where they can retain their power. If you are a flamekeeper, this is a good time to bless candles for that purpose. Cleanse and purify all your flamekeeping tools and candleholders, freshening the energy for the coming year.

This is also a powerful time to make protective and strengthening talismans. One traditional talisman is the *brat Bhríde*, Brigid's cloak. This is a length of cloth that is left outside overnight on Imbolc Eve for Brigid to bless as she passes by. It can then be worn, used for healing, or simply placed on your altar, and used each year to be blessed again and again. Irish linen or wool is traditional. I also tie a length of green silk ribbon to a tree and just leave it there all year, to blow in the wind and disperse Brigid's blessings as the seasons turn.

On Bride's Morn

There is some disagreement in the Pagan community about the date for Imbolc—is it February 1 or 2? Because Saint Brigid's feast day is February 1 and so many of her customs are connected to the goddess Brigid, my feeling is that February 1 is the better choice. Since Celtic holidays start at sunset, I put out my *brat Bhríde* and ribbon on the evening of January 31, and take the *brat Bhríde* inside the next morning, making sure I give special thanks to the morning light, which is strengthening day by day.

The theme of light returning continues on Groundhog Day (February 2). Its origins are linked to the snake, an oracular animal associated with Brigid. A traditional invocation for Imbolc says:

> *Early on Bride's morn*
> *The serpent shall come from the hole.*
> *I will not molest the serpent,*
> *Nor will the serpent molest me.*[28]

Some folktales say that after the snakes left Ireland, the job of coming forth on Brigid's day was taken over by the badger or the hedgehog. From hedgehog to groundhog isn't much of a leap! You may wish to do some vision questing with one of these chthonic creatures at Imbolc (see page 100). Their folklore speaks of weather divination—if the day is sunny so their shadows can be seen, it means the Cailleach is gathering firewood for more weeks of winter. For divination of a more personal nature, Lady Wilde (Oscar's mother) cited an Imbolc custom of lighting a candle for each member of the household and then seeing whose candle went out first. That person would be the first to die, and then the next and the next, ending with the final candle burning, representing the survivor of all. For a more cheerful augury, Lady Wilde also said that whoever hears a lark first thing on Imbolc morning will have good luck that whole day.[29]

----

28. *Carmina Gadelica*, commentary for verse 70.
29. Lady Wilde, *Ancient Cures, Charms, and Usages of Ireland.*

Seasons of Light and Dark

The ancient Celtic year was separated into lunar months, each with a light half and a dark half. This idea of the months being divided into dark and light can extend to other ways we reckon time. Thinking of the year in terms of Brigid, she brings us two seasons of light, spring and summer, and two of dark, autumn and winter. Just as our own concerns and activities vary with the seasons, so Brigid changes and moves with us around the turning of the Wheel.

BRIGID IN SPRING

Brigid in springtime is the life force embodied. She is midwife to the world, drawing it forth from winter's dark enclosure into the light. This is her best-known aspect, the one who breaks winter's hold on the earth. The light has been growing since winter solstice, but it is only now, beginning at Imbolc, that we really begin to notice and to see its effects on the wakening world. The restlessness and increase in energy that we call spring fever is part of Brigid too, for she is a wanderer at this time of year, moving over the land and bringing green growth everywhere her cloak touches the earth.

With the increasing warmth comes the birthing of animals. Brigid is the protector of all newborn creatures, and she blesses new mothers with abundant milk and the instinctive knowledge of nurturance. Nesting birds come under her protection too, and the spawning water-life, and the serpents stirring underground. Her watchful eye is everywhere at this time of year as she ensures the continuity of life. The world is waking up, called by the sweet song of Brigid.

> *Brigid of the lambs,*
> *Brigid of gentleness,*
> *Brigid of the new milk,*
> *I welcome you in.*

Springtime Activities to Honor Brigid

- Purification is a theme associated with Imbolc, making this an excellent time to begin a new health regimen or cleanse.

- Use the brightening energy of the returning light to do some spring cleaning, literally and metaphorically! Sweep away what no longer serves you.
- Plant some shamrock seeds to invoke Brigid as the Triple Goddess. You can buy seeds from Ireland online if you can't find them locally, and you can even buy some Irish soil to plant them in!

BRIGID IN SUMMER

Brigid loves to feed the world, and in summer she raises the vegetables from the soil, ripens the fruit on tree and bush, and teases the grain upward toward the sun. Her oak trees provide a shady shelter in which to contemplate the bountiful gifts of the earth. Brigid as healer is especially active in summer, pouring her power into herbs, roots, barks, and all the wild plants that contribute to wellness. As protector of bees, she guides them to their hives, increases their productivity, and provides them with sweet blossoms.

On summer mornings, the dawn light touches the dew-bedecked world with diamond brightness. Brigid is associated with both dew and sun, and her guidance has been called *imbas gréine*, wisdom from the sun, in which dewdrops are "impregnated" by sunlight and whoever consumes them is touched with poetic inspiration. The custom of rising on the morning of Beltane (May 1) and washing your face in the morning dew may stem from this, though now the recipient is generally said to receive beauty, not genius. Brigid would like you to have both, so take full advantage of her light-filled summer offerings.

> *Brigid of the noonday sun,*
> *Brigid of wellness,*
> *Brigid of the shining shield,*
> *I welcome you in.*

Summertime Activities to Honor Brigid

- If fireworks are legal in your area, use them ceremonially as a fire offering to Brigid. Tuck some away to be used at winter solstice—honor Brigid then with sparklers in the snow!

- If fire is a danger in your area, create a ritual invoking Brigid as god-dess of both the flame and the sacred well waters. Ask her to bless and protect the land and its people in this season of wildfire.
- Use the power of the sun at its peak to draw down creative fire for any projects that you want to bring to fruition now and in the months to come.

Brigid in Autumn

The season begins with a blaze of glory as Brigid's beloved oaks turn to gold and the scarlet rowanberries tremble in the rising winds. The hazel trees of wisdom release their nuts, their branches shaken by crows whose harsh warnings foretell the coming cold. Brigid begins to welcome the dark months of the year by inviting us to draw closer to hearth and home. Ever practical, she energizes us now to prepare for the months to come. The summer's bounty of food is preserved and stored away. The wool that was shorn and washed in the spring is spun into yarn for the winter's weaving.

Brigid as the protector of the home urges us to make sure all is in good repair before the storms arrive. In the glowing days of autumn, she fills our hearts with thankfulness for the blessings of comfort, shel-ter, friends, and family. The harvest of food is safely in, and it's time to assess the harvest of the inner life as well, as we prepare to descend into the time of deepening wisdom. Brigid is invoked for her discern-ment, for this is the time of gathering what nourishes and winnowing out what no longer serves.

Brigid of the acorns,
Brigid of the fox cry,
Brigid of the twining root,
I welcome you in.

Autumnal Activities to Honor Brigid

- As you put your garden to bed, invoke Brigid's blessing. Envi-sion the energy of new life and growth safely slumbering under-ground.

- Create (or buy) a grain dolly at Lughnasadh that can be used as your Bridey doll at Imbolc.
- Lay in a store of books to be read through the colder months, and make plans for study and creative endeavors.

BRIGID IN WINTER

In winter, bare branches trace stark black patterns against the pale sky. When distractions are minimized, clarity is enhanced. Senses are acutely awake as the winter cold touches skin and breath and bone. Brigid isn't slumbering through these months—she is deepening, gathering and reserving her strength for the tasks ahead. She blesses and protects the pregnant animals; they too await a new life emerging. She gives her attention to homespun arts, weaving, knitting, discerning the patterns as disparate pieces come together to make a whole. In the long darkness, her flame burns brighter still, its warmth more welcome than ever. In the hush of a deep winter's night, her voice can be heard and her guidance revealed.

The gifts of Brigid's winter are contemplation, introspection, and intuition. Sight adjusts to darkness, and our inner sight does too. Look thoroughly and slowly, and move with care over the frozen earth. Whether you sit with Brigid beside a blazing hearth or the smallest glimmering candle flame, give thanks for the beauty of her light. She isn't absent, not for a moment. Her emergence at Imbolc is just a change of intention, a shift of energy and focus. Reach out your hand in the darkest night and she is there.

> *Brigid of the iron pot,*
> *Brigid of comfort,*
> *Brigid of the poet's flame,*
> *I welcome you in.*

Wintertime Activities to Honor Brigid

- Remember those less fortunate than you and invoke Brigid's qualities of compassion, charity, and hospitality. Give generously in every way you can.

- Use the long, cozy nights to write some personal or family history. See page 182 for ideas.

- Be creative with your fire offerings. You can enhance your hearthside fire gazing with additives that make the flames change color. You can buy commercial colorings or easily make your own (look online for instructions). Make some green fire for Brigid!

Brigid in the Land
Sharon Blackie

Sharon Blackie is a writer, storyteller, psychologist, and editor of EarthLines *magazine. She lives in a riverside cottage in a small wood in County Donegal, Ireland.*

———

For four years, until recently, I lived on a working croft by the sea on the Isle of Lewis in the Outer Hebrides, just before the last road south and west gives out at the abandoned village of Mealista and melts into the stony mountains of Harris. From the back of our croft-house we looked out (on a clear day) to St. Kilda, forty miles west; from the front we looked out onto Lewis's highest mountain, Mealasbhal, and the very clear figure of a reclining woman in profile in the mountains beside it. The first time I saw her there, I knew I was home; I had looked out onto a similar reclining woman in the hills to the front of the house I'd moved from, on the mainland coast of north-west Scotland.

There are a number of locations in Scotland in which the shapes of specific mountains or ranges represent the silhouette of the reclining goddess; the best-known of them is Lewis's Sleeping Beauty, visible on the southeastern horizon from Callanish stone circle, but many others exist. In the Outer Hebrides, the old Celtic mythologies speak of the goddess of the land in two aspects: Brigid and the blue-faced Cailleach (the Gaelic word for old woman, crone, or hag). The story is that the old woman of winter, the Cailleach, dies and is reborn as Brigid (or Bride), the spring maiden, on the festival day of Imbolc. She is fragile but grows stronger each day as the sun rekindles its fire and turns scarcity into abundance. There are many stories about this battle for the seasons that takes place between Brigid and the Cailleach, but they can clearly be seen as two aspects of life in balance. The reclining women in the hills and mountains are constant reminders of these two very potent spirits of place and seasons.

And so Brigid, to me, represents the land: its fertility, its life. Protector of domestic animals, she looked down from the hills onto our croft—possibly the most windswept in the country, with nothing between us and the prevailing gales in two directions. She watched over us, and over the lambs born to our beautiful black, horned pedigree Hebridean sheep in the damp chill of a Lewis spring. A black Kerry milk cow, who came to us first at Imbolc, was named after her. When spring in the polytunnel greenhouse offered unseasonably early salad and broccoli, it was Brigid I thought to thank. Each morning, as I walked the dogs along the wild salt-splattered and windswept coastline just beyond the croft, it was Brigid, silhouetted in the mountains, who kept me company. I told her my stories, and she told me hers. Hers were older, deeper, wiser, manifested in the *to-wheep* of oystercatchers and the slow, graceful dance of the resident wild red deer. In our last year there, when many things began to fall apart and there were many small deaths, it was Brigid's rocky bones that supported me, Brigid's green arms that cradled me, Brigid's whispered promise of a new spring that sustained me. And now, called home to Ireland, and a beautiful old cottage by a waterfall in a small grove of trees, it is Brigid's wells and waters that quench my long thirst.

For more about Sharon, see the Contributors appendix.

BRIGID OF THE WHITE MOON

The ancient Celtic calendar was lunar, and the start of the month was most likely marked at the full moon, rather than at the new moon as most Pagan systems now use. This makes sense—it's easier to notice the full moon rising than it is to be aware of the absence of moon, or even the arrival of the first slender crescent, which hangs so fleetingly on the horizon. More modern Celts held the first greeting of the crescent moon as fortuitous, as recorded in the dozen or so invocations to the new moon in *Carmina Gadelica*, a collection of folk prayers and incantations. Here's one of my favorites:

> *Hail unto thee,*
> *Jewel of the night!*
> *Beauty of the heavens,*
> *Jewel of the night!*
> *Mother of the stars,*
> *Jewel of the night!*
> *Fosterling of the sun,*
> *Jewel of the night!*
> *Majesty of the stars,*
> *Jewel of the night!*

The Celtic lunar cycle has a mystical and poetic quality: marking the new month with the full moon, observing the descent into the dark moon, watching for the first appearance of that "jewel of the night," and then watching her wax full again until the beginning of the next lunar month.

You're probably familiar with names given to the full moons, drawn from various traditions: Wolf Moon, Rose Moon, and so on. Many people adapt these to fit with the seasonal qualities of their own locations—for example, Winter Rains Moon rather than Snow Moon. Where the Celtic holy days fall in relation to each month's full moon influences the energy of the moon cycle: a full moon near the beginning of October has a very different mood than a full moon at Samhain. Brigid is often considered to be a sun goddess, but her passage through the seasons can also be observed moon to moon, with each full moon and its lunar cycle dedicated to one of her attributes. I invite you to explore the lunar year with Brigid, as she walks through the seasons under the full moonlight.

The Spring Moons

FEBRUARY: MILK MOON

This is the full moon closest to Imbolc, also known as Oimelc, "ewe's milk." As the lambs of early spring are born and their mothers swell with milk, dedicate this moon cycle to the birthing of your own new projects, hopes, and aspirations. Nurture them with tender care, and feel Brigid's presence sustaining you in your endeavors.

MARCH: BUDDING MOON

The first blossoms of springtime make their way to the surface now, blessed by Brigid's warming breath. Dedicate this moon cycle that encompasses the spring equinox to the observance of the quickening of life everywhere. The more you pay attention to the beauties of the world around you, the more you will be filled with grateful wonder.

APRIL: MUSIC MOON

Birdsong fills the air, awakening each day with melody. The winds of spring turn the trees into Aeolian harps raising a song in praise of life. Dedicate this moon cycle to the celebration of music and of Brigid as the matron goddess of song. Make music yourself in every way you can—even by whistling!—and explore other people's musical offerings, listening with all your heart and soul.

The Summer Moons

MAY: BONFIRE MOON

This is the full moon closest to Beltane, traditionally the festival when cattle were freed to graze in the summer pastures. The cows were walked between two bonfires to bless and protect them in the months to come, and surely Brigid was invoked, both as fire goddess and as protector of cattle. Recreate this ritual for yourself (with bonfires if you can or symbolically with smaller flames) and receive Brigid's blessing for all your summer activities.

JUNE: POETRY MOON

The world is filled with loveliness this month, with flowers at their peak, the weather warm and soft, and the cares of winter long forgotten. Give thanks to Brigid with the reading of poetry that praises the beauties of the natural world and its creatures, or perhaps with a reading of love poetry, if you are so moved. Poetry read aloud by moonlight touches the soul and may inspire creative offerings of your own.

JULY: GREEN OAK MOON

Trees are at their most full and lush, and Brigid's oaks are green sanctuaries where her wisdom can be sought in cool shade. As the full moon rises, seek out a favorite tree (oak or any other) and sit beneath it to watch the moonlit world for a while. Let silence enfold you. Listen for Brigid's voice as she teaches you earth lore.

The Autumn Moons

AUGUST: BLACKBERRY MOON

This is the full moon nearest the festival of Lughnasadh, the beginning of the autumn season. Lughnasadh is sometimes called the "feast of first fruits," when berries in particular are at their most perfectly ripe and luscious. The blackberry is sacred to Brigid; invoke her by baking Bridey's Brambly Crumble (see page 49) and sharing it with your dear ones.

SEPTEMBER: SUNBEAM MOON

While the weather may still be saying summer, the slant of sunlight confirms that this is the season of autumn. The angle of the sun's rays in the late afternoons evokes the story of Saint Brigid hanging her cloak on a sunbeam to dry. What would you like to hang on a sunbeam? Hand over your sodden spirits and moist moods to Brigid, and let her warm them in her healing golden light. Then go watch the sunset and moonrise with a peaceful heart.

OCTOBER: HARVEST MOON

This is the full moon closest to the autumn equinox, and it's often the brightest and largest moon of the year. Brigid as both goddess and saint finds satisfaction in feeding people well. Honor her with a harvest home supper in the full moonlight. Make a special point of inviting those who may be in need of the comfort of a home-cooked meal. The next day, share your bounty through a donation to a local food bank.

The Winter Moons

NOVEMBER: PROPHECY MOON

The moon closest to Samhain draws out the wisdom of the ancestors that is always within you. Make an offering shrine to them and then use your favorite divination methods to see what lies ahead in the next turning of the Wheel of the Year. Invoke Brigid's gifts of seership and clarity of vision to understand your readings.

DECEMBER: MIGRATION MOON

The great flocks of migrating birds fill the air with their haunting calls, pulling your attention skyward. They and all migrating creatures have a deep instinctual knowledge of their rightful place in every season. As the full moon rises over the frosty earth, ask Brigid to bless you with this knowledge, that you may always be headed in the right direction and always find your way home.

JANUARY: HEARTH MOON

Whether you have an actual hearth in your home or not, the spirit of the warming center is strong now. Tend that fire well with whatever traditions truly feed your inner flame. Remember, Brigid awaits you in the quiet moments, so be sure to make space for those amid your seasonal celebrations. As the moon rises, open your spirit to midwinter's mysteries.

BRIGID'S EARTHLY ALLIES

Exploring the creatures, plants, and stones that are associated with Brigid is another way to know her, just as you learn about your friends as you discover the things they enjoy. The affinities you share draw you closer together.

As I mentioned in the last chapter, books often list certain plants or animals as belonging to Brigid, but you may need to use your intuition and knowledge of symbols to understand why (or if) this is so. Remember, your relationship with Brigid is uniquely your own, and she may very well introduce you to other allies that strengthen a particular aspect of your soul work in this lifetime.

As you explore Brigid's allies, first get to know the ally on a personal level. What are your own feelings about it? What do you understand about it intuitively? What gift can it bring to you or bring out in you? Make a prayer or charm based on what you feel you need from this ally: "Speed of the salmon be mine" or "Strength of the oak be mine" and so on. After this initial intuitive exploration, you may want to do some research—using books as well as the Internet—and become acquainted with what other people have felt about the stone, plant, or creature. Seek out myths and folklore, and interpret their symbology. Question everything to see if it feels true to you. This is Brigid's way of teaching: a combination of lore and the inner wisdom that adds to that lore.

If you can interact with the ally tangibly, by all means do so (some will be easier than others—wild boars, for example, should be approached with caution). Visualizations and meditations will connect you with the ally's spirit. All allies can be visited on the astral plane; be sure to keep watch for them on the physical plane too. Once you establish a connection with an ally, it may appear in unexpected ways. These are all beings that Brigid blesses, protects, and calls her own, just as she does with you.

Birds, Beasts, and Fish

Brigid has so many aspects and qualities that it's no surprise she is associated with such a variety of creatures. Let's meet a few of them.

SWAN

The fairy swan of Bride of flocks...[30]

When I hear the thrilling call of migrating flocks overhead, it echoes in some longing part of my heart. The wisdom offered by all migrating birds is to heed that heart-call and follow it home. In Ireland swans migrate at Imbolc, and their departure is a sign of spring approaching. They return at Samhain, bringing the winter. The swan's instinctive knowledge of where it needs to be in every season is one reason it is Brigid's bird. This is the knowledge of Home in its deepest sense, where your soul finds peace. It's about timing, direction, courage, and grace.

The swan is also Brigid's bird because of its association with poetry and music. Master bards wore the *tugen*, a ceremonial cloak of swan feathers, to invoke the soul's flight toward poetic inspiration. Swans dwell at the liminal places between the worlds, and in Celtic lore they transport souls to the afterlife, the shining land of Tir na nOg, to await rebirth. As midwife of souls into and out of life, Brigid guides this journey.

Swans are often considered a symbol of peace because of their graceful, calm appearance. They bring a note of peaceful beauty to a rural scene. But swans are powerful and fierce, especially when protecting their nests. Invoke the protection of Brigid's swan for your own nest, her white wings spread wide to repel negative energy.

The two birds that appear most often in Celtic tales of shapeshifting are the swan and the raven. The transformation from human form to raven is voluntary, but human-to-swan can be the result of a spell or curse. Enchanted swans wear silver or golden chains as a sign of their otherworldliness, and if you encounter these swans or follow them, you may be taken into the Otherworld yourself. Some swan maidens cast off their feathered form and become human at dawn or twilight—again, the theme of liminality, the between-times and the between-places. The swan is a threshold creature.

....
30. *Carmina Gadelica*, 114.

RAVEN

At Imbolc, ravens are the first birds to nest in Ireland, their presence a sign that Brigid is bringing spring back to the land. That alone would be enough to associate ravens and crows with Brigid, but there are other affinities as well.[31] Brigid's mother and aunts (the Mórrígan, Badb, and Nemhain) are all shapeshifter goddesses who take on crow form, so there is a familial fondness for these birds. Although the Mórrígan and her sisters invoke the warlike aspects of carrion crows, the connection between Brigid and ravens is more peaceable. Ravens hold the spirit of sovereignty over a place, asserting the owner's right to dwell there and guarding all within. Ravens point out injustices and tell the truth, no matter the consequences. They are among the most intelligent of all creatures, the keepers of memory, the historians of the mythic world. All these are aspects of Brigid.

Ravens and crows are also Brigid's birds of divination, offering warnings and oracular messages, and drawing your attention to matters of interest. I have many crows around my house, and they always have a lot to say. Count the number of crows you see flying by, or count the number of caws you hear, and consider what significance that number has for you. When a crow caws in a way that seems meant especially for you, take it seriously.

Cow

> Give the milk, my treasure,
> With steady flow and calmly.[32]

Brigid is protectress of both the earthly cow whose milk sustains the body and the white red-eared otherworldly cow whose milk sustains the soul. Her mother, the Mórrígan, is also a keeper of these faery cows, just as Saint Brigid's mother was a dairywoman and taught her daughter the skills of caring for cattle.

....

31. Crows and ravens are both corvids, and the names are used interchangeably in Celtic lore. Both are associated with Brigid.
32. *Carmina Gadelica*, 374.

Milk and butter were two primary sources of nourishment in traditional Celtic life. For rural Celts, the cow was a treasure, ensuring against starvation. The loss of a cow was ruinous for country folk, and Saint Brigid was known to magically restore cows to their owners. She also turned well water into milk, caused cows to give three times their usual milk, and blessed vessels to contain milk until the last hungry person had been satisfied. The milk from her own white cows was so nourishing that no other food was needed. The goddess Brigid's otherworldly white cows give milk that can bestow poetic prowess or imbue the drinker with knowledge of healing lore.

The cow also represents the goodness of the green land that sustains it—the land that Brigid awakens to fertility by her warming presence. A family cow (or a herd of cattle for a tribe) meant wealth and security. Brigid's fire was invoked for their protection, such as walking cows between two bonfires, waving torches over them or embers under their udders, and sprinkling them with ashes from the hearthfire.

Brigid's qualities of constancy, generosity, and nourishment are called forth when you align yourself with her cow ally. Calmness is another of Brigid's most-mentioned qualities, and a placid cow is the very embodiment of calm. It is easy to envision Brigid walking in deep contentment alongside her cows and resting in their quiet company. When you ruminate over a problem or a choice, taking your time with thoughtful deliberation, you are moving at cow speed. But calm doesn't mean passive or complacent. Cows can move fast when they feel like it, and great energy is required to generate milk. Milk is a symbol of the sacred feminine and of wisdom passed from mother to daughter. The cow is symbolic of Brigid's constant nurturing, her care that never ceases. The cow must always be milked, no matter what. People must be fed. The milk must not be wasted.

SHEEP

Brigid's association with sheep is simple and sweet. In the early days of spring, she guards the lambs when they are born and acts as midwife to protect their mothers. She brings on the milk to sustain the young ones. (Brigid's holy day of Imbolc is also called Oimelc, "ewe's milk.")

She blesses the fields where her sheep graze and protects them from predators. When it is time, she blesses spinners and weavers of wool and all who work with woolen crafts. Her healing gifts can be invoked by bringing three sheep into your house to sleep for three nights. (If you do this, I want pictures.) The qualities Brigid offers with this ally are peacefulness, community, and trust. Cozy up to Brigid's sheep when you feel the need for comfort.

BOAR

Brigid is not just mistress of the contented cow and the peaceful sheep. The fierce wild boar is part of her nature as well. Though boars are often thought of as symbolizing masculine power, this may be because strength and leadership have been considered male traits in patriarchal societies. Not so for the ancient Celts, who honored power in both men and women. Brigid does not shrink from righteous battle, nor does she hesitate to act swiftly in the defense of the weak. The king of all boars, Torc Triath, is her companion in these causes.

The boar was the symbol of the Celtic warrior spirit. Boar imagery adorned jewelry, weaponry, battle trumpets, coins, ceremonial offerings, and helmets. In parts of Celtic culture, eating the wild boar was forbidden, and some individuals had a *geis* (a ritual taboo) upon them to never taste the flesh of a boar. But for most Celts, boars and domestic pigs were symbolic of prosperity, and their meat was considered the finest food in this life (and the afterlife). There are magical tales of pigs that were roasted for the night's feast but were alive again in the morning, in a never-ending cycle of abundance. Saint Brigid's miracles often included bacon as one of the foods she magically provided. Boars and pigs eat acorns fallen from Brigid's sacred oak trees, imbuing them with oak-wisdom that passes along to those who consume their flesh.

Is it wrong to honor an ally of the Goddess by eating it? You must listen to your own inner guidance here, as in all things. Ask Brigid how she feels about it for you personally, and ascertain your own *geis* about meat-eating, with no judgment about others. Thankfulness and respect are at the core of this matter. Coming from that point of view, taking in an ally's body to become part of your body is profound magic—you could even see it as a type of shapeshifting.

CHTHONIC CREATURES: SERPENT AND BADGER

Animals who live in both the dark and the light pass over that liminal threshold place where both worlds are known and understood. Their deepening time is balanced by a time of action. Two creatures from this world who belong to Brigid are the serpent and the badger.

Wait a minute—how can the serpent be one of Brigid's creatures when there are no snakes in Ireland and never were? First of all, remember that Brigid is not just an Irish goddess. The Celtic tribes were far-ranging and their beliefs are part of many lands. But beyond that, Brigid is present *today*, all around the world, and as such her lore will always be expanding, as long as we don't become stultified and dogmatic about it. There are snakes in many of the places where Brigid is known and loved.

As I mentioned earlier, the serpent comes forth on Imbolc as a sign of warmth returning:

Early on Bride's morn
The serpent shall come from the hole.
I will not molest the serpent,
Nor will the serpent molest me.[33]

The serpent's entire body touches the land and feels its energy and seasons through that intimate connection. Its knowledge of transformation and regeneration makes Brigid's serpent her ally of healing. The serpent is a guardian of sacred wells; seeing a snake near one of these holy places is a fortuitous sign indeed. Watchful and silent, the snake observes the well's visitors and judges their conduct.

The badger also emerges on Imbolc morning and works some rather counterintuitive weather divination: a sunny day that reveals its shadow means more wintry weather is ahead, while stormy and cold conditions mean warm weather will soon follow. This is because if Imbolc is fine

....
33. *Carmina Gadelica*, commentary for verse 70.

and sunny, the Cailleach sets out to gather dry firewood before hunkering down to brew up more winter. If Imbolc is stormy, the Cailleach and Brigid are meeting to exchange seasons, and the Cailleach is having one last blast in farewell before retiring to her long sleep. Beyond this seasonal connection, the serpent and the badger are both symbols of wisdom, lore, and knowledge shared only with initiates. This is the teacher aspect of Brigid, she who guides you toward understanding your own potential—if, like serpent and badger, you are willing to go deep.

SALMON

According to Celtic legend, the oldest creature in the world is the Salmon of Knowledge. This venerable salmon lives in a well that is surrounded by nine sacred hazel trees, whose nuts of wisdom feed it.[34] There is (as always) some variance in the details of these legends. Some say there is a single Well of Knowledge and a single Salmon of Knowledge. Others say there are several such wells and each of them contain a salmon of knowledge. Some lore says that every river in Ireland has such a well at its head, and the salmon that come from these waters carry their knowledge throughout the land. It is also said that the well and its hazel trees are in the Otherworld, and the water is a portal between the worlds. All of these feel true to me at their core.

The salmon's knowledge comes to humans by receiving the gift of a hazelnut from the salmon, drinking or bathing in the water that flows from its well, or eating the salmon itself: "And whoever could catch and eat one of these salmon would be indued with the sublimest poetic intellect."[35] The links between Brigid and salmon are strong: sacred waters, poetic gifts, and knowledge mystically obtained and divinely inspired. Salmon is also a symbol of plenty; indeed, at spawning time the salmon runs may be so plentiful that the fish seem to leap right into the fisherfolk's arms. As we know, one of Brigid's greatest joys is providing

....

34. A "well" in the Celtic sense isn't a deep humanmade hole in the ground (the kind you don't want to fall down), but a natural pool of fresh water that is fed by a spring.

35. Lady Wilde, *Ancient Legends, Mystic Charms, and Superstitions of Ireland*.

more than enough food to nourish the body and cheer the spirit. Her salmon ally contributes to this generosity.

The salmon holds the knowledge of seasonal death and rebirth as it returns to its birthplace to spawn. It is a keeper of memory and ancestral wisdom, blessed by Brigid with a powerful instinct that tells it how to find its way home.

WOLF

Here is a tale of Saint Brigid: In Ireland long ago, a man was sentenced to death for accidentally killing the king's tame wolf. Always an advocate for prisoners, Brigid traveled to the court to ask the king to be merciful. As she drove her cart through the woods, a huge grey wolf rushed toward her. But Brigid had no fear and reached out toward the fierce animal, calling it to her. The wolf leaped into the cart and lay down beside her, licking her bare feet. She went on her way to court, and the sight of her walking with the wild wolf at her side amazed the king. Brigid asked for compassion and clemency for the prisoner, and offered the wolf in exchange for the one that was killed. In some versions of the story, the wolf stays happily with the king, and in other tellings the wolf leaves with Brigid. In any case, the prisoner was spared.

I almost didn't include the wolf in this section about Brigid's animals. The story above is the only "official" connection between Brigid and wolves, and in some versions the animal is a fox. But I felt she strongly wanted the wolf included, which can be seen in artwork depicting Brigid—the wolf is often included in her iconography, as if she put the idea into the artist's mind as strongly as she put it into mine. In meditating on why this might be, I was guided toward Celtic tales of wolf packs magically helping to herd sheep and pigs into shelter, of wolves returning lambs unharmed to their mothers, and of wolves shapeshifting into humans and back again. In each resource I read, "Though wolves are now extinct in Ireland…," and that plaintive phrase resonated like a keening howl on the wind.

A Celtic symbol of strength and courage, Brigid's wolf companion counters the ferocious stereotype of the big, bad wolf with the reality of its noble nature. Her wolf walks beside those who fight for the protection of its earthly kin. Invoke its presence in prayers for the earth, and invoke Brigid's eloquence and vision as you work in practical ways for the survival of all endangered creatures.

A Shapeshifting Journey

In *The Once and Future King*, by T. H. White, the future King Arthur is educated by the great wizard Merlyn through being transformed into various creatures and living among the creatures' societies. He learns about power and courage, freedom and honor, beauty and wildness. Brigid, too, offers the gift of shapeshifting. It is an ancient part of Celtic myth and spirituality (which is of course why Merlyn the Druid knew of it), with countless tales of both mortals and immortals turning into birds or animals, or even grain or ocean waves. While you may not possess the magic to shift your physical form, you can shift your consciousness to align yourself with Brigid's allies and receive their teachings.

This is a visualization to be done at bedtime. The misty edge of sleep is one of the liminal between-times when magic is potent. If you usually share your bed with someone, you may want to spend this night on your own, or simply wait until your bedmate has fallen asleep.

In the dark, in your soft bed, begin by breathing slowly and deeply. Keep your eyes closed and open your inner vision so that you willingly see what will be given to you. You sense a presence, soft as a whisper, and feel Brigid's hand passing over your closed eyes. She places in your mind an image of one of her creatures—perhaps one mentioned in this book or perhaps another that she wishes you to learn from.

Observe the creature for a moment, and then begin to feel yourself shapeshifting into the same type of creature. Feel the shape of your body, the weight or lightness, the abilities you do not have as a human, and the human abilities you no longer have. Notice how the world looks through your new eyes, and how your other senses work. Join the creature-guide that Brigid has sent to you, and go where the guide and the vision take you. It may be a time of connection between just the two of you, or you may join the creature's flock or herd or school. Don't try to

consciously direct the scenario—the whole point of this journey is to
teach you things you don't know in your usual human state of mind.

Unlike other visualizations where you bring yourself back to full
awareness at the end, in this shapeshifting you move directly into sleep.
Don't fight the pull of slumber, as each visit with Brigid's allies will
take just as long as is needed, and there will be other visits. Float easily
into the dreamworld.

In the morning, make note of any dreams you remember, but don't worry if you don't recall any. According to Celtic shapeshifting lore, the essence of the creature you became is always with you. You don't need to strive or strain for understanding of the allies' lessons—they are part of you now and will reveal their gifts in good time. Just give thanks to every ally you come to know, and to their benefactress Brigid.

Plants

Brigid is associated with many plants and trees, including dandelion, oats, angelica, mint, watercress, cowslip, fennel, flax, mugwort, figwort, all brambles and thorns, the rowan tree of protection, and the hazel tree of poetic inspiration. You could spend a lifetime getting to know her green allies and what they have to offer you magically, medicinally, and symbolically. Here are some to get you started.

OAK

Today the oak is mainly associated with Brigid because of Kildare, *cill dara*, church of the oaks, but the connection goes back much further. The ancient Celts practiced their rites in sacred oak groves known as nemetons, from the Old Irish *fidnemed*, a shrine in a forest. According to the Celts' Roman chroniclers, there were also fearsome oak groves where light never penetrated and where no one—not even the Druids—set foot, where "the glare of conflagrations came from trees that were not on fire, and serpents twined and glided around their stems."[36] This combination of otherworldly attributes speaks strongly of Brigid—fire that has

....
36. Cunliffe, *The Ancient Celts.*

no earthly source and oracular serpents entwined with the trees of wisdom. Could these groves that were forbidden to priests have been where Brigid's priestesses kept her flame? It's an intriguing thought. Oaks have another association with Brigid's illuminating fire; folklore says that oaks attract lightning more than other trees, and that wood from a lightning-struck tree holds divine inspiration. Above all, oaks are associated with wisdom—the wisdom that comes with age and endurance.

RUSHES

Rushes represent Brigid's blessings of shelter, hospitality, and protection. In Celtic country cottages, rushes were used for roof thatching and were strewn on the dirt floors, bestowing those blessings on the home from top to bottom. Rushes were ceremonially placed across the threshold at Imbolc to make Brigid welcome and to welcome others in her name. Rushlights were also made and burned in honor of Brigid. These are the dried pith (the center part) of rushes, dipped in tallow or other fat and used in place of costly candles by country folk. This was one of those household tasks that needed to be done faithfully and often, as rushlights burned for no more than forty minutes or so. Brigid's crosses (see page 25) are traditionally made from rushes, and the leftover bits can be saved for charms to tuck under mattresses for healing or carry for protection when traveling, especially on water. Rushes are a water plant associated with holy wells and springs—Saint Brigid was known to cause wellsprings to arise where rushes were pulled from the earth. Rushes grow in wetlands, one of the liminal places blessed by Brigid. Faeries may be found there too, hiding among the rushes. If you come upon one, apologize and depart as quickly as possible.

SHAMROCKS

Oh the Shamrock, the green, immortal Shamrock!
Chosen leaf
Of Bard and Chief,
Old Erin's native Shamrock! [37]

....
37. Moore, "Oh the Shamrock," 1868.

The name shamrock is an Anglicization of *seamair óg*, young clover. Saint Brigid is said to have to have chosen Kildare as the site for her monastery because of its glorious green fields of clover, which would serve well for grazing purposes. There is a lively debate about what plant is the true shamrock, and there are half a dozen varieties of clover that vie for the title. Some people say that the shamrock isn't clover at all but a distinct plant that grows only in Ireland—not true, but it shows how passionately the Irish have embraced the symbol. The usual explanation of the shamrock's significance is that Saint Patrick used it to illustrate the idea of the Holy Trinity to the Druids, who couldn't grasp the concept of a deity who was three in one. This is ridiculous, of course, as triune deities were well known to the Celts. I like to imagine the scene was something like this: Patrick held up the shamrock and pointed to the three leaves on one stem, and the Druids said, "Oh, you mean like Brigid!" In any case, that story wasn't told until 1,200 years after Patrick's time, and it doesn't appear in any of his own writings. (The Internet didn't invent the concept of perpetuating misattributed quotes!) We can embrace the shamrock as a symbol of Brigid's triplicity. The four-leafed clover is considered lucky because of its rarity, but to me the three-leafed *seamair óg* holds the true luck—the luck of knowing Brigid.

Stones

Although the Celts revered stones both great and small, there are no specific stones or crystals traditionally associated with Brigid, as far as I know. But I've been working with stones since the crystal craze of the 1980s, and I like to include them in my devotions. I've made my own associations for Brigid's stone allies, and I encourage you to find some too. All stones have intrinsic qualities and energies that are brought forth when held or worn. There are lots of books that give the generally accepted properties of stones and crystals. You may agree with these books, but don't be limited by them. Sometimes you will establish your own connection with a stone that tells you something completely different.

To get you started, here are stones that invoke Brigid. You can work with these stones singly or in combination (rather like jelly beans). All of them are easy to find in raw or polished/tumbled stones, as well as in jewelry.

- *Healing: Garnet.* This rich red stone promotes and affirms your natural state of healthy well-being. It restores balance and subdues chaos (such as viruses) throughout your body and outward through your aura. When you wear or hold garnet, you can feel Brigid "setting things to rights."

- *Courage: Citrine.* This is the golden variety of quartz crystal, and its energy feels like holding a sunbeam in your hand. It is one of the few stones that never takes on negative energy but radiates pure optimism and invincibility. Fear cannot touch you when you wear or carry citrine, a stone much beloved by Brigid.

- *Self-esteem: Amber.* Amber was held in high regard by the ancient Celts. Not technically a stone, this fossilized sap calls forth your Brigid-given strengths and personal power, helping you aspire to excellence. Amber is a jewel of leadership, confidence, and nobility.

- *Peace: Moss agate.* This stone with its soft greens and grey-blues evokes Brigid of the well waters. Its mineral inclusions resemble moss and ferns that seem to float in its translucence. When you wear or hold moss agate, the soft murmur of water over stones echoes in the deep places of your heart…the deep peace of Brigid.

- *Transformation: Rainbow obsidian.* Born of fire, this volcanic-glass stone blasts through stuck patterns of grief, despair, blame, addiction, anger…whatever no longer serves you or perhaps never did serve. Within its black depths, iridescent fires gleam. Obsidian is reflective, acting as a dark mirror to reveal what you may have been refusing to see. With Brigid at your side, you have nothing to fear.

Besides wearing and carrying these stone allies, you can also make elixirs charged with their essence. Pure spring or well water, whiskey (*uisce beatha,* water of life), or a mix of the two may be used. Simply place the stone and liquid in a glass or pottery vessel, seal it, and let it sit for a period of time that feels right to you, such as a moon cycle, from holy day to holy day, or over a nineteen-day flame vigil. Even just twenty-four hours will make a potent potion, especially if empowered by sunlight and moonlight and prayer. You can sip these elixirs to infuse your being with the energetic blessings of the stones.

BRIGID'S SACRED PLACES

As I was starting this book, a friend was preparing to leave for Ireland, with the intention of visiting sites dedicated to Brigid. I had two glimmering golden calcite stones on the Brigid altar in my home workspace, and I gave her one to place somewhere in Ireland for me, to energetically tie the two places together, which she very kindly did, at Brigid's well near Liscannor. One morning, while lighting my morning candle on my altar, I took in my hands the stone that remained behind, closed my eyes, and envisioned that other stone, seeing the energies between them as a luminous light stream. I thanked Brigid for such a strong link to a place that was sacred to her, and heard a clear reply: *This too is a place that is sacred to me.* But of course! Brigid isn't just in Ireland or in those ancient and revered spots. She is everywhere, in every place where she is loved. The Celts took their deities with them when they moved from place to place, and so it is with me, and with you. As with my two stones, wherever we make sacred space for Brigid, we connect our energy with the well-known places that hold her essence.

Kildare

The name Kildare is from *cill dara*, church of the oak, but the oaks were there long before the Church. The Druids practiced their rites there beneath great oaks, their most beloved tree. Legends say that the goddess Brigid was worshiped there, her perpetual flame tended by nineteen priestesses, each for one day. On the twentieth day, Brigid herself kept the flame burning. These few things are commonly told, but the history of Kildare is filled with gaps, and as with much of Brigid's lore, we must piece it together with guesswork as the glue. The website for the town itself says that Saint Brigid may have been a convert from the group of priestesses who tended the flame of the goddess on that spot, which is an interesting version of Brigid's tale. Maybe Saint Brigid wandered from her home to Kildare, met the priestesses there, became one of them, and then converted to Christianity (perhaps because her mother was a Christian).

If the perpetual flame was tended by Saint Brigid in the fifth century, and was reported to still be tended by sisters of her monastery as late as the twelfth century, that's at least six hundred years of unbroken devotion added to perhaps thousands of years before that. *This is where we tend the flame of Brigid*, the women of Kildare may have said to those who brought the new religion. Call her goddess or saint or what you will—the flame shall be tended.

How Saint Brigid got the land on which to build her monastery is a story that has several versions, and this is the one I like best, dating back to the early Middle Ages. The king of Leinster had lands and wealth and power, but he had something else too: the ears of an ass. Having heard from many sources of Saint Brigid's miraculous deeds, he asked her to heal his asslike ears. Brigid agreed, and in return asked the king to give her "a bit of land" for the monastery she was establishing in Kildare. The king was reluctant to give up even a bit of his precious holdings, so Brigid said that she would only ask for as much of his land as her cloak would cover. The king agreed, and Brigid performed a miracle that gave the king perfectly beautiful human ears. He then visited her at Kildare to complete the bargain and plot out the amount of land as measured by her cloak. Brigid smiled, took off her emerald green cloak, and laid it on the earth. The cloak magically expanded, spreading wider and wider over the land, until the king begged her to stop, which she willingly did, having attained what she needed for her purpose—and taught the king a thing or two about generosity in the bargain.

Brigid's monastery became a center for scholarship. She founded a school for art, particularly illuminations and metalwork of surpassing excellence, so fine that some viewers declared them to be the work of angels, not humans. By the time of Saint Brigid's death, the community she established among the oaks was a mighty cathedral city, renowned throughout Europe.

Today, Kildare is Brigid Central, the heart of worship for devotees of the goddess and the saint. The Cathedral of Saint Brigid dominates the town, built on the same site as Brigid's monastery. Brigid's Well is about a mile from the town center. The Brigidine Sisters of Solas Bhríde have a center dedicated to Brigid (see page 127), and on Imbolc 2006, Ireland's President Mary McAleese lit Brigid's flame in a permanent sculpture at the center of the town square. The sculpture is a tall column opening into a group of oak leaves, at the center of which is an acorn cup that holds the flame. The design was intended to honor both Saint Brigid and the Druidic worship that long preceded her, in recognition of the fact that Kildare, *cill dara*, has always been a sacred place.

Dedicating a Well in the Name of Brigid
MICKIE MUELLER

Mickie Mueller is an artist, illustrator, author, Reiki Master, and Pagan. She works with the spirits of nature and several deities, including Brigid, for the healing of self, loved ones, and the earth.

———

When my family moved to our country rural home, for the first time ever we had a well. This was a fascinating idea to me: natural water, filtered through its limestone bed. When I lived in the suburbs I used to gather rainwater to cleanse my stones and crystals and for spellwork, but now I had a natural source at every faucet.

I do a lot of healing work as a Witch and a Reiki practitioner and one of my favorite deities for this work is Brigid. I thought about her sacred wells, especially the one at Kildare, and what made them sacred. I dreamed of ley lines that connect power places on Earth, the concept of oneness, and the scientific fact that all water molecules on Earth have been here since the beginning, evaporating into clouds and falling back to Earth again as rain as the cycle continues endlessly. It occurred to me that the water molecules in my well have been part of the ocean, glaciers, and even Brigid's sacred wells in Ireland! I decided that on Imbolc I would bless our well and dedicate it to the goddess Brigid, thus awakening that energy and empowering the water with her mighty blessing and healing.

Imbolc in Missouri is often icy, and that day we had freezing rain. Using rosemary and lavender oil, I anointed a white candle and surrounded it with rowanberries. I put my candle in a steel and glass lantern to shield it from the wintry mix falling from the sky. I placed my Brigid statue on the fireplace mantle so she gazed out the window directly at the well but was safe from the elements. The sun set as I bundled up and headed out, my candle in one hand and a written blessing in the other.

I placed my candle on top of the well and lit it. Pulling in all of my thoughts about connections, oneness, and the goddess Brigid herself, I began. I felt her power swirling through the air, in the land, living in the flame and in the water beneath my feet, as I spoke my blessing:

I bless this well in the name of the goddess Brigid on her feast day of Imbolc.

May these waters be filled with her power, light, and grace. As with her holy well of Kildare, so shall it be in the waters of this land.

May all who touch these waters be filled with healing for mind, body, and spirit.

May the waters of this well be filled with the blessings of the goddess Brigid on her feast day of Imbolc.

By the power of earth, air, fire, and water, I name this well Brigid's Well. May her loving energy bless and preserve us with her healing, protection, and grace.

As I will it, so shall it be!

The candle in its lantern flickered on as the ice fell all around it. I retreated into the warmth of my home, and my family shared a meal of creamy soup and dessert of blackberry cobbler in honor of Brigid.

Now our every shower and bath is filled with sacred energy. Our dishes that serve nurturing food are washed clean with blessed water. Our clothing that shields our bodies from the cold are infused with protective energy of the Goddess. The water we drink fills us with healing energy. I plan to rededicate our well every year on Imbolc.

I wish I'd thought of blessing our water earlier. There's no reason why you can't do the same thing if you have city water. Locate the main pipe that leads into your house, and tie a white ribbon around it, knot it three times, and with each knot say, "In the name of the goddess Brigid." Inside the house, place a white candle in a jar candleholder, then tie another white ribbon from the same spool around the jar, knot it three times, and with each knot say, "In the name of the goddess Brigid." Now the candle and the incoming pipe are energetically connected. Put the candle in the kitchen sink and perform the same blessing I did for my well. All the pipes that bring water to our homes are the modern equivalent of a well, in the same way that the gas or electric range in the kitchen is the modern equivalent of the hearth. It's the concept that's key. Remember that all water molecules have been everywhere: sacred wells, the vast ocean, and floating above us in the clouds. Why not turn all the water that comes into your home into a blessing to all who live there and mindfully share Brigid's blessings every single day?

For more about Mickie, see the Contributors appendix.

Holy Wells and Springs

Brigid is a water goddess as well as a fire goddess—Celtic spirituality doesn't shy away from such paradoxes. Water is Brigid's element of healing. Throughout the Celtic lands, there are thousands of wells that have been honored as sacred and magical for millennia. There may be as many as 3,000 holy wells in Ireland and Britain alone. Some are traditionally associated with Brigid—such as Kildare and Liscannor—but those who seek her have found Brigid at countless other places where fresh waters spring from the earth. As with other ancient pagan places, many wells have been rebranded to honor saints. To me, this merely confirms their power. Sacred is sacred and magic is magic, whatever you call it. As with anything having to do with Brigid, look beyond the religious differences and find the common spiritual roots.

The custom of tying ribbons or strips of cloth to trees near a well is a form of healing magic. These cloths, called clooties, are dipped in the water and touched to the afflicted part of the body. The clootie absorbs the ailment and then is tied to the tree, where it will gradually rot away, taking the ailment with it. Some wells have large stones with carved or natural indentations where in times past seekers could lie down and sleep beside the well to receive additional healing. Women who hoped to get pregnant or faced a difficult delivery could rest there in the arms of Brigid the midwife. One such stone, known as Saint Bridget's Chair, would forever after protect the sitter from accident or sudden death.

Metal offerings to the well waters are traditional—and appropriate to Brigid as goddess of metalcraft. Metal cups were a favorite offering in the past, as were metal figurines, buttons, and pins. Today people offer coins to "wishing wells" everywhere without realizing they are keeping the ancient sacred tradition alive. The next time you pass by that fountain in the shopping mall, take a moment to connect energetically to the holy wells and offer a bright penny to Brigid.

Given in the proper spirit, the gaily colorful clooties blowing in the breeze are much more than a mere "I was here." They say that you are surrendering your trust to Brigid. In Celtic lore, sacred and magical wells are openings between the worlds, and as at every such portal, Brigid is there. Thresholds are places of choice—will you cross over? At her holy wells, Brigid asks you whether you choose healing. She will work miracles on your behalf, but you must commit to that choice. It may not come in the form you expect, but Brigid will never leave you unhealed.

In Every Rock and Whisper of the Wind
MARA FREEMAN

Mara Freeman has been teaching Celtic spiritual and magical tradi-
tions for over thirty years, both in person and through her books and
distance learning program, the Avalon Mystery School. She leads sa-
cred journeys to ancient sites in the Celtic lands.

———

One of my favorite of Brigid's wells is in the far west of Ireland on
the Dingle Peninsula. It's actually known as Gobnait's Well: Gobnait was a sixth-century saint whose feast day in early February co-
incides with Brigid's, and they share many similar legends. For instance, she was one of three sisters who carried fire in their aprons
without getting burned. At the coming of Christianity, so the legend goes, the sisters disappeared into the ground and sprang up
as sacred springs. It looks like Gobnait may have been a historical holy woman who became conflated with Brigid. One reason
I love this well is that it is halfway down the slope of a steep cliff
overlooking the wild blue ocean. A modern sculptor has carved a
woman's face out of stone at the well, which is very beautiful. It's
a stark and elemental little shrine with none of the religious trap-
pings you get at more frequented places—just the cry of the gulls
and the boom of the sea against the rocks far below.

In the West of Scotland, Brigid was often called "Bride of
the Isles" and was particularly associated with the sacred isle of
Iona. The energy of Brigid is surprisingly strong on this little island, despite the fact that both the modern restored abbey and the
medieval ruins are not associated with her but with a male saint,
Columba. When I take groups there, we make Brigid's crosses
from the reeds and take them up to the top of an old Celtic hill
fort called Dun I, a very pure and powerful place that commands
a spectacular view of the whole island and surrounding sea. Here
we bless the crosses in a sacred spring known as the Well of Youth.

Legend tells how the old goddess called the Cailleach flies over mountains and sea to visit the spring at the end of each winter. When she drinks the waters, she turns into her youthful aspect of Bride, the maiden of spring. I've also spent time alone up there and have particularly fond memories of one early June when I sat dabbling my bare feet in the shockingly cold water, which was surrounded by the most beautiful wild purple orchids. It's a truly magical place, and the power of the Sacred Feminine is in every rock and whisper of the wind.

For more about Mara, see the Contributors appendix.

WORSHIP, DEVOTIONS, AND PRAYER

In the writing of this book, I found myself hesitating over using the word *worship*. Worship has a lot of connotations overlaying it in the context of mainstream religion. At worst, it has nuances of subservience or a giving-over of power. Sometimes looking at the root meanings of words can help us reclaim them in a way that is healing and empowering. Worship is a good word, a strong word, with its root meanings of "worthiness" and "respect." When you offer your worship to Brigid, you are respecting her as worthy of praise and trust—and also proclaiming your own worthiness as her worshiper. The love flows both ways.

A word I tend to use more than worship is *devotion*. Worship seems to me to be the feeling that motivates devotions. Devotions are active ways of offering worship, and they are limited only by your imagination. When you create an altar to your goddess, that is an act of devotion. When you light some incense there, that is another act of devotion. When you say a blessing over your morning porridge or put on a piece of jewelry you've dedicated to Brigid or immerse yourself in a lustral bath—these are all devotions. You can live your life every day as a devotee simply by shifting your consciousness toward the sacred.

Léitheoireacht Diaga: *Divine Reading*

Reading for illumination is a simple devotional practice that has four parts. It can be your entire daily practice, especially in hectic times, and provides a welcome oasis of quietness when you are busy. It also has the advantage of mobility: you can do it anywhere you happen to be. This is a practice borrowed from the Benedictines, who call it *lectio divina*, divine reading—in Irish, *léitheoireacht diaga* (LAY-hee-racht JEEAH-gah).[38] It's well suited to devotees of Brigid, as it is all about drawing forth deeper meaning from the written word.

The first part is *léitheoireacht*, reading. Simply open a book and read for a paragraph or two. The book can be anything, really. You may want to keep a small stack of books near your altar or in another place where you do this practice, or you could just go to a bookcase and pull one at random. I don't recommend that you use one of the many excellent books that offer a reading for each day. Use a more random and varied selection for your *léitheoireacht* practice, so that Brigid can work with you to provide what is needed for that moment.

So … you open your book and read, with full attention, for a couple of paragraphs. Maybe you read a whole page. Or maybe you only read one line. Be present with the words; let them reach you.

Then comes the second part: *smaointeach* (SMIHN-tyach), which means thoughtful. Set the book aside and move peacefully into reflection. Your own heart and Brigid have drawn you to these words today. Why? Let your soul soar on the words you just read. Let them take you as far as they will.

You will know when it is time to move on to the third part: *urnaí* (UHR-nih), the prayer of the heart. Speak your own words now, to Brigid or whomever you are moved to address.

The last part is *rinnfheitheamh* (RIHN-neh-ehv), contemplation. Here you could write in your journal or just simply sit with your thoughts for a few moments. Feel your wholeness of spirit, mind, and being. Give thanks. Return to the day.

....

38. Thanks to Domi O'Brien for translations and pronunciations.

A Book of Devotions

Sacred reading is a great way to ground yourself in a daily practice and open your spirit to a deeper connection with Brigid. Taking it to the next step, creating your own book of devotions is itself an act of loving devotion—and it's fun too! Don't be daunted if this seems like a lot of work. It may not appeal to everyone, and even if it does appeal to you, consider it a multi-year project, something you add to when you feel moved to do so.

Start by buying a blank book, or two, or four—for example, four seasonal books to begin on Imbolc, Beltane, Lughnasadh, and Samhain. Unlike a journal, where you want to feel free to scribble and make a mess, a devotional book that is intended to last a lifetime can be a bit more fancy. Blank journals come in a gorgeous array of sizes, papers, and covers. Do you want lined or unlined sheets? A small, thick book, like an medieval breviary, or a leather-bound notebook stamped with a Celtic design? If you know a bookbinder, you could have a special book made for you, perhaps using the gilded cover of an antique book whose pages are crumbling. Or take a bookbinding class and make it yourself! (I took a Coptic stitch workshop and loved the process, which is easy to learn and has a satisfyingly ancient feel, both in the making and in the finished book.)

Add dates to the top of the pages—just the month and day, not the year. You might want to also include pages for days that change dates, such as the solstices and equinoxes or full moons and new moons. These dates make it easy to find your place, in case you skip a day when reading from your devotional (trust me, you will). Create a framework that suits your own devotional practices or what you would like them to be. Within this loose framework, your imagination can take flight. Here are some things you might include:

- *A reading, prayer, or poem that inspires you and prepares you for your day.* Even though the inspiration for your devotions is Brigid, the readings don't have to be Celtic. Brigid loves all language, all poetry, all the ways word-weavers create their offerings of beauty.

Any words that speak of spirit to you will do. Write these in by hand or paste in a printed version.

- *A guardian or an ally for the day.* This could be an ancestor, a role model or soul teacher, an animal ally (or tree or stone), a nature spirit, or perhaps one of Brigid's sister goddesses. For me, these change with the seasons. For example, on a day deep into autumn, I might call upon the golden ripe energy of pumpkin to surround me with fruitfulness.

- *Something for which you are grateful.* Be sure to make it something you will always be grateful for, such as the beauty of the rising moon, the simple goodness of bread, or the recognition of your talents by others. Think in terms of coming across that entry year after year and saying, "Yes, I am still grateful." (Giving thanks for your boyfriend might not have such lasting meaning!)

- *A challenge or a task.* In many religious traditions, holy days and seasonal cycles offer opportunities for spiritual growth through such activities as fasting, observing a day of silence, making specific offerings, making amends and atonement, and stretching the mind in a new direction. Draw upon the qualities of Brigid to include such things in your devotional book—not every day, perhaps, but here and there: a day to offer charity, a day to learn a new craft, a day to find a new poem to love, and so on.

- *Suggestions for other resources.* There will be days when you are feeling inspired and days when you will need an extra boost of inspiration. Make notes of books, music, artwork, and activities that fit the seasons and cycles of your devotional year.

You can include just one of these on a page or more than one, as you're inspired to do. Remember that you can (and will) add to this book over the years. Here is an example of a daily page that includes several of these suggestions:

December 16

○ *My tidings for you: the stag bells,*
winter snows, summer is gone.
Wind high and cold, low the sun,
short its course, the sea running high.
Deep-red the bracken, its shape is lost;
the wild-goose has raised its
accustomed cry.
○ *Cold has caught the wings of birds;*
season of ice—these are my tidings.[39]

On this day, I ask the blessings of
the Cailleach, crone of winter.
Today's ally: Granite, for stability
and courage.
I give thanks for resilience—
in spite of all challenges,
○ I am still here.
Music for the day:
Zingaia, *Beneath the Veil*

The Pleasure of Prayer

Through daily practice, in ritual, in holiday celebrations, and in the
spontaneous reaching out to Brigid in moments of joy and pain, we
offer our prayer. Like *worship*, the word *prayer* can be a hot button, and
some Pagans prefer not to use the word at all, associating it with power-
over, dogma, and authoritarian control. This is unfortunate, as prayer is
one of the most beautiful creations of humankind. It can be as simple
as a whispered "thank you" or as elaborate as a high mass. It can be
silent or spoken, sung or danced, written or improvised. Prayer comes
from the depths of despair and the heights of ecstasy.

I differentiate between "prayer" and "prayers," as I've found that the
objection some people feel toward prayer has to do with established
prayers that are spoken by rote, rather than an act of spontaneous *prayer*
that comes from the heart. It's true that simply rattling off a composed

....

39. "The Coming of Winter," Irish, author unknown, ninth century, in Jackson, *A Celtic Miscellany*.

prayer can be meaningless, but that doesn't devalue such prayers in and of themselves. Brigid is the goddess of poetry, after all, and she loves the written word. Reading and (especially) writing prayers is a powerful component of Celtic spirituality. The beauty of language sings through the spirit when prayers are spoken aloud.

> *Thou art the light of the beam of the sun,*
> *Thou art the surpassing star of guidance,*
> *Thou art the step of the deer of the hill,*
> *Thou art the step of the steed of the plain,*
> *Thou art the grace of the swan of swimming,*
> *Thou art the loveliness of all lovely desires.*[40]

It's all about your intention. If you truly hear every word, comprehend the prayer with your full mind and seek to understand its wisdom, you need not fear that it will be humdrum. You bring the words alive with the fire of your love.

As I mentioned in the section "Brigid's Sisters" early in this chapter, prayers to Mary often work well for Brigid, as the qualities and gifts invoked run strongly through them both. Here is my adaptation of a prayer in praise of Mary:

> *Brigid, thou shining woman of gentleness,*
> *Thou glorious woman of kindness,*
> *Shield of every dwelling, shield of every people*
> *Who call upon you for courage.*
> *Thou art the well of compassion,*
> *Thou art the root of consolation,*
> *Thou art the living stream of the maidens,*
> *And of them who bear child,*
> *And of women of aged years.*
> *Thou art the vessel of fullness,*
> *Thou art the cup of wisdom.*
> *Thou art the well-spring of health,*
> *The wished-for visitant of the homes of the world.*[41]

....
40. *Carmina Gadelica*, 3.
41. *Carmina Gadelica*, 256.

When you seek out written prayers, don't limit yourself to just Celtic (or Pagan) sources. Prayers from every faith throughout recorded time can be adapted to your devotions. Many of them need little more than a change of gender, if that. This medieval prayer is one of my favorites— I just changed "God" to "Brigid":

> Brigid is over all things, under all things; outside all;
> within but not enclosed; without but not excluded;
> above but not raised up; below but not depressed;
> wholly above, presiding; wholly beneath, sustaining;
> wholly without, embracing; wholly within, filling.[42]

Isn't that lovely? When I speak it aloud, I feel Brigid's pleasure in the words as well as my own.

The language of prayer is purely a matter of personal taste. Sometimes I use what might be called the "high language" (thee, thou, thine) and sometimes not. In the Goddess-spirit community over the years there has been argument about using such language, with the objection being that it is "patriarchal"—a catch-all word that sometimes means that a bruised place from a childhood religion is being poked. I like the high language especially for prayer that moves into very deep places, trance, and visioning. I certainly don't think Brigid demands it, but it is both an offering of my respect and a portal that takes me out of the mundane and into the otherworldly. I don't address my fellow humans as "thee" and "thou," after all. But far from being more formal and distancing, the use of these other terms actually feels more intimate, rather like the difference between *vous* and *tu* in French, where only those who are within the closest circle of connection are invited to use the more familiar word. "I am one with thee, Goddess, and thou art one with me" is a different flavor of prayer than "I am one with you…" Not better, not worse, just different. Brigid hears you no matter what language you use.

Prayer can be structured and improvised at the same time. Celtic prayer lends itself especially well to this. Create a basic rhythm structure with a repeated phrase and then let the words flow forth in spontaneous gratefulness:

42. Hildebert (1055–1133), Archbishop of Tours.

I arise with inspiration, thanks be to Brigid.
I work with excellence, thanks be to Brigid.
I provide food with joy, thanks be to Brigid.
I face the night with no fear, thanks be to Brigid.

When I find myself in a funk or a wave of pessimism, a prayer like this will help me regain my perspective. It's a good style of prayer to say out loud in the car—get your kids to join in with a call and response!

Connection with the Goddess can be formal liturgy or as casual as a conversation with a friend. Brigid may offer you revelations as part of a vision quest, or she may caution you to be extra careful going down the stairs. She may tell you to make a major life change, or she may tell you to eat more protein. As the saying goes, "I am the Mother of All Things, and All Things should wear a sweater." Your life decisions are not trivial to Brigid.

All this is a way of saying, don't ever worry about doing prayer "right." Prayer is dialogue, not monologue. It is connection, not performance. Especially if you were raised with a religious upbringing that only used formal prayers, you may feel a little self-conscious about just chatting with Brigid over a cup of tea (or a pint of beer!). Take a deep breath and remember that she always welcomes you.

The Genealogy of Brigid

The poem known as the "Genealogy of Brigid" has become beloved liturgy for many devotees and flamekeepers. This invocation can be used on a daily basis—every day and every night, as the poem says—or it can be recited when you are feeling caught in a fear vortex and need a powerful affirmation of Brigid's protection:

Every day and every night
That I say the genealogy of Brigid,
I shall not be killed, I shall not be harried,
I shall not be put in cell, I shall not be wounded,
No fire, no sun, no moon shall burn me,
No lake, no water, no sea shall drown me:
For I am child of Poetry;

Poetry, child of Reflection;
Reflection, child of Meditation;
Meditation, child of Lore;
Lore, child of Research;
Research, child of Great Knowledge;
Great Knowledge, child of Intelligence;
Intelligence, child of Comprehension;
Comprehension, child of Wisdom;
Wisdom, child of Brigid.[43]

I feel a mystical sense of moving inward as I recite this incantation of protection—layer upon layer of mystery pull me deeper. Let's walk together back through the generations and explore the genealogy of Brigid.

We begin with Brigid herself. She is the source of this lineage of deepening. She is the mother of Wisdom, the innate inner knowing that is in all women, if we will only trust and heed it. For many women, this trust in our own wisdom comes as we age, and it's no surprise that crones are considered wise. Some wisdom does indeed come with time, but it's also a matter of coming to accept what you know. You hear the voice of Brigid, and you know it is true.

Wisdom is the mother of Comprehension. Drawing from your deep inner knowing, you come to understand the things you contemplate. The word *comprehend* means "to grasp," and from the place of wisdom, you grasp the meaning and pattern of life's experiences. Wisdom feeds your understanding as a mother feeds her daughter.

Comprehension is the mother of Intelligence. You understand on an intuitive level, and then you begin to analyze it, break it down, and solve the problems of life from a more logical place. The wisdom given you by

....

43. The first part of the prayer appears in *Carmina Gadelica*, listing the names of Saint Brigid's father, grandfather, and other generations in her patriarchal line. The last part is a section of the twelfth-century "Colloquy of the Two Sages." Caitlín Matthews may have been the first to associate the two, in her book *The Elements of the Celtic Tradition*. *Carmina Gadelica*, 70, and Stokes, "The Colloquy of the Two Sages."

Brigid has been deepened, expanded, and now it is sharpened and made useful in the ways of the world.

Intelligence is the mother of Great Knowledge. This reminds me of the proverb "The fox knows many things, but the hedgehog knows One Big Thing." Intelligence is your fox-mind, seeing many things, taking it all in, strategizing. Then one day you may have an epiphany, a Great Knowledge moment, where something vital is made clear to you, something on which your passion turns.

And this hedgehog moment leads to Great Knowledge's child, Research. Research isn't a drudgery but a joy when it is spurred on by passion. Brigid blesses all true scholars, because they pursue excellence according to their heart's delight. When you delve into topics that beguile, your inner flame of curiosity is fed. The curious mind loves to learn, and Brigid's daughters have a strong appetite for learning.

Research is the mother of Lore. Along the winding paths of your serendipitous learning, you find the stories that feed your imagination and explain your cosmology—myths, tales, history, all the ways we express and record the great mysteries of life. When you take time to explore Lore thoroughly and with your full awareness of metaphor, symbol, and language, it becomes more than mere words. It leads you to Lore's child, Meditation.

Meditation releases you from scholarly and intellectual pursuits. Now you simply *are*, letting thoughts float through your consciousness and away, trusting that what Brigid most wants you to see will linger. The vast, beautiful world of Lore has become part of you now, adding to your dreams both waking and sleeping. In meditation, you accept both what you know and what you will never know.

Meditation is the mother of Reflection. In meditation, you encourage thoughts to come and go. In reflection, you encourage them to stay. You are thoughtful—full of thought—yet your mind is as calm and serene as a reflecting pool. From these deep waters is born Reflection's child, Poetry.

Poetry, welcome! Child of Reflection, grandchild of Meditation, offspring of all the qualities of ancestral Wisdom going back to the spark herself, Brigid. Poetry, in its fullest sense, is how you express yourself in this lifetime. Some women express their poetry in words, but all women express it in deeds. From your life's poem is born awareness of your place in the universe, your sacred path, and your relationship to Brigid. No fire, no sun, no moon shall burn you. No lake, no water, no sea shall drown you. The genealogy is complete.

BRIGID'S ETERNAL FLAME

As I sit down to write today, I light a candle to invoke Brigid's blessings and inspiration. I ask her to show me how best to serve her and to help me make my word-offering with love. In the act of flame-lighting and prayer, I am one woman in a long line of women who have performed the same simple act of connection and devotion. Or perhaps "line" isn't the right word—Brigid whispers in my ear, puts an image in my mind's eye—it is a spiral, a series of spirals, coming forth from a central flame that has burned since before measured time.

When we feel ourselves connected in this way, it's as comforting as Brigid's soft lambs-wool cloak draped over our chilly, lonely shoulders. We are part of a continuum of faith. The things we have in common are far more powerful than our differences. My desk candle burns in a pottery candleholder made in Ireland. Around the base are the words "Saint Brigid's Cathedral, Kildare." The flame dances and glows through stylized flame-shaped cutouts edged in deep, warm orange. It is both ancient and modern in feel, as it should be. Kildare, the flame, the flamekeepers, Brigid herself—are all timeless. When we step back and take the long perspective—or come in very close and see only the flame—then small matters like saint and cathedral, goddess and grove, fall away. There are women who worship Brigid as goddess and there are women who revere Brigid as saint, and Brigid clearly wants it this way. From the great flame that is her spirit, women light their individual and community flames and carry them out into the world to inspire and illuminate. Brigid wants only the fire, in whatever container of faith you choose. She blesses and loves all her daughters of devotion. And we are all sisters in her name.

"Brigid's Fire: The Offering," by Joanna Powell Colbert, 2014.

Offering the Flame

JOANNA POWELL COLBERT

Joanna Powell Colbert practices creativity as a devotional path, whether expressed through artwork, writing, nature connection, or calling circles of women to gather on retreat.

———

As an artist, I know what it's like to be filled with *awen*—that mysterious elixir of inspiration that flows through you like a river of fire, pushing everything out of its way until you've poured your vision out on paper or canvas with paint or ink.

The initial spark comes in many ways. Sometimes an image or idea comes in meditation, and sometimes a palette of colors captures your imagination. Sometimes you're moved by words you read or hear, or you want to capture a feeling or experience.

And sometimes, the Muse (the Goddess, the Holy One) wakes you up in the middle of the night with firm, clear instructions.

One night in mid-January, I woke up around 3:00 A.M. with this distinct thought: *I have to paint a portrait of Brigid, where she is offering us her sacred fire, holding it out in her hands.* I got up and made some thumbnail sketches, then fell back asleep. When I woke the next morning and looked at my notes, I felt an electric jolt move through my body. I recognized the dream-thought as a mandate from Brigid. A calling. And I knew it had to be done in time for her holy day of Candlemas/Imbolc on February 1.

I had no choice but to respond.

I hadn't had any plans to paint a new image of Brigid—in fact, I had no plans to paint at all. My focus and intentions for the year were all around writing.

But when the Lady calls, I answer.

So I cleared my calendar, canceled quite a few projects and appointments, and got to work. The next ten days were in turn exhilarating and exhausting. I felt a bit like I'd been whisked away by the faeries, caught up in a creative vortex as I painted her portrait, experiencing "flow," where hours slip away like minutes.

I played with new techniques, paints, inks, and colored pencils. I did pencil sketches and color studies. I listened to Celtic music, especially harp music, hour after hour after hour. I took breaks for ecstatic dance, but I barely left my studio for sustenance and sleep.

Then finally she was done.

And I felt Brigid accepting my offering with a slow smile and a twinkle in her eye.

In the image I painted, we see Brigid offering us her sacred fire—the fire of creativity that brings forth poetry, music, and art; the fire in the head that is the hallmark of shamans, seers, and bards; the fire of the forge that symbolizes transformation; the fire of healing in the hands; the fire of medicinal and magical herbs; the fire of the sun emerging from its winter slumber; the fire at the center of the earth waking up once more to spring.

And she asks us:

Will you accept my offering?

And what will you offer me in return?

I do accept the offering of her sacred fire, and in return I offer: my heart, my skills, my life.

For more about Joanna and a link to her painting in color,
see the Contributors appendix.

Brigidine Sisters

From ancient days, women have gathered to tend Brigid's perpetual fire and to do good works inspired by her example. First as priestesses, then as nuns, and now again as priestesses, these sisters persevered through many hardships to follow in her footsteps and serve the world through sacred vocation. We've already talked about Saint Brigid and the monastery she founded at Kildare. In the twelfth century, the monastery was destroyed, and from then until 1807, we don't know for sure what happened to the women who worshiped Brigid. In times of oppression, religious communities often go underground, continuing to live and work together in secret. Surely the flame did not go out within the hearts of those who loved Brigid, and when the time was right, she called her daughters forth again.

On Imbolc 1807, in Tullow, County Carlow, six women became the first Sisters of Saint Brigid and took up residence at the house their priest-sponsor had found for them. The sisters declared that this wasn't a new congregation but a reestablishing of the Order of St. Brigid of Kildare. This is where our thread of continuity picks up. The priestesses who tended the holy flame of Brigid at Kildare and the nuns who took up that flame in the fifth century were now linked in spirit with these first six women who called themselves Brigidines. Let us bless their memories: Eleanor Tallon, Bridget Brien, Judith Whelan, Margaret Kinsella, Eleanor Dawson, and Catherine Doyle.

Though the sisters were nearly illiterate, their enthusiasm was boundless, and they opened a school soon after their founding. An oak sapling was brought from Kildare which the sisters ceremonially planted on the convent grounds. As the tree grew, so did the nuns' community. The sisters educated themselves as they taught others. It was a life of austerity and discipline, long hours and few comforts, but the women persevered and more joined them.

Over the next decades, the Brigidines branched out with as much vigor as their now well-established oak tree. They founded new convents, took in orphans, started a button factory to earn money to fund their projects, and created two boarding schools. Educated women joined the sisterhood, as did accomplished musicians and artisans. The reputation of the sisters for educational excellence grew, and the congregation was given formal approval by the Vatican as a religious order.

In 1883, six Brigidine sisters set sail for Australia to found a school and convent. They were greeted with cheers and bells, an auspicious beginning, but their life there was hugely challenging and five of the women died young within a few years. Nevertheless, more foundations were made in Australia, then in New Zealand, and then in locations around the world, including the United States. Today, in addition to teaching, the sisters run retreats, do counseling work in prisons, and work with indigenous and special-needs children. The spirit of Brigid is evident in their passionate involvement in human rights activism and environmentalism worldwide. The Brigidine motto, *Fortiter et Suaviter*, "Strength and Gentleness," affirms the power of women to change the world.

Solas Bhríde

In 1992, two Brigidine sisters, Mary Minehan and Phil O'Shea, set up the small Centre for Celtic Spirituality in Kildare. They named their new endeavor Solas Bhríde, "Brigid's light." The following year, they co-hosted an international conference called "Brigid: Prophetess, Earthwoman, Peacemaker." At that conference the perpetual flame of Brigid was relit, which the Brigidine sisters at Solas Bhríde have tended ever since. From 1992 to 2005, the flame also burned in Kildare's town square during the annual Féile Bríde (Brigid's Festival) celebrations. The sisters were invited to conduct a ritual with the flame to open the 1995 United Nations World Conference on Women, and Celtic singer Nóirín Ní Riain carried the flame to Beijing for the conference itself. Since then, the flame has been carried to peace conferences around the world.

In a wonderful example of how Brigid works to weave the cloth of commonality between faiths, the Brigidine sisters of Solas Bhríde participated in the 2004 Goddess Conference in Glastonbury, England. They brought Brigid's flame from Kildare to be added to five other sacred flames: the conference flame, lit by the sun; the Hiroshima Peace Flame, lit by a woman survivor from the embers of the nuclear aftermath; Bridie's Flame from the Isle of Lewis in the Hebrides; and the Children's Flame and the Madonna Ministry Flame from the United States. The conference attendees were invited to light a seed candle from this flame and take it forth into the world. You can still do this today if you visit Solas Bhríde.

To celebrate the bicentennial of the founding of the Brigidine Order, the Brigidine Congregation purchased a site for a pilgrimage center and hermitage in Kildare. Seven oak trees were planted there on International Pilgrimage Day, July 7, 2007 (7/7/07), and after a fundraising campaign, construction on the center began in 2013.

The Brigidines at Kildare emphasize Brigid's qualities of hospitality, care for the earth, contemplation, and women's leadership. Along with their outreach community Cairde Bhríde, "friends of Brigid," they offer retreats, rituals, and pilgrimages, share the lore of Brigid, do circle dancing, and hold an annual weeklong festival at Féile Bríde, as well as gatherings at Samhain, Beltane, and Lughnasadh. In September 2013, a gathering at Solas Bhríde set an official Guinness World Record for the most Brigid's crosses made at one time—357!

In their words, the Brigidine sisters "seek to unfold the legacy of Brigid of Kildare and its relevance for our world." They welcome "people of all faiths and of no faith." The sisters welcome those who seek Brigid as goddess or as Saint Brigid, and feel that the two are inextricably interwoven. In the words of the Brigidines in Australia, "There is mystery at the heart of what holds us together, expressed in shared faith, symbols, stories, and experiences. We engage with the issues of our time, stand in solidarity with the oppressed, and seek to build a more inclusive community." [44]

Ord Brighideach

Ord Brighideach International is a Brigidine Order of Flamekeepers (not affiliated with the Catholic Brigidine Order). Founded in 2005 by its abbess, Kim Diane, the order now has around 700 flamekeepers worldwide, each of whom vows to faithfully tend a flame in Brigid's name for a daylong shift. I've been a flamekeeper with the order since 2007. Their website says, "Our belief is that Brighid the goddess and Brigit the saint are inseparable." Abbess Kim explains, "It's hard not to see her as the same entity morphed by homespun traditions and migrating religious belief systems transcending centuries. Seeing her as one entity gives me a sense of comfort that there has been a continuous thread through the spiritual ebb and flow of a Celtic theological journey. Ord Brighideach is, therefore, an interfaith order."

You can choose to join as an individual flamekeeper or join a cell. The cells each contain nineteen flamekeepers, in the ancient tradition of nineteen priestesses or nuns tending the flame of Brigid. Each cell is named for a sacred tree or plant, such as Cill Abhaill (Apple), Cill Caorthann (Rowan), and Cill Coll (Hazel). There are both all-female and mixed-gender cells, and at this writing there is also one all-male cell (Cill Drualus, Mistletoe). You can also join as a complete cell, if you have nineteen people committed to tending together.

44. www.brigidine.org.au.

The order's website has a calendar that shows the shifts for each month. If, for example, you have the eighth shift in the nineteen-day cycle, you can see what day that shift falls on. The shifts run from sunset to sunset, in the Celtic tradition.

When a new member joins Ord Brighideach, she is asked to swear an oath of her own devising that she will faithfully tend her flame. As each flamekeeper has a personal relationship with Brigid, the terms of that oath are individually determined—it's between you and your goddess. The order asks that if you find you can't fulfill your oath and tend your shifts as flamekeeper, you withdraw and let someone else fill that shift, to keep the energy flowing strongly. If you wish, you can ask for a candle that was lit from the flame at Kildare. These candles carry the energy of that flame, and when you relight the candle and use it as a seed candle for other flames you light, you are linking energetically with Kildare. The Ord Brighideach website contains personal stories from flamekeepers, shared prayers and blessings, and Brigid lore.[45]

Brigit's Daughter
MAEL BRIGDE

Mael Brigde, cat-lover, plant-lover, and writer of hidden poetry, founded the Daughters of the Flame in 1993, thus helping to initiate the modern Brigidine flame-tending movement.

———

In 1993, I did two things that changed my life, giving it a focus and an element of devotion that would strengthen over time. I decided to relight the perpetual flame of Brigit and share that dedication with other women. And I became initiated into her service (my name, Mael Brigde, means servant of Brigit), offering her my life.

....
45. www.ordbrighideach.org.

That January, I prepared myself and invited women—Neopagan and Christian—to take shifts as Daughters of the Flame. Beginning in Canada, we've tended her fire from Indonesia to Italy. As Brigit's daughters, we are blessed with the charge of keeping her flame alive in ourselves and in the world. We take part in the exuberant awakening that commitment to her brings.

On Imbolc 1993, I lit her candle for the first time, and went with two sisters-in-the-spirit to a glacial mountain stream. There I undressed and plunged beneath the waters of death, leaving my old self behind. When I emerged, amazingly warm after the icy dousing, I dressed in a new garment, and a new consecration. I met the Hag at the far side of the stream:

Mael Brigde: Great Goddess, I am your daughter, contemplating your mystery. Grant me entrance into the River of Death, that it may cleanse me and be the womb of my rebirth.

Hag: In whose name do you ask?

Mael Brigde: I ask in the name of the Goddess of Green and Blue and Gold. I ask in your name, Dark Mother, fire of the sun, water of the moon, warrior, gravedigger, mourner. Tender mother, strong daughter, loving sister. Mediator of disputes. I ask in the name of you, the Unbroken Vessel from whom all life comes and through whom all is unified.

I ask in the name of Brigit the smith and the Morrigan, whose feet are in the River of Death, who cleave flesh from bone, soul from body; in the name of Brigit the nourisher and guide, Danu, Anu, whose fine hands placed the steppingstones across the stream; in the name of Brigit the healer and consoler, liberator and inspirer.

Brigit of the Poets, initiate me. As you loosen the grip of the coldest season, so loosen and liberate me. Breathe life into me this Imbolc as you breathe life into the mouth of the dead winter.

When I was allowed to pass and had been welcomed by the Mother Goddess, I was asked by her to commit myself.

Mother: What do you pledge, Daughter?

Mael Brigde: I pledge myself to the fire of life, to the poetry of the soul, to the forging of our strongest, supplest, most radiant selves, to the healing of my life, ever forward, gently, to the mending of all hurts and conflicts, to the healing of those around me, to the protection and healing of your living planet through word and deed and joy.

If I should break faith with you,

May the skies fall upon me,

May the seas drown me,

May the earth rise up and swallow me.

I was unaware of it then, but on Imbolc 1993, when we Daughters of the Flame kindled Brigit's fire in Vancouver, Canada, the Catholic Brigidine sisters in Kildare, Ireland, relit her fire as well. Over the years that followed, numerous groups have sprung up to keep Brigit's flame, and more will follow. One woman who passed through our midst has changed the face of Brigidine worship. Kim Diane joined the Daughters in our fifth year, with the idea of starting an online flame-tending group and an email discussion list available to all followers of Brigit; the next year she initiated Ord Brighideach.

It's been more than twenty-one years since I kept my first shift with Brigit. In that time I've met many who are drawn to her, nourished by what she symbolizes and what we can bring forth in offering to the world on her behalf. We've sung songs, written poems, and created jewelry, drawings, and books. In her name we've done ritual and performed services of reconciliation, empowerment, and compassion. We've sat with the dying, prayed with the suffering, shared our celebrations and our pain, given birth, married, grown discouraged, emerged from heartbreak, endured illness, and died.

My practice has changed a great deal since I began this journey. I have moved from a largely Wiccan approach to a Celtic Reconstructionist worldview, with glimmers of the Catholic still shining through. I am immensely grateful to Brigit for bridging, for myself and others, the Pagan and Christian worlds, for leading me into communion with my ancestors, and closer to myself and my fellow seekers. Within and without our communities, we attend more to our differences than to our similarities, and this has brought great harm. When I prayed with the Brigidine Sisters in Kildare, the sister leading the devotion added "or however we see divinity," with a glance to me after saying the word "God." I was moved by the grace and gentleness that Brigit's flame can bestow on people who have so long been divided from each other. Brigit stands above us all, reconciling Protestant and Catholic, Christian and Pagan, atheist and seeker. Her presence is a never-ending blessing in my life. The long darkness is over. Her blaze is reignited. I give great thanks.[46]

For more about Mael Brigde, see the Contributors appendix.

FLAMEKEEPING: TIME AND TIMELESSNESS

What does it mean to be a flamekeeper? It means slowing down, stilling your chattering mind, breathing in peace. It means being completely in the moment, a moment that is distilled down to its essence. When you touch the living flame to its waiting fuel—whether that be honeyed beeswax, fragrant oil, or sacred wood—you are enacting a ritual that is both ancient and immediate. There is a mystical aspect to flamekeeping, something indescribable and individual, a shiver that runs through you in the act of making holy fire.

Flamekeeping requires attention, even if your flame burns for only a few moments. Dedicating yourself as a flamekeeper can range from simply lighting a candle to Brigid on a particular day to maintaining a perpetual flame to her. Whichever you choose, your small fire is added to the collective fire. This element of fire has life, energy, movement,

....
46. Portions of this essay were previously published in Murphy-Hiscock, *Out of the Broom Closet.*

power, and yet it calms and quiets the spirit. Within that quiet, Brigid is beckoning. Within that quiet, she hears your call.

> Come over the hills, O Brigid bright and fair,
> Come over the hills to your daughter,
> Kindle the flame that illuminates your name
> And I'll keep that flame bright forever.
> For strong grows the oak in Brigid's ancient grove,
> And fair glide her swans on the river,
> Clear runs the water within her blessed wells,
> And bright burn her fires forever.[47]

Temporal Flames

The word *temporal* has to do with earthly time, as opposed to eternity. When you tend a temporal flame, you choose a particular period of time for your flamekeeping. The priestesses (and nuns) who tended the sacred fire of Brigid did so in twenty-day cycles—nineteen women each took her turn to watch over the fire for a day, and on the twentieth day Brigid herself kept the watch. This shift was a time when the woman's focus was on the flame, on her sacred purpose and her path, a time when prayers were offered and the connection with Brigid was made stronger through dedicated hours spent in her service.

Dedicating a special time to light a flame to Brigid and offer your prayers creates a glow in your soul that lasts long after the temporal flame is extinguished. Many of us light candles on our altars all the time, whether as part of regular devotions or for special purposes or magical workings. But there is something comforting about having a particular flamekeeping time. Brigid is a goddess who likes rhythm, the steadiness that cycles and seasons and patterns bring. Listen and she will guide you to a practice that fulfills and feeds you.

---

47. Sing to the tune of "Red Is the Rose" or "The Bonnie Banks o' Loch Lomond" (same melody).

DAILY

Lighting a candle every day is a beautiful act of devotion. But let's be realistic—some of the time you just won't be able to, and some of the time you just won't want to. Don't set yourself up to feel a sense of failure if you drop the ball—or the match, as it were. While it's good to push your boundaries and deepen your spiritual path, a wise woman will make a practice that fits her real life. If you feel strongly called to tend a daily flame, find a way to make it easy. There are two good ways to do this: make the flame brief, or make it part of your regular daily routine.

A brief flame is just as powerful and meaningful as a flame that burns for hours or days. Giving yourself over to one minute of profound prayer is fine. You don't even need to use a candle or lamp—in a pinch you can simply light a match and connect to the energy of Brigid's flame for that ephemeral moment you hold the tiny torch in your hand.

Making flamekeeping part of your regular daily routine requires some creativity. First, think over the things that you do every day, no matter how mundane, beginning when you wake. Then ask yourself if flamekeeping will fit in with those activities and what form it could take. For instance, in my morning routine, one of the first things I do is put water in a kettle for tea. As I wait for the water to boil, instead of checking my email, I could light a dedicated candle that I keep in the kitchen and extinguish it when the kettle whistles. On mornings when I have a bit more time, I could take that first cup of tea and sit with the candle, gathering my dreams from the night and my hopes for the day. A simple daily flamekeeping doesn't have to happen in the morning, of course. Just run through your day in your mind and make note of the things that happen every day, no matter what. Those are the pockets of time where you can offer a flame to Brigid.

SABBATH

The word *sabbath* means "rest," something we need more pressingly today than ever before—not so much a rest from labor as a rest from the pressures of the roaring world. Taking a day once a week to tend Brigid's flame offers an opportunity to tend your flame within as well. Turn off all electronics and let time expand into slow time. As you watch over your sabbath flame, move thoughtfully through the day with full attention. Let your activities be restful ones that replenish you. Make art, do needlework and other slow crafts, read, cook, write letters (actual paper letters!) to loved ones. Watch the clouds drifting overhead, and listen to the sounds of your environment. Tune in. Breathe deeply. Regain your perspective. Gaze into your flame and feel the approving presence of Brigid as you care for yourself in this quiet way. Rest in her warm embrace.

NEW MOON AND FULL MOON

Women are strongly connected to and influenced by the moon. Our cycles mirror her waxing and waning, physically and emotionally, long after our bleeding years are over. Making a special time of flamekeeping in accordance with the moon is an act of woman-power. You might choose to do this at new moon, at full moon, or both. The energies are quite different at new and full moons, and you will experience these energies in ways that are unique to you.

New moon could be considered the time when the moon is completely dark (not visible). This is how it's marked on calendars, and modern Pagan practice usually calls this the beginning of the lunar cycle. Personally, I like to call this "dark moon" rather than new moon. To me, it feels crone-like, a time of dissolution and ending rather than newness and beginning. In the moonless night's darkness, tending Brigid's flame offers a time of deepening. This is a good time for inward journeying, journal writing, divination, and connecting with Brigid for advice and guidance.

What the Celts called new moon was almost certainly the sight of the first slender crescent in the early evening sky, perhaps two days past what we call new moon today. Traditional prayers to the new moon praise her appearance, not her absence:

I am raising to thee mine eye,
I am bending to thee my head,

I am offering thee my love,
Thou new moon of all the ages! [48]

Tending a flame that you light when you see the first crescent connects you to those ancient Celts, to the priestesses of Brigid who gazed up at that same moon and felt the stirrings of the waxing light. That quality of Brigid—light-bringer—can be evoked with a simple ceremony in which you light a flame and spend devotional time with it until the moon slips below the western horizon. Bid her goodnight as you extinguish your flame.

Full moon was the beginning of the Celts' month, and I like the idea of the extra energy and oomph that the full moon brings in the context of starting a new monthly cycle. Tending a flame to Brigid at full moon, from moonrise to moonset, can be a time when you offer prayers for projects, intentions, positive outcomes, and other ways you ask Brigid for her practical help. As you light your flame, hold its container in your hands and make a ritual gesture of offering the flame to the moon, feeling the connection between the two lights, and envisioning Brigid in that stream of brilliance. You needn't be awake all night during your flamekeeping, as long as the flame is in a safe place. If you awaken early enough to see the moonset, extinguish your flame then; otherwise, just extinguish it when you wake.

BRIGIDINE CYCLE

We don't know why the number nineteen was chosen for the priestesses who tended Brigid's fire. It may have been as simple as there were only nineteen women in the initial group, and from there it became a tradition. I like the symbolism of nineteen being a prime number—it can't be divided. An auspicious number for a dedicated sisterhood! Modern flamekeepers also form groups of nineteen to take the flamekeeping duties in turn. For a period of twenty-four hours, each person holds the intention of being the flamekeeper for that shift. Being part of a flamekeeping circle can be greatly rewarding, but you can also observe a nineteen-day cycle on your own.

....
48. *Carmina Gadelica*, 308.

1. Using your regular calendar, choose a beginning date within the calendar month (the simplest choice would be the first of the month) and mark a period of nineteen days.

2. On the first day, light your devotional flame and ask Brigid to bless you over those next nineteen days. Take your time and have a good talk with her, telling her your concerns, your hopes, and your intentions for that time period. Feel her closeness and her love, and know that she will continue to be with you in the days to come. When you are ready, extinguish the flame and set it aside. Leave the flame unlit.

3. On the nineteenth day, relight the flame. Again, spend some time with Brigid, looking back over the days past, giving thanks, asking for clarity, coming to a greater understanding of the lessons learned. When you extinguish the flame, do it with the awareness that Brigid herself will be tending it for the twentieth day. The flame is no longer alight in your presence, but it burns steadily in Brigid's heart, and you are a precious part of that flame.

4. You can repeat this nineteen-day cycle throughout the year, which would amount to about thirty-six flamekeeping days in a calendar year (always counting the twentieth day as Brigid's day).

Another way to observe the Brigidine cycle is to perform a ritual in which you tend a flame for nineteen consecutive days, lighting a new candle every night. (Remember, the Celtic day starts at sunset.) Tealights are perfect for this. They burn for about three hours, so they will be safely out by the time you go to bed. Each day can be dedicated to a particular quality of Brigid or a focus for her blessing. I've offered an example of this, using a simple invocation for each day's lighting, on page 242. I'm sure Brigid will inspire you to create others! Even though this is a ritual that takes nineteen days, each day's devotions can take just as much time as you wish—and that may vary from day to day. You may take just a moment or two to light your flame and invoke Brigid, or you may end up spending hours in contemplation, inner journeying, journaling, art-making, or whatever Brigid inspires you to do in her honor.

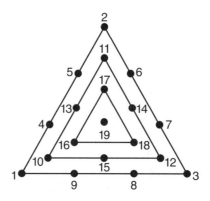

If you wish (and if you have the space), you can lay out nineteen
tealights in this pattern and light them in the order shown (follow the
dot-to-dot!). This pattern moves you around the triangle several times,
moving toward the center. Such shapes and movements have magical
power, which can add to your flamekeeping meditations. At the end
of your nineteenth day, as you extinguish your flame, offer the fire to
Brigid and envision her taking it from you, to keep it burning bright
forever.

VIGIL

Tending a flame for a full night can carry you to unexpected places.
In the wee hours, when the world is quiet, every subtle and symbolic
nuance can be seen and contemplated in depth. Time passes slowly,
with no electronic interruptions. Your body is experienced in unfamil-
iar ways through its cycle of weariness and wakefulness and perhaps
euphoria. The mystical becomes probable. Watching your flame burn
low, then lighting a new candle or replenishing your lamp's oil, you may
feel a particularly intimate sense of devotion. If you have been going
through a time of feeling scattered or ungrounded in your faith, setting
aside a full night with your flame can put things in brilliant perspective.

Start your vigil at sunset, having made all preparations ahead of
time for solitude, sustenance, and security. Release all expectations and
goals—don't set yourself a bunch of tasks, such as divination or journal
writing. Follow your impulses of the moment, as Brigid guides you. At

sunrise, bless and thank your flame, extinguish it if you wish, and spend the day in peaceful contemplation and rest.

Perpetual Flames

Temporal flames are lit and extinguished according to earthly time, in honor of Brigid's connection to our daily lives. Perpetual flames burn without ceasing, honoring Brigid's eternal presence, such as the flame that burns in the town square in Kildare. I've been a perpetual flame-keeper for many years. Wherever I've lived, I've had a candle that is always lit, unless I'm away from home overnight. Because it's at the center of my house, I see it when I pass from room to room, and I can see it from my desk as I work every day. As one candle burns down, I ceremonially light the next one. My Brigid flame has become a beloved part of my everyday life, a little beacon of blessing glowing in my shadowy dining room.

I use tall jar candles for my perpetual flame, which burn for about three days. When the wick gets close to the bottom of the jar, I light the next one, saying the same prayer I always use for this purpose. I bless the new candle, then thank and bless the old candle and extinguish its flame. As I do this, I envision the energy of the flame passing from one container to the next with no interruption. I reach out to sense a connection between my flame and all other devotional flames around the world.

There is great power in perpetual flames, just as there is power in tending a temporal flame. I experience these in different ways. My perpetual flame feels protective and serves as a visible affirmation that my faith is strong, no matter what. I light daily candles on my workspace altar to Brigid, to bless my day and ask for her help as I do my work. I also light a devotional candle at my desk if I am working on something that has to do with spirituality (such as this book). These temporal flames call my mind to attention much more than the perpetual flame. They need to be lit more often and watched more closely. There is an opportunity to note the passage of time and what has happened in the time since I lit the candle and the time it has extinguished itself. If I'm using a bigger candle or lamp that needs to be extinguished by hand, it's an opportunity to thank Brigid, to bring my mind back to her gifts and blessings in my life.

Invoking the Fire

There is a moment when you have an unlit candle and a moment when your candle burns bright—and a moment in between, when you pause at the edge of time and are one with eternity. Take that moment.

Saying a prayer to bless the lighting of your flame focuses your attention and dedicates the flame to Brigid as it burns. By invoking her with the action of creating fire, you are acknowledging that she is present in that flame. She has been made welcome to your sacred space and to the sacred center of your being. The Celtic style of rhythmic triads works well for flame lighting (see page 172). You might start with the symbolism of the flame and how it represents Brigid for you, and then just improvise:

> *Brigid of the spark,*
> *Brigid of the flame,*
> *Brigid of the embers,*
> *I call you in.*
> *Brigid of inspiration,*
> *Brigid of shielding,*
> *Brigid of comfort,*
> *I call you in.*
> *Be in my flame, O Brigid of courage.*
> *Be in my flame, O Brigid of grace.*
> *Be in my flame, O Brigid of beauty.*
> *This night and every night, this day and every day.*

You may prefer to have a regular prayer you say with every lighting, establishing your own tradition, such as:

> *From the fire of Kildare to my altar fire,*
> *The flame is eternal, the flame is one.*

Ending your prayers with a closing phrase or word is a nice touch that signifies you are turning to other tasks now, with respect for Brigid and for the conclusion of your devotions. I usually end my prayers with "Blessed be," in the Pagan/Wiccan way. The word *amen* could also be used—an Irish translation of amen is *áiméan* (pronounced awe-mayn). Find the closing words that feel right for you—you could even use "hey-hey!" in a merry Irish style. Spirituality is always respectful, but it doesn't always have to be solemn.

Faithfulness and Compassion

Being a flamekeeper is a sacred task, and one that you will take seriously. Your faithfulness to that task will feed your spirit and enhance your sense of self-worth. You are honoring the Goddess and honoring yourself in her service. Be sure to extend compassion to yourself if, as will certainly happen, you don't meet your intentions perfectly. A candle will gutter out because of a faulty wick, or you will forget to notice when a jar candle is getting low, or the day of your flamekeeping shift will slip by you. Remember that you are aspiring to excellence, not impeccability. (If you *are* aspiring to impeccability, you will need an extra helping of compassion!) Do the best you can. The other day as I was lighting the daily candle on my Brigid altar, I silently apologized for not lighting it first thing that morning, and instantly heard clear as a bell: "You have too many rules." The thought was so antithetical to my usual Virgo mindset that I knew I'd been lovingly cuffed upside the head by Brigid.

If you find that in time you no longer feel called to be a flamekeeper, stop—with respect and in a conscious manner. Thank Brigid for the opportunity to have tended her fire, and envision the many others who will continue to keep the flame burning bright. There is no shame in stopping and no danger that you have failed. Trust that Brigid understands.

Circle or Solitary?

Joining or creating a flamekeeping circle can provide encouragement and accountability—both helpful especially when you are first starting out as a flamekeeper. As Mael Brigde says on page 129, true sisterhood can develop among women who have a common devotion to Brigid. If you are creating your own circle, you certainly don't need to have the traditional nineteen women! Be creative in the way you work together.

A circle of just three women, for instance, might meet at the full moon to bless the new lunar cycle and kindle their seed candles from a common flame. You could also come together to do a flamekeeping vigil for a special purpose, such as a crisis of healing, an upcoming journey, or a national or international incident. The more you work together, the more you develop a sort of spiritual shorthand that lets you create ritual and prayer on the fly, drawing from the store of material you share with each other throughout the year or extemporizing and just speaking from the heart. Doing devotions in the presence of others solidifies them, and if you feel sometimes that you are not doing it "right," having others to practice with can take away that feeling of doubt.

Tending a solitary flame requires strength of spirit, but it gives great rewards. It's just you and Brigid, so close, so connected. It's not lessthan. The tradition of hermits and anchorites is strong in the Celtic tradition. Religious folk have always practiced their faith apart from community, whether literally dwelling in a little stone hut on an island or just keeping their devotions to themselves while living in the midst of the busy world.

Let's talk a moment about online communities. At its best, the World Wide Web lives up to its name—it weaves strands of connection that vibrate and sing. It helps us find like-minded souls who may become true friends. At its worst, it creates the illusion of connectedness without truly feeding the spirit, and the result can be a hollow bewilderment, a lonely wandering in the fog of the etheric realm. For the solitary flamekeeper, the desire to connect with others through the Internet is perhaps especially strong. It can be comforting to know that there are so many out there who are also tending their fires of devotion. But this can become a distraction, or even an addiction, insidious as any other. If you find that you can't focus on your real-world devotions, or you are reluctant to meet with or talk on the phone with people in your immediate circle, or you can't go a day without checking in online, it's time to get back in balance.

Remember that the practices of spirituality that deepen require the *willingness* to go deep. Clicking to light a digital flame can't compare to touching living fire to a candle wick. Watching the digital flicker onscreen won't carry you to the profound places found by candlelight. By all means, feed your mind and soul with the words of others, but keep it in proportion. Stay in the real world.

Practical Flamekeeping

The type of flame you choose will depend on your style of flamekeeping. Here are some suggestions to get you started.

CANDLES

Tealights are good choices for flamekeeping sessions of two to five hours, and they self-extinguish, so you can light one, perform your devotions and prayers, and then safely leave it to burn out on its own (as long as it's in a container). Tealights are available with the usual paraffin as well as with beeswax and vegetable-based waxes such as soy. Soy-based candles have a lower melting point than other waxes and therefore don't burn as long. Beeswax burns hotter and faster, and the flame can be a little higher. Beeswax is a magical golden substance that is perfect for special-occasion flamekeeping. It holds the essence of ancient wisdom—there is an old saying: "Ask the wild bees what the Druids knew."

Small *votive candles* that are placed in glasses have been overcome in popularity by tealights, which are tidier and don't require scraping out the old wax as with votives. But there is something very cozy and comforting about an old-fashioned votive candle. It melts to fit the shape of its container before it is consumed in the burning, so it lasts much longer than a tealight. Tiered racks that hold multiple votive glasses, traditionally used in churches, can be used to light candles for various intentions at the same time, such as prayers for friends in need, for your own needs, and for the world.

Jar candles come in several shapes and sizes. The most stable is a bulbous-shaped candle sometimes called "Victorian," such as are seen at restaurants or bars. These have a broad base, so they are unlikely to tip over (you really have to try hard), and the flame is sheltered well inside the jar. They burn for about five hours. Tall, narrow jar candles burn for seventy-two hours. One of the nice things about the tall jars is that you can easily add images to them. Just print out or photocopy artwork that inspires you, trim it to fit the dimensions of the jar, and glue it with a regular glue stick. If you want to add glitter, just keep it on the body of the jar, not around the lip, as glitter can pop and fizzle if it gets too close to a flame.

Wood-wick candles are a delightful addition to flamekeeping, with their gentle crackling sound that invokes a tiny cozy hearth. Burning times vary depending on the candle size. *Floating candles* can last from eight to ten hours, and they burn well in groups. The combination of fire and water is evocative of Brigid's sacred wells. And here's a good place for that glitter—sprinkle it across the surface of the water and watch it sparkle in the dancing candlelight. *Tapers* are such lovely candles, with their open flame that seems to aspire toward the heavens. Depending on their length, they can last quite a long time and are a good choice for vigil candles, as they require, well, vigilance! Any open flame (that is, a flame that is not housed within a container) should be burned with full attentiveness and thus can be a compelling focus for longer meditational devotions.

Oil

Oil lamps have a sacred lineage in many religions. Ceremonial pottery lamps have been found that date back thousands of years. We don't know what kind of flame was tended by the Celtic priestesses and nuns of Brigid, but it wouldn't surprise me if it was oil. It may be more practical to use candles for your regular flamekeeping, but the ambiance of an oil-fueled flame has a magical energy all its own. Small oil lamps may burn only an hour or two, and others can be fed with more oil and kept alight. Larger lamps can hold enough oil for many hours or days. You can find beautiful ceramic and hand-blown glass oil lamps on websites such as Etsy, and instructions for making your own lamp can easily be found. Most food-grade oils can be used as fuel, so don't feel that you need to use chemical-heavy and artificially scented lamp oils. Consider the symbolism of the oils you use, such as olive for peace or sunflower for strength. Burning clarified butter (ghee) is especially auspicious for Brigid, goddess of the dairy!

CAMPHOR

Burning camphor is a Hindu devotional custom, one of several ways of blessing by fire, collectively called *aarti*. The small aromatic pellets are held with metal tongs or tweezers and lit, then placed on a plate and waved through the air, or set gently in a bowl of water, which is my preference as a flame offered to Brigid. The floating flames skitter across the surface of the water in a mesmerizing dance, lasting only a few minutes. The essence of the camphor is purifying, dispelling negative energy and opening the spirit to the sacred. The first time I used the floating camphor, I was moved to tears. As with floating candles, the energies of fire and water evoke Brigid's presence in a mystical and beautiful way. The water from either of these offerings can be used to bless and purify; sacred water created in combination with fire is called lustral water.

ALCOHOL

Alcohol offers a fleeting but dramatic and inspiring ceremonial flame. You will need a fireproof metal bowl or chalice. If this container has feet or a stem, make sure it is all one piece, not soldered, as the heat of the flame can cause these to come apart. (I learned this the hard way, as my charming little three-footed cauldron suddenly plopped down on its tummy.) Even a very small container will work, and I recommend that you don't use anything wider than about three inches, especially your first time when you are getting to know this type of flame. The curved interior of the bowl is what creates the graceful shape of the rising flame. Put about half an inch of Epsom salts in the bottom of the bowl, and place the bowl on a heatproof surface, such as a trivet or brick. Add a tablespoon or two of 91 percent isopropyl alcohol. (Lesser percentages of alcohol will not burn well, if at all. You can get this alcohol at any drugstore, though some may keep it behind the counter in the pharmacy department.) Light a wooden match and carefully drop it into the bowl. Do not use a lighter! Depending on the size of your bowl, the flame may reach as high as eight inches or so, and it will burn for several minutes, until the alcohol is consumed. There is no need to extinguish the flame; it will go out on its own.

If you wish, you can create this type of flame without the Epsom salts, which have a purifying effect similar to camphor but aren't necessary. Resin incense can also be used, such as copal or frankincense, and it will release its fragrance upon the air when the flame dies out. This kind of flame is wonderful for blessing an altar space and invoking Brigid's presence in ritual. If you wish, have prayers and invocations on hand to speak as the fire burns, or just gaze into its depths and listen for the voice of the Goddess. The bowl will remain hot for some time after the flame is finished, so use an oven mitt if you need to move it. And always keep a damp towel nearby in case you need to smother the flames. I've performed this kind of fire ceremony many times with no mishaps, but it's wise to take precautions.

Flameless Candles

Nothing will ever take the place of living fire, but I'm including flameless (battery-operated) candles as an option for your flamekeeping for several reasons. You may want to keep a flame dedicated to Brigid at your place of work, where an actual candle might not be allowed. Or you might want to offer a flame to Brigid in a place where fire is not only prohibited but dangerous, such as a hospital room. Personally, I always go ahead and light candles in hotel rooms, but if you are better about following rules than I am, that's another place where a flameless candle could be handy. If you are not comfortable leaving a flame burning when you aren't there to watch over it, a flameless candle could be used to hold energy for a special purpose, such as asking Brigid's protection for a loved one who is traveling.

When you use a flameless candle, it can be more challenging to find the deep sense of connectedness to Brigid's eternal fire. Think of it in terms of energy—as you turn on the switch, you are initiating the *energy* of light. Be sure to do all the prayers and invocations you would do with a living flame. When you turn off the switch, bless and thank the candle as you would with a traditional one. For normal usage, I advise against using the timer that comes on some flameless candles, as your presence and intention are important. But if you do want to use the timer, be mindful of the time so you can be present on the etheric plane with the flame as it goes on and off, holding it clearly in your mind and asking Brigid to be present as well.

Matches vs. Lighters

Pay attention to the act of creating your flame. I prefer wooden matches rather than a lighter. Each flame is born anew, unique, for a match is only used once. The act of striking it against the box or another surface requires a bit of force—just a bit!—so my energy is involved in the flame-making in a more personal way than when just clicking a lighter. A wooden match makes a satisfyingly dramatic hiss and sizzle as it flares to life, and as it burns there is a tiny crackle like an infinitesimal hearthfire. Unlike a lighter, which will keep on burning as long as you hold down the switch, a match flame has a limited lifespan, so your full attention must be brought to its application. Time both speeds up and slows down as you bring match to wick and transfer the living fire from one to the other. Now blow out or shake your match to extinguish it, and observe the fleeting wisp of smoke, the glow of the dying match head. Thank this tool, so commonplace but so valuable. Thank the people who made your matches and the person who invented them. Send a blessing back through time to all your foremothers who had to make fire in far more difficult ways.

Aesthetics

Flamekeeping is a beautiful practice, both internally and externally. The beauty of the flame itself is never-ending, and even if you just light a humble tealight in its little cup, you have satisfied your soul. But do pay attention to what satisfies your senses as well. You don't have to spend a lot of money to find lovely candleholders—after-Christmas sales are a great time to stock up on sparkling candles and holders that you can use in your flamekeeping throughout the year. For instance, I recently saw a votive stand that held multiple glass holders, each adorned with three metal oak leaves. What could be more perfect for Brigid?

When you experience beauty in the act of tending your sacred flame, you will be even more drawn to it. You will give your flamekeeping more attention and focus if you vary the aesthetics from time to time, perhaps with the seasons. It's not trivial or self-indulgent if it gives you pleasure, for delight should always burn at the center of your devotional flame.

CATS AND OTHER CAUTIONARY CONSIDERATIONS

I'm not going to insult you with condescending warnings about never leaving a flame unattended. I know you will keep your wits about you and not set yourself or anything else on fire. Mostly I want to reassure you. With common sense at hand, there is no need to be afraid of fire. It is your friend and ally, and Brigid will be protecting you in your devotions.

An exposed flame such as a taper candle obviously requires more care than a jar candle, where the flame is enclosed by glass. Pillar candles are beautiful, but they are unpredictable in terms of their burning patterns and can easily result in a pool of melted wax that you will spend a lot of time picking out of that nice Irish lace altar cloth. Speaking of cloths, obviously you won't burn your flame anywhere near curtains or other hangings, but also be aware of the type of cloth you set your candle on. A draft could lift the hem of a wispy cloth and float it over an open flame.

Scented candles should only be used when you are nearby to keep an eye on them, as they contain scent oils that can be more volatile than typical unscented candles. They are generally safe, and I've used hundreds of them with no mishaps, but I did have one soy jar candle overly scented with essential oils ignite in a sheet of fire across the surface of the molten wax, with a flame about five inches high. Exciting! Fortunately, no harm was done.

Working safely with fire isn't so much a matter of being cautious as it is being conscious. Be aware of your surroundings, and take the room's activities and occupants into account. Perform tests if you are concerned about a container's safety and stability. When I first started keeping a perpetual flame, I covered the shelf surface in aluminum foil to protect it from melted wax and then shook the bookcase as hard as a rattling earthquake would shake it, to see if the candle would tip over.

(It didn't.) Then I actually did tip the candle over to see what it would do. (It went out.) Even so, I keep my perpetual flame jar candle inside another glass lantern, for two layers of safety.

Keep in mind that if you have several candles burning closely together, they will generate lots of heat and be consumed fast. Groups of glass containers, such as for votive candles, can overheat and crack, and grouped pillar candles will melt all over the place very, very quickly. (They don't show this part in those romantic movie scenes where the room is lit by hundreds of pillar candles.)

Now, what about those cats? Cats have individual personalities, and only you can predict whether your cat will bother a flame. But don't just assume it will be a problem without trying. I've had many cats and many flames, and they've always coexisted peacefully. A tealight that sits deep inside an external container should not be at risk of any feline interference. An open flame will be more problematic if fluffy tails and curious whiskers come close. If your concern is that your cat will knock over a flame, you might consider a hanging lantern or a candle jar inside a larger jar, with water in between. In a pinch, you can always burn your flame in the bathtub!

EXTINGUISHING THE FLAME

How you extinguish your flame is as important as how you light it. This is the moment for thankfulness. Thank Brigid for the honor of serving her sacred fire. Thank the flame itself for blessing your home. Be fully present with the flame before you extinguish it—things are often most powerfully real to us just before they vanish. Think about how the energy of your prayers and intentions continues even when the visible flame is gone.

The manner in which you extinguish your flame is up to you. Some people believe you should never blow out a spiritual or magical flame; others (including me) feel that the breath is sacred too. You may want to use a special candle extinguisher and dedicate it to your flamekeeping practice.

Take a moment as you blow out your candle to watch the last glow of the wick, the spiraling of the smoke. Listening and watching for auguries at such moments and learning how to interpret them is part of being a flamekeeper. Once when I was preparing to light my next perpetual candle, I noticed that the old candle's wick had entwined itself into a triple knot—a powerful affirmation of Brigid's presence in my flame.

CHAPTER FOUR

FORGE:
THE TRANSFORMING FLAME

Three jewels adorn my shield:
The red jewel of passion,
The black jewel of wisdom,
The white jewel of faith.

Within the forge blazes the roaring fire of purification. What no longer serves us is burned away, revealing what is shining and true. The forge is where we are tested by fire, soul-strengthened and challenged to become our most authentic selves. Here is found the spark of creativity, the flame that ignites passionate self-expression. In Brigid's forge we are tempered, melted down, and melded together again, integrating the fragmented parts of ourselves into something that is whole and holy. Here, we are healed. Come, draw near the forge and be transformed.

BRIGID THE CREATRIX

What does it mean to be divinely inspired in a creative process? It means that in the act of creation itself, the ego is set aside. You make yourself a conduit for whatever your beloved deity wants to bring forth upon the earth. The pen moves like lightning over the page, the paintbrush dances across the canvas, the voice lifts in song that comes from a place deep within the soul's knowing. When you can bypass your inner critic and just let Brigid have her way with you, your creativity will flow forth in all its endless brilliance. Refining and revision have their time too. But begin with that initial openness. As with prayer, approach your creative projects with no expectation. You may have past experiences of creative success you can look back on, but they can't be recreated. Indeed, if you try, you may lose the vital gift of the moment that is waiting to fall into your open hands.

All art and craft are blessed by Brigid three times: in the inspiration, during the creation, and at completion. This means that at any stage during your creative process, Brigid is with you—and she *loves* what you are doing. She's the proud mommy who puts your work up on her cosmic refrigerator door. Your job is to love it too.

Now, this doesn't mean that you won't work hard or run into blocks or find yourself staring at a blank canvas, page, or screen. But at your core—in the fiery heart of the creative forge—your passion must burn red-hot. And that means you must find creative outlets that really fire you up. Everyone needs them, and you probably already have some. You may not think of, say, knitting as being a wildly passionate pursuit, but that excitement you feel as you start a new project, the delight in colors and textures, the ways you challenge yourself to excel—these are all symptoms of creative passion. Surrender to it, glory in it, seek it out! Brigid is with you as creatrix and craftswoman.

Blessed Are These Hands
Marvelle Thompson

Marvelle Thompson is the co-creator with Susan Kullmann of Blessed Are These Hands, *a book of photographs of women's hands, each woman holding something that represents her deepest values. She is thankful to live in a canyon that blesses her with its beauty every day.*

———

Numinous threshold—that is what Brigid is for me. She is the guide between the inner and outer, leading the way to my deepest self, the whole of me. When ideas and events begin to fall into place, I know Brigid is present. At those times, I need to listen deeply. That inspiration occurred many, many times in the process of birthing *Blessed Are These Hands*. Brigid is my sacred threshold, guiding me to creative transformation.

At autumn equinox 2001, I made a vow to honor women in a creative way. That seed lay dormant all winter as my musings took me in different directions. On Imbolc 2002, I asked Brigid for inspiration. A poem from one of my favorite books of poetry (*Earth Poems*) spoke to me that day. The author, Dian Neu, begins this untitled poem, "Blessed be the works of your hands…" Her writing inspired me to photograph women's hands holding objects that they found sacred. It's not a coincidence that one of Brigid's aspects is poetry and it was a poem that inspired me.

In *Blessed Are These Hands*, themes are often repeated: ancestors, mothers (birth and earth), family, and love. Brigid can be seen working through women's strength in nurturing and deepening connections to the people and things they care about. Their hands reach out to embrace life on many levels. They often become the keeper of memories, collecting realia freighted with meaning and capturing personal moments with photos, words, and other media. Angela Villalba, while describing the traditions of the Day of the Dead, writes, "I live bravely when I feel the warmth of those who came before me."

Brigid is present when hands reach with passion to life and the miracle of creation: holding a newborn, planting a garden, and birthing art in many forms. Many of the women are indeed artists, but we see creativity shining through on every page from everyone. Olwyn states, "We hold within our hands the subtle magick of creativity. It is within every touch of love and comfort, in words written for inspiration and encouragement."

Brigid comes to the forefront when women's hands cradle objects of spiritual devotion: religious symbols and statues, holy books, prayer beads, and, quite powerfully, the very earth, fire, and water that sustain life. In the photo of Susun Weed, well-known author of many books on herbal medicine, it seems her hands are giving energy to and receiving energy from the ground they rest on.

Brigid's voice is heard in the words of more than one hundred women in this project and in the rising voices of all women the world over.

For more about Marvelle, see the Contributors appendix.

Soul Windows: Icons for Brigid

An icon is more than just an image of a deity or saint. A true icon is a window into the sacred, an opening between the worlds. It does not *depict* the holy personage, it *represents* her. An icon will often seem to be looking directly into the viewer's soul, opening a channel for wisdom and teachings to flow. Creating an icon for Brigid is an act of intimate communication with her from start to finish—and beyond.

Making an icon doesn't require special artistic skill. In my women's spirituality programs, one of the first things I encourage participants to do is make a collage. Quickly. Without over-thinking it. Setting a time limit and using minimal materials (I recommend thirty minutes, one magazine, and one glue stick) allows you to blast through any resistance that says you can't make art. Sometimes you have to sneak up on your creativity! Once you are comfortable with collage, your confidence will grow.

The most important part of this work is (as always) not the product but the process. You will be spending quiet time assembling an image to honor Brigid, and in that quiet she will speak to you. As you work, keep in mind that you are opening a window between the worlds, between the sacred and the mundane, between the seen and unseen. Let Brigid guide your fingers.

Bless your workspace and ask Brigid to be with you as you create this icon in her honor. Take a moment to anticipate the creative enjoyment to come. And then begin.

STEP ONE: GATHER YOUR IMAGES

Gather images that speak of Brigid to you. You're going to make this icon with paper, not digitally. (Yes, Brigid loves her electronics too, but the tangible process is essential here.) Ask and listen for what Brigid wants in terms of symbology—it may surprise you. For example, in one Brigid icon I made, I didn't feel like including any images of fire, even though I am a flamekeeper. My finished collage showed a red-haired woman wearing a bronze torc and a dress made from the stone spirals at Newgrange. She was accessorized with Irish soda bread, fronds of fennel, and fragments of ancient gold Celtic knotwork.

STEP TWO: ARRANGE AND REARRANGE

When you've gathered your images, start to arrange them on your base. I use 8½ by 11 cardstock, but if you intend to put your icon in a frame or a shrine (old cigar boxes are great for this), cut your base to fit that. Push your images around, layer them, trim them, remove one, put in another one, but do not—do not!—stop working at this point and go find more images. The world is so full of pictures, especially now when you can find anything and everything online, that you can easily shatter any creative rhythm by searching to find that elusive perfect whatever.

STEP THREE: COMMIT!

This is often a tense moment: committing to the placement of your images and gluing them down. Since you have to work from the bottom up in your layering, you might feel more comfortable if you snap a quick photo of your arrangement before you take it apart. (Don't get distracted by whatever might be on your phone if you use it to take the photo. It can all wait. Really.) On the other hand, sometimes trying to exactly reassemble your design takes some of the fun out of it. Listen to your intuition. *There's no way to do this wrong.* (That should be your mantra for all creative projects. Say it a few times right now.)

STEP FOUR: EMBELLISH

Decorate your icon with ribbon, shells, twigs, buttons, lace, jewels, glitter, sequins, beads, tinsel, or anything else that appeals to you. In *Carmina*

Gadelica, Carmichael says: "Customs assume the complexion of their surroundings, as fishes, birds, and beasts assimilate the colours of their habitats. The seas of the 'Garbh Chriocha,' Rough Bounds in which the cult of Bride has longest lived, abound in beautiful iridescent shells, and the mountains in bright sparkling stones, and these are utilised to adorn the ikon of Bride." [49] He is talking about the making of a Bridey doll, but it applies to your icon too. Embellishing it with natural objects from your surroundings draws Brigid even closer to you and your home.

When I made my first icon, I glued a piece of tulle to the cardstock, which had to be lifted to unveil the Goddess. That first icon was made at a workshop in which each woman had her picture taken and included it in her icon. (This was in the days before digital cameras, so someone had to run to the one-hour photo shop.) It is a powerful experience to include your own image with that of your Goddess, an affirmation that you too are sacred.

When your icon is complete, just sit with it for a while. Light a candle or two. Spontaneously speak whatever words of blessing come to you, or simply commune silently with Brigid. With your palms facing the icon, feel your energy radiating toward it. Know that this energy is in every part of this creation of your hands.

Spool and Spindle

Brigid was revered by the Celts as the goddess of all domestic arts. Some of those arts are things that we take for granted in the modern world. We think of needlework as a hobby, a pleasurable pastime, or a form of art. To our foremothers, it was a vital primary task. The sheep must be raised and tended, and their wool must be sheared, cleaned, and spun into thread. The threads must be woven into cloth, and the cloth sewn into garments. Every. Single. Time. Women's prayers to Brigid must have invoked her skill and strength for endless domestic tasks. In the seventh century, Saint Eligius admonished Celtic women to stop invoking "Minerva" (as the Romans had called Brigid) when they engaged in spinning and weaving. What do you want to bet they didn't stop?

....
49. *Carmina Gadelica*, commentary on verse 70.

I was at a crafts fair recently and admired some extraordinary felt hats at one booth. "Felting has really become like an artform," I said to their creator, meaning it as a compliment, but as soon as the words came out of my mouth, I regretted them. "It IS art," she replied, and she was right. Everything that we associate with art—imagination, skill, dedication—is part of craft too. The distinction between art and craft is fuzzy and getting fuzzier. The word *craft* in its highest sense means the thing that you do well, the thing you create that your soul finds satisfaction in.

The old rhyme "Man may work from sun to sun / But woman's work is never done" is still true for many women. In our crazy-busy lives, it's satisfying to have some work that *does* get done. Crafts give us the satisfaction of finishing something. That's symbolic and empowering. This is a feminist issue. So-called women's work has been demeaned for far too long. Woman-craft is essential for the well-being of the world. Women's work is women's magic.

Connecting Threads
RUTH TEMPLE

Ruth Temple is an editor, beekeeping gardener, dancer, musician, spinner, weaver, and fiber artist in the sacred tribe of curious folks who do Stuff with sacred intent.

———

I am a spinner and weaver, and sew and wear fine garments from my handwoven cloth, as well as making simpler garments and household goods of wool. The weaving came first; it's something my artist mother was studying and teaching in the 1960s–70s as I was growing up. The spinning, having come later and along with teaching from folks who incorporate it in their daily sacred practice, has always had sacred connections for me.

I keep a personal Brigid-honoring practice; I am, alas, a little removed from the actual practice of sheep-raising. A nearby friend with a steep hillside keeps cashmere goats, and tells of her deepening connection with the seasons; February, around Brigid's Day, is not only the start of lambing/kid season, it's also the time in California when that valuable second coat, the cashmere down, comes loose and can be brushed or plucked from the goats.

I start each project with honoring intent, and ask a blessing for the person for whom I'm making it. Even when I set out to make yardage, there's sacred intent in the planning and setup. I reach back to notice the source of my materials and give thanks for every step along the way.

I use a lot of different fibers, and come back to wool and wool blends for the texture, the feel of it in the spinning, and all the different fine details one can bring to the spinning practice by preparation and technique. Wool is aesthetically pleasing, flexible and forgiving to work with, and in a garment is warm and sheltering. It can hold up to thirty percent of its weight in water before feeling wet and will still keep a person working out in the elements warm. At the end of the day, though, it's the sheer delight in beautiful, good materials where wool both draws and answers my pleasure.

Since the fiber arts, like many hand arts or home arts, have done a couple of generational skips in this past century, I find in my fifties that some of my favorite teachers and weaving buddies are in their eighties and nineties; it's also exciting to see the next ones coming along in that whole younger not-much-arts-instruction-in-the-schools-yet-we-must-have-art DIY generation. Textile and fiber arts are part of a continuum, connecting threads across generations. Older textiles, gifts that have been handed down, and practical items made by other artists bless my home. There is a joy that comes with pulling something out to use, and mentally greeting the maker or giver, that deepens that connection across time or distance.

Weaving basics go back millennia, and spindle spinning as well; look back just a few generations or up into rural countries now, and everybody spun, about all the time, just to have clothes. Whether I'm weaving on a jack loom, a technological innovation from this past century, or turning a pack of tablet-weaving cards identical in structure and technique to those pulled from Egyptian tombs or found in northern Iron Age culture burial sites, or working with a rigid heddle loom whose global origins go very far back in the archaeological record, I have a sense of acting within a continuing history of makers using similar tools to make sacred and everyday items as I do.

Setting sacred space and intent when sitting to spin wool into a thread that will become something down the road gives a very tangible result to one's efforts. That immediate feedback is powerful, and helps strengthen efforts in the perhaps less immediately tangible parts of one's practice. Making, crafting, creating art, whether for ritual use or for use in what my love and I call the Sacred Quotidian—an everyday sort of use that reminds one to be mindful—is as necessary to me as breathing. It is nothing less than a sacred act to wear a pair of hand-knitted socks.

For more about Ruth, see the Contributors appendix.

BRIGID THE JEWELSMITH

When you think of Brigid as goddess of smithcraft, your thoughts might go to swords and shields, or pots and pans, but her craft also encompasses jewelry. Wearing jewelry that has ritual or spiritual meaning is a practice that goes back as far as humans have been adorning themselves. Jewelry that is worn with devotion and reverence holds power that remains in the item over its lifetime, which may be hundreds or even thousands of years. The Celts were famous for the magnificence of their metal jewelry, and the most important of these was the torc.

A torc is a circular Celtic necklace made of twisted metal (the name comes from the Latin *torqueo*, "to twist"). The circle is left open, and the ends often have ornamental finials with symbolic shapes such as knot-work or animals, especially boars (*torc* is also the Irish word for boar). While I was doing research for this book, I came upon a photograph of first-century gold and silver torcs found buried in a pit, part of a larger archaeological find. Their power and energy were evident even in a photograph; they were far more than just pretty trinkets meant for mere decoration. The torc was a sign of sovereignty, indicating a person with strength and nobility of character. Both men and women wore torcs, and depictions of deities were shown wearing or holding a torc. Many have been found buried with other funeral tokens, or just buried on their own in what may have been ritual offerings. As goddess of met-alcraft, Brigid would have been invoked in their making and wearing. Wearing or making one today ties you to that long lineage in a very tangible way.

Torcs are worn with the opening in the front, the finials resting on the collarbones at either side of the base of the throat. On a metaphysi-cal level, this leaves the fifth (throat) chakra open. This chakra is the energy point in the body that governs communication, so symbolically one way to see the torc is as a supporting framework that strengthens the head, the seat of sovereignty, while allowing for eloquent communi-cation and expression of your own voice.

Another symbolic aspect of the torc is that it's not easy to put on or remove. The circlet must be slightly untwisted, fitted closely around the neck, and then twisted back into shape. It requires a certain commit-ment to wearing it for a while, which can be symbolic of moving with intention into a new field of challenge, committing to an undertaking or a project, or generally affirming your own strength and stability.

When you dedicate any piece of jewelry to combine its essential en-ergy with your own, the act of putting that jewel on your body will instantly strengthen your connection to the sacred. It holds the light of your inner flame. Some people feel that such dedicated items should never be removed; if that feels right for you, then by all means leave them on. Others (like me) find it meaningful to wear different pieces for different purposes. Always treat your ritual and magical jewels with re-spect, putting them on with your full attention and putting them away with thanks. The most humble iron ring can hold as much power as the most elaborate gold torc.

The Magics of Metals

Metal is created by the application of heat or fire, imbuing the raw materials with the transformative energy of the forge, so a piece of metal jewelry has Brigid power even before you add stones or a design with symbolic meaning. (See page 103 for some stones associated with Brigid.) The various metals have their own qualities, just like stones do. Here are some of Brigid's powerful metals.

Gold

The essential energy of gold is incorruptible purity, though most of the gold we interact with isn't pure gold; it is blended with other metals for strength. This has a metaphorical significance too—purity must be combined with strength to endure the challenges and roughness of the world. Wearing gold affirms a pure intention and nobility of character that cannot be corrupted. It confirms your faith in the eternal goodness of creation.

Visualize a golden shield, forged by Brigid herself and intricately engraved with a circle of knotwork that has no beginning and no end. The shield glows with warm radiance and hovers just before you, at the center of your chest. The purity of the gold repels harshness and crude ugliness. With each beat of your heart, the radiance grows.

Silver

The essential energy of silver is intuitiveness. Silver's soft luminosity is evocative of the moon, and it is considered a metal with feminine power. Unlike gold, silver will tarnish and requires care to keep it shining. This aspect serves a metaphorical purpose: when you attend to your emotions and intuition and respect their insights, they reward you with increased clarity and vision. Wearing silver enhances your psychic gifts and connects you to the sacred feminine.

Visualize a clear stream running from a wellspring among mossy rocks. This sacred site has been dedicated to Brigid for thousands of

*years. Beside the water's source is a pure silver chalice, engraved with
the triple spiral. Dip the chalice into the icy water and drink, feeling the
purity of water and metal combine to cleanse your body and your soul.*

Copper

The essential energy of copper is connectivity. Copper conducts energy
and amplifies it when combined with your own intention and the qualities of any stones you include. Copper is a wonderful metal for healing
purposes because it keeps the energy moving, working through stuck
places both emotionally and physically. Use it for amulets dedicated to
love, sexuality, and feminine power.

*Visualize a wand made of strands of gleaming copper, twisted and
entwined like Brigid's flowing hair. Green stones at either end seem to
radiate light from within their depths. Take up this wand, holding it
at the center, and feel your own energy connect with the metal, flowing
to both ends and shining healing light where your will directs it to go.*

Iron

The essential energy of iron is protection. Wearing iron jewelry or carrying iron as an amulet creates an energetic barrier that repels negativ-
ity. There are many myths and folktales about the magical uses of iron,
some contradictory, so (as always) use your own intuition to determine
how the energies of iron work for you. In general, iron is best for everyday protection and less useful for vision-questing and otherworldly
workings, as it is so intensely earthbound that it may be hard to get off
the ground, as it were.

*Visualize an open hearth, banked with glowing red embers and
flickering with tiny flames. Suspended above the fire is an aged iron
cauldron, containing a gently bubbling brew. Gaze into the pot and invoke Brigid's blessing as you add ingredients for protection. Stir and
envision iron's protective energy infusing your potion. Sip and feel the
strength of Brigid flow through you.*

PLATINUM

The essential energy of platinum is timelessness. Platinum is the metal of eternity and universal wisdom that shines through the ages. When you wear platinum, you are pulled energetically to a higher plane of vibration. Lesser concerns fade away so you can see what is at the heart of things. It is an excellent metal to wear while doing shamanic and ancestral work. Platinum is also a powerful metal on which to make sacred vows that will transcend this lifetime.

Visualize a platinum torc that hangs in the air before you, silver-white and gleaming. It is perfectly round, and at the opening between the two ends, a tiny flame flickers on the air. Looking closer, you see that the torc is engraved with a flame design that reflects this timeless fire. The torc fits perfectly around your neck, and you become one with Brigid's flame.

BRONZE

The essential energy of bronze is healing. Bronze is an alloy of copper and tin, and so combines the qualities of both. Tin (a crystalline metal) clarifies your intention, and copper directs that intention where it needs to go. Bronze is a good metal to wear and carry as an amulet when you want to do long-term healing of either body or spirit, as its vibration is steady and enduring.

Visualize a door at the end of a hallway, and hanging on a peg at the back of the door is a deep green cloak, hand-woven of softest wool. You take the cloak from the peg and wrap it around you, feeling the comforting weight of it upon your shoulders. At the throat is a bronze penannular brooch, its ring and pin delicately carved with spirals. You thread the pin through the woolen fabric to close the cloak securely, and Brigid's healing magic is sealed.

STEEL

The essential energy of steel is courage. Steel is another alloy, combining the protection and groundedness of iron with the strengthening and stabilizing qualities of carbon. Steel breaks negative energy and thought-forms, dispels or contains fear so it can be dealt with properly, and invokes victory in righteous causes. When you wear or carry steel, Brigid fights on your side.

Visualize a glowing forge and before it, an anvil upon which a shining steel sword is laid. Brigid herself strikes the sword with her hammer, and sparks fly into the night air. Plunging the sword into the water beside her, Brigid cools and tempers the blade, then puts it into your outstretched hands. You feel the courage of all your foremothers running through you, and your fears fly away like those ephemeral sparks.

Fire's Fierce Power
Wendy Alford

Wendy Alford is an award-winning blacksmith and a member of the Worshipful Company of Blacksmiths. She is the owner of St. Mary's Forge in Norfolk, England, which lies upon the mystical Mary Ley Line.

————

Looking back, I believe that Brighid has always been in my life, although I was not conscious of her presence by name or of the significance of her attributes until she showed herself to me through Gina McGarry's book, *Brighid's Healing*, which shone out from the catalogue pages of *Cygnus* (how typically and beautifully apt!) magazine about seven years ago. When I began reading the book, I experienced a shower of revelations, each one aligning me closer to Brighid. I was filled with wonder that all her amazing aspects linked somehow to the qualities I valued and was experiencing along my journey.

I feel I have been led by Brighid, from my love of nature as a child, my fascination with the spiritual and esoteric, being drawn into blacksmithing apparently quite by accident, learning about plant medicine and other forms of natural healing, to my enduring compulsion to write poetry. Brighid is a constant presence in my life, guiding, protecting, and inspiring. I offer up a prayer or incantation to her (which I found in Gina's book and chant in Gaelic, hoping that Brighid has guided my pronunciation!) every time I light my fire. If for any reason I forget or am interrupted, I later notice that I feel incomplete or that things have not been going very well, and then I realize why. Brighid's patronage and influence permeate the forge, her energy manifesting through my mind and body as I work.

The elemental aspect of fire is held in Brighid, with its associated properties of heat and light, comforting warmth and fierce power. There is this huge energy, which we as smiths try to harness to make useful and beautiful objects, transforming cold, inert iron or steel into miraculously malleable material, upon which we can apply our hands and tools to shape and create infinite forms. So the process of transformation is central, as our creations arise out of the fire like a phoenix.

But it is not only the fire—we smiths work with all four elements, which again holds us close to Brighid, as well as contributing to the historical association between shamanism and blacksmiths: fire in the hearth, air in the bellows or blower, water in the bosh, and earth in the coal and iron. Another prayer or incantation I use when lighting my fire is in medieval French, calling upon the spirits or gods of the underworld and the four elements—fire, air, water, and earth—to rise up and help me in my work. The symbolism and the physical reality are inextricably bound up together. The process of forging is spiritual and magical, yet at the same time material and very practical.

For more about Wendy, see the Contributors appendix.

Metalwork as Meditation

You don't have to have a home forge to connect with Brigid as the goddess of metalcraft. Bead stores offer classes in simple metal techniques such as chain-making and wire-wrapping, and online video tutorials are widely available. Many women haven't had much experience with metalwork, although this is changing with younger generations. I've found a warm sense of satisfaction when I use my jewelry-making tools. They are small and fit my hand well, yet are strong enough to easily cut through wire, twist and coil it, and punch through sheets of metal. I feel competent and confident—just how Brigid wants us all to feel!

Coirníní Paidir Bríd: Prayer Beads for Brigid

When I first became aware of Brigid, one of the things she inspired me to do was work with my hands, not just my head. As a writer and editor, I was always immersed in words—drowning in them might be more accurate—and I badly needed to get in balance with something that was word-free. I had made jewelry when I was younger—delicate web-spun necklaces of tiny seed beads—so I went to the bead shop thinking I'd do something along those lines. Brigid had other ideas, and she steered me over to the findings section to add some metal to my beadwork. ("Findings" are all the little bits and bobs used to put jewelry together.) The next thing I knew, I was making goddess rosaries.

I didn't have any buttons to be pushed about the word *rosary* being applied to Pagan prayer beads, but in those early days it was a rather radical concept. "How can a *rosary* be for the Goddess?" was something I heard a lot. Now you see goddess rosaries everywhere! It was also unconventional in those early days to wear rosaries, and I intended mine to be worn as necklaces. The word *rosary* comes from the Latin *rosarium*, garland of roses. Mala, the name for Hindu or Buddhist prayer beads, also means garland. A garland of prayer beads is a portable sacred circle that encompasses you as you move through your world. Rosary is the word we know best in the Western world, so I will use that here.

Prayer beads are traditionally used to keep count of a cycle of prayers, mantras, or the recitation of your deity's name(s). The rosaries you make for Brigid can have many purposes. Healing rosaries invoke her care during illness and provide a focus for affirmations of wellness to speed the healing. Rosaries for Brigid are also powerful at any transitional time. I was once privileged to make a rosary for a woman who was approaching her death and who found holding the beads as she communed with her goddess to be comforting; the rosary was buried with her. Rosaries can be made as memorials for a specific person or in honor of your ancestors. I once made a custom rosary using beads that had been part of a necklace belonging to the woman's grandmother, and it was such a pleasure to work with the old crystal spheres with their patina of time and love.

But you don't need to dedicate your rosary to any purpose other than accompanying you in prayer. You know how when someone is talking to you and reaches over to lightly touch your arm as she makes a point? It's the same idea—using prayer beads adds a tactile element to your spiritual practice. The Celtic bards' memorization of lore was helped along by the use of counting rhythms in their poetry and song. When you use prayer beads with a numeric pattern, touching each bead as you pray or chant grounds your thoughts and words in the earthly realm. The power of your faith remains within the beads, and over time you will feel that power grow.

So let's make a Brigid rosary!

I Come into Thy Presence: A Brigid Rosary

The first step is choosing your beads. Beautiful rosaries can be made with natural stones, which add the qualities and energies of that stone ally. But don't feel that you always need to use stones or crystals. I make most of my rosaries with glass beads. Along with the gorgeous range of colors to play with symbolically and aesthetically, the energy of glass is quite neutral and pure, so the magical or spiritual intention can be set by the wearer. Glass (especially red glass) was often used in ancient Celtic jewelry and ritual items such as decorative shields.

Glass is made with fire, which contributes to the purification process, and this fire aspect connects glass beads to Brigid. Czech glass beads called "fire-polished" have a sparkle that can't be beat. Glass artisans make dichroic beads that fuse precious metal into the glass in glorious patterns. When glass is combined with metal, the connection with Brigid is powerful indeed, which is why I link my rosary beads with metal eyepins (thin wires with a loop, or "eye," at one end). You don't have to make yours this way—you can simply string the beads one after the other—but I find the metalworking to be more satisfying, in part because it's slower and more meditative. It's also repetitive—in a good way—conducive to trance and going within as you work.

If you have a specific prayer you want to use with your rosary, it will determine how many beads you'll need. For example, with a triad prayer, you can use a repeated sequence of three beads separated by a larger bead. The mystical Celtic three-times-three is what I use as the base number for most of my goddess rosaries, which have multiple sets of nine beads. When I make Brigid rosaries specifically for flamekeepers, I use three sets of nineteen beads, for the number of priestesses who tended the perpetual flame at Kildare.

Our rosary will be an unbroken circle intended for use with this prayer:

I come into thy presence,
Goddess of the hearthfire,
I come into thy presence,
Goddess of the threshold.
I come into thy presence,
Brigid of brightness,
I come into thy presence,
Brigid of grace.
[Pattern begins again.]
I come into thy presence,
Goddess of healing,
I come into thy presence,
Goddess of light...
etc.

As you can see, there are two sets of four lines each: one set has alternating lines that start with "Goddess" and the other has lines that start with "Brigid." The idea is that you can fall into a trancelike rhythm by improvising the end of these lines as you pray. Moving around the rosary reinforces the prayer's pattern as your fingers note the shape and size of each bead.

You will need:
Round-nose jewelry pliers
Jewelry nippers / cutters

OR

Rosary pliers (which combine the two tools in one; this is what I use)

21 gauge eyepins (about 70, so you have some to mess up)

40 8mm beads (we'll call these the "heart beads")

5 beads in a different shape, size, or texture than your main beads
    (the "breath beads")

5 10mm or 12mm beads (the "liminal beads")

Bless your workspace and ask Brigid to be with you as you create this
rosary in her honor. Take a moment to anticipate the creative enjoyment to come. And then begin.

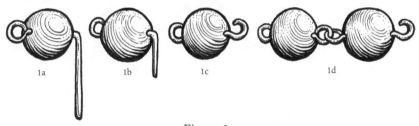

Figure 1

Figure 2

Figure 3

1. Prepare all your beads by putting each one on an eyepin and bending each pin 90 degrees, flush against the bead (figure 1a).

2. Clip the eyepin "tails" to about ¼ inch (figure 1b). Having all the beads prepared this way makes putting them together flow more easily.

3. Pick up your first heart bead and grasp the very end of the tail with the tip of your round-nose pliers. Roll the pin slowly around the tip, back toward the bead, making a loop. It should be about the same size as the premade eye on the other end of the pin. Leave the loop open a bit (figure 1c).

4. At this point, you can congratulate yourself for successfully learning a new skill! Or you can congratulate yourself for having patience and humor as you take it apart, insert a fresh eyepin, and try again. (I promise, it gets much easier.)

5. Pick up your second heart bead, and attach its eye to the open loop of the first bead (figure 1d). With the tip of your pliers, close the loop.

6. Repeat for heart beads 3 and 4. You should now have a strand of four linked beads.

7. Use the same process to add one of your breath beads here, then do another set of four heart beads. You now have a strand of nine beads.

8. Repeat these steps until you have five strands with nine beads each (figure 2).

9. Connect the five strands with the five liminal beads, which mark the transition from one strand to the next. Close the circle (figure 3).

You're done! Isn't it beautiful?

Now close your eyes and move from bead to bead with your fingers. For each *heart bead*, say a line of your prayer. At each *breath bead*, note that the pattern changes from "Goddess" to "Brigid." At each *liminal bead*, note that the pattern begins again. Let the rosary take you from line to line, so that you can lose yourself in the emotion of deep connection with Brigid. Let the words pour forth from you in spontaneous devotion.

There's no limit to the ways you can work with prayer beads. How about a rosary that invokes the three Celtic elements of earth, sea, and sky? Or the three realms of underworld, middle world, and otherworld? A rosary for safe travels or a rosary for inner journeying. A rosary for the triple aspects of Brigid: healer, poet, smith. A rosary for Brigid's mother, the Mórrígan, perhaps made with beads from your own mother.

It's good to support artisans who make their living through creativity (I'm one of them!), but do try making some jewelry yourself, especially when it has a spiritual intention. Remember that Brigid likes you to be hands-on, so the more ways as you can find to tangibly honor her, the better.

BRIGID AND THE POWER OF WORDS

Language is a complex and powerful tool. It is a gift given to humans by the Goddess. Words preserve our history and our lore. They give expression to our joy and our grief. Words are our offering to the Divine, in thanks, in supplication, in worshipful delight. Words can be art, and words can be a weapon. We use words in magical workings, choosing carefully which arrangement of letters will best serve our intention. Brigid is the goddess of poetry, and in the metaphorical sense of the word, "poetry" is all written and spoken language. Let's explore some of the ways Brigid blesses us through the power of words.

Triads

The power of three is vividly seen in the Celtic poetic triad, a short saying or verse that combines three elements to make a whole. It was used by the Celts as a learning tool, summarizing an idea in three parts for easy memorization. This was highly prized in a society that handed down its lore through the spoken word, and it is surely blessed by Brigid, goddess of eloquence and poetry.

I love these little prayers, invocations, and meditations on the spiritual life. Often the smallest things can be the most profound, because we can simultaneously examine them in detail and comprehend them as a whole. Just as gazing at a single flame can open you to your most profound knowing, reading just a few words can add to your store of wisdom.

Hundreds of triads have been collected over the past centuries—each one a tiny window peeking into the Celtic spirit. Some triads were about facts, such as history or geography:

The three dark places of Ireland: the cave of Knowth,
the cave of Slaney, the cave of Ferns.[50]

Others were meant to inspire:

Three profitable labors in the day: praying, working, reading.

Some hold deep mystery:

Three dead ones that are paid for with living things:
an apple-tree, a hazel-bush, a sacred grove.

....
50. These traditional triads, gathered from manuscripts dating back to the fourteenth century, are all from Meyer, trans., *The Triads of Ireland.*

Many are practical and domestic:

Three excellences of dress: elegance, comfort, lastingness.

Here's one of my favorites:

Three woman-days: Monday, Tuesday, Wednesday.
If women go to men on those days,
the men will love them better than they the men,
and the women will survive the men.

In devotions, the power of three intensifies and affirms:

As it was,
as it is,
as it ever will be.

Reading, reciting, and writing triads adds a Celtic flavor to your spiritual practice. Prayer is often spontaneous—connecting to the Goddess from the depths of your spirit—but having a collection of prayers and invocations to draw from creates your own tradition. You may find yourself creating triads in the moment, as Brigid inspires you with her gift of eloquence. Let's create some together, as practice. To begin, complete these simple triads:

Three tokens of a blessed site:
Three candles that illumine every darkness:
Three signs of wisdom:

Next, try your hand at creating a longer triad. Complete this blessing with a last line:

Threefold blessings of the cat:
Lithe speed be thine,
Calm grace be thine…

Here's another one; finish each line as you are inspired to do:

Stir the cauldron of life three times:
Once for… ,
Twice for… ,
Thrice for… .

Now invoke Brigid with a triad of praise:

Brigid of the...,
Brigid of the...,
Brigid of the...,
I bid you welcome.

One last triad for you to complete:

As plentiful as the...,
As bountiful as the...,
As beautiful as the...,
So are the blessings of Brigid.

Brigit be n-éces: *Brigid the Woman-Poet*
Erynn Rowan Laurie

Erynn Rowan Laurie is a poet, professional madwoman, student of filidecht, and devotee of Brigid. She talks to spirits, and sometimes they talk back. This isn't as mad as it sounds.

———

My central devotional practices for Brigid are twofold. First is the ritual of flamekeeping, which honors her and brings her visibly to mind as the spark in the well of wisdom. My second devotional practice connected to my creative work is reading and research. As Brigid is a scholar, so I study as well. It is my joyful duty to learn and to understand the kinds of things that a traditional *fili* (poet) would have known. Myths and history, ogam and poetry, symbolism and ritual, law and folklore and language are all a part of this body of knowledge.

I have too often heard it said that practitioners of reconstructionist paths "don't have spirituality," only books, but I think the people who say this don't understand that the study itself is a devotional act, and that books are ritual tools for us. Without our study, we would have very little upon which to base our personal spiritual work as contextualized in a particular culture. If you're not doing research work, you can never know the joy of discovering that an inspired insight you're using in ritual has historical precedent.

If I respect and honor Brigid, then I must also respect and honor what she does, and one of the things she does, one of the things she is, is the work of the scholar. If I wish to devote myself to her and become more like her, I must cultivate that scholarly aspect of myself and develop the talents of discernment and synthesis. One of the goals of devotional work is to become more like what one has devoted oneself to and to bring those qualities into one's life. If I am to live authentically as a devotee of *Brigit be n-éces*—Brigid the woman-poet—then I must devote myself to learning and to the poetic arts, and I must cultivate the pursuit of wisdom.

An early Irish law text says that all things are connected by a thread of poetry. Poetry is about how we live in the world, about who we are as human beings. Do we strive for truth and beauty and compassion? Do we work on ourselves to become better human beings, and to leave the world a better and more just place for our having existed? We must become poems, become words of power, become moments of beauty in the world. Even our roughest and most painful experiences, our sharpest edges, our night terrors, can be used to bring forth something profound and poetic if we are willing to do the work. This takes looking at ourselves with honesty and knowing that we will never be perfect, and understanding that we can still at least attempt to act with grace when we have a choice.

For those who wish to practice poetry as an art as well as a metaphor for life, tapping into those experiences, the things that generate the most powerful emotions, is a place to begin. Learning to put those things into words that are both strong and artful takes time and a great deal of work, but it is rewarding, and there is deep and powerful transformational magic in the process.

Sitting down and putting words on paper, or on a screen, is a fundamental part of the process. If someone is serious about poetry and practicing the art of poetry, it's very useful to try composing different kinds of poems, whether they have specific types of rhyme and meter or they are attempting to achieve a particular artistic or emotional effect. Over the years I've read and worked with dozens of books on writing and poetry, playing with exercises and trying new things. I've studied with other poets. I've also read hundreds of volumes of other people's poetry, both translated from other languages and by poets writing in English. I've done some reading and translation of poems from other languages myself. We need the examples of both good and bad poetry in order to understand what works when we're dealing with the rhythms and sounds of language. Every good poet I've ever read has been a wide reader of poetry. It takes exposure to art to refine our own art.

In a spiritual sense, I think it's necessary to find something to devote ourselves to and to immerse ourselves in it. If there is no particular passion in your life, look to Brigid for a spark of inspiration, look to the land around you, reach into history and myth and see what presents itself. Carry a notebook and scribble down thoughts and images and overheard scraps of conversation. Record dreams. Read everything. Look at works of art. Listen to music. Walk with your eyes and your heart open, and observe the vast world around you. Look deeply into your own heart and explore the things that you love, and the things that ache and tremble with your pain. Breathe slow and deep.

Now write.

For more about Erynn, see the Contributors appendix.

PEN VS. COMPUTER

One of the things people tout about writing with a computer is that typing on a keyboard can move "at the speed of thought." There is certainly a time and place for that, and I would never give up my keyboard for most of the writing I do. But there is something to be said for writing at the speed of *thoughtful* thought. Slowing to a measured musing, letting your pen set the pace, there is time for silence—a pause to allow for consideration of what remains to be written. Lifting the pen from the paper and gazing out the window or into the candle flame feels natural. The page doesn't demand your return as does the glowing screen, the blinking cursor. And there is no interruption—the paper will not flash an incoming message at you, and the pen won't "helpfully" suggest a different word. Much of this book was written on a computer, but when I felt fuzzy or overloaded with information, I knew it was time to turn off the machine and uncap the fountain pen. When you are writing in your journal or any of the other spiritual and intentional writing that Brigid inspires you to do, take a moment and ask her what medium she would like you to use. Brigid is the bright arrow, swift and brilliant as words typed onscreen. And she is also the glowing embers that draw you closer and slow you into quietude, and the words that come forth from that banked fire of wisdom within.

Oaths and Vows

There is a saying that a person is only as good as her or his word. This goes beyond the casually spoken word, or even a promise that must be kept or an intention that must be followed through. A Word in the highest sense encompasses integrity, honesty, dependability, and ethical virtue. To have a Word means holding certain things to be inviolable. Living by your Word doesn't mean being perfect—we all fall down and we all mess up, and that's part of growing wiser. But holding true to what you know is right—for you—is always part of a sincere spiritual path.

In the Celtic tradition, the taking of oaths is a sacred act. I mentioned earlier the personal nature of such oaths as the Celts acclaimed their vows to the deities they knew intimately, the protectors of their tribe: "I swear by the gods my people swear by." Brigid is invoked as a protector of oaths in an invocation to *Brigit Búadach* (Victorious Brigit): "…righteous person, perjury's peril…" [51] To take an oath of some action under the name of Brigid is to know that she will oversee its completion and hold the oath-taker accountable for all deeds done in her name—or deeds left undone. It's both promise and prayer.

In modern times, the occasions for formal oath-taking are fairly rare. For most people, the vows they take when they marry may be the only solemn oaths made, and even then, the solemnity is sometimes short-changed, as weddings have shifted from sacred ceremonies to expensive parties. You may be asked to give your word in more mundane circumstances, such as swearing to tell the truth in court, signing non-disclosure agreements at work, or even something as trivial as agreeing to a website's conditions of use. Every time you put your name to something, you are using the power of words to affirm your Word. And your Word is under the auspices of Brigid, goddess of wordsmithing, goddess of truth-telling.

I see oaths and vows as two different things. An oath is a single statement of intention, support, or commitment, something that could even be done spontaneously in the need of the moment. You may not use the words "I swear by…," but the intensity of your oath is in whatever words you use, and your whole soul is behind the speaking of them. When you tell a friend in crisis that you will be there for her, no matter what, that is an oath and Brigid is your witness.

I think of vows as a collection of oaths made in a more formal setting and with a considerable amount of thought beforehand. Marriage vows are the ones we know best, of course. Writing your own vows offers an opportunity to really think about what you're swearing to (and whom you are swearing by), but traditional vows hold great power too. It's all in the degree to which you dive deep within your soul and breathe truth into each and every word you speak. "'Til death us do part" is intense stuff.

Religious vows are made to your deity as to your beloved and sometimes to your spiritual community. There may come a time when you

....
51. Anonymous, probably tenth century, from Meyer, ed. and trans., *Miscellanea Hibernica*.

feel you want to take vows as a priestess of Brigid or as a flamekeeper. This is a serious, sacred act. Vows are for life. They are a specific expression of some part of your Word. Yes, marriage vows are broken all the time, and it's easy to think of any vows as just good intentions—a promise to do the best you can, and hey, if it doesn't work out, no hard feelings. Vows to your goddess are beyond even vows to your spouse. When you make a vow to Brigid (or any aspect of the Goddess), you are offering your life to her. You are expressing your deepest love and trust. There is no divorce from this. These vows are lived every day in your heart and soul, and death will not part you from them.

The marriage analogy is apt when it comes to religious vows. When I took my priestess vows and offered myself in service to Brigid, I didn't know what that meant other than she had proposed and I had accepted. We can never know what the future holds in terms of challenges to our vows. We take those vows so that whatever happens, we will hold true to our Word. I vowed to honor the gifts that Brigid has given me, to listen for how she wants me to use those gifts, to be of service to others, to hold true to my inner guidance, to not lose my faith. Your vows will be uniquely your own. My only advice about their content is to recognize that because vows are for life, you should be able to grow with them, and never outgrow them. To use a rather silly example, don't vow to drink milk every day as a libation to Brigid, as your aging body may object to this at some point. More seriously, a vow to serve your goddess as a writer may change over the years if she decides that she'd like you be a painter for a while—or a healer, or a mother, or a trainer of guide dogs, or Brigid only knows what. My wise priestess sister Bryn included in her vows "a willingness to whatever."

Oath-breaking and the breaking of vows have dire consequences. In ancient times, oath-breakers were exiled and rejected by their tribe—or worse, put to death. We have legal and financial repercussions now, but that's not what I'm talking about when I use the word *dire*. Breaking your Word is damaging to your spirit. It is a soul-wound that is not easily healed. As women, we are often far harder on ourselves than any other person would ever be to us, and as spiritual women, there is a danger of falling into a deep pit of unworthiness if we break oaths or vows made to the Goddess. She will always understand and forgive, because she takes you at your Word—moment by moment, year by year, lifetime by lifetime. But from a mortal perspective, breaking spiritual vows causes a real crisis of faith and leads to a dark night of the soul. I've seen this in women who come to doubt that they can continue to call themselves a priestess, and it's not the loss of the title that tears at them, it's the feeling of having failed. Unlike a marriage between two people, there is no one else to blame.

In truth, there is no blame. If you have a clear and innocent heart, if you do the best you can, if you are kind and generous, if you use the gifts Brigid gave you, if you are grateful, if you are true to your Word, then you will never be forsworn.

> *Three things that are impossible:*
> *That hope should be lost,*
> *That life should be meaningless,*
> *That faith should be in vain.*

Oíbel Ecnai: *Spark of Wisdom*
DOMI O'BRIEN

Domi O'Brien served as Preceptor in the MotherGrove of Ár nDraíocht Féin: A Druid Fellowship; since 1996 she has been with Grove of the Golden Leaves of Druidic Association of North America. She teaches beginner and intermediate Irish for Conradh na Gaeilge Shasana Nua.

———

I use Irish (and sometimes Scottish Gaelic) in my own ritual work and incorporate bits of it into group ritual. I use some of the hymns, charms, and incantations from *Carmina Gadelica* regularly in ritual, in both their Scottish Gaelic originals and in translation. Some of them I edit to take out obviously Christian references. The litanies and lineage of Brighidh given in the volumes are full of wonderful imagery. At Imbolg, we always use a version of that in our ritual, with each person who wishes to pulling out three strands of hair by the roots and feeding them into a flame while putting themselves anew under the protection of Brighidh. And if a new initiate has not been clearly claimed by a different High One, he or she is placed under Her guardianship and guidance.

I am somewhat saddened by the apparent inability of some of my younger students to memorize and recite even what seem to me to be fairly simple things, like the nine elements of the body and their correspondences in the universe. Technology means they can look anything up; they are not used to simply retaining information in their own memory. That has profound effects. I tell the same tales from the tradition at the same times of year, and only a few seem to recognize them and get new insights into their meaning as they come around again.

This is an Old Irish traditional prayer:

Brigit Búadach,	*Victorious Brigit,*
Búaid na fine,	*Glory of kindred*
Siur Ríg nime,	*Heaven-King's sister,*
Nár in duine,	*Noble person*
Eslind luige,	*Perilous oath,* *
Lethan breo.	*Far-flung flame*
Ro-siacht noí:bnem,	*She has reached holy heaven,*
Mumme Goídel,	*Gaeldom's foster mother,*
Riar na n-oíged,	*Support of strangers*
Oíbel ecnai,	*Spark of wisdom,*
Ingen Dubthaig,	*Daughter of Dubthach,*
Duine úallach,	*High-minded lady,*
Brigit búadach,	*Victorious Brigit,*
Bethad béo.	*The living one of life.*

*Swearing by Brighidh is very dangerous for perjurers.

For more about Domi, see the Contributors appendix.

Preserving Your History

We know that Brigid is a goddess of poetry, but the word *poetry* in the Celtic tradition isn't limited to what we now think of as poetry—a lyrical expression of thought or emotion. It also encompasses history, biography, and all the preservation of the culture's lore. In a society that depended upon oral tradition, it was crucial to have bards and *fili* who specialized in handing down this lore from generation to generation. Poetry was an efficient way to preserve it, as poetry was usually sung, and it's always easier to remember a song than the simple spoken word. But it wasn't just the professionals who held the tales and passed them on. Stories of humor, travels, mystical encounters with the fae, and ancestral adventures have always been told at the hearthside, spun out like wool to warm the winter nights. Personal histories weave the fabric of a society as much as heroic epics.

At first glance, it might seem that we are in a position to preserve our personal histories in detail that would have astonished our foremothers. Many people always have a camera with them and record every activity. Social media speeds these images—and our every random thought—to the wider circle of friends and family. But paradoxically, because we have this instant connection, we often don't bother to tell the longer tales or preserve them in a more lasting way. The goal has become to make communication ever more brief and fleeting, sometimes disappearing as soon as it is read.

The reality is that our histories are just as ephemeral as the tribal Celts' oral tradition and in similar danger of being lost. At some point, if stories are not written down, they are forgotten. Not every story, perhaps—the larger adventures, the funniest anecdotes, and the most tragic experiences may be remembered. But it is the more intimate and heartfelt moments that make up a lifetime, and these are often lost, forgotten, or just overlooked.

This is particularly true for women. Most written history over the centuries has been about men, because it was written *by* men. The memories and tales of women need to be recorded as part of the history of our civilization. The poet Muriel Rukeyser wrote, "What would happen if one woman told the truth about her life? The world would split open." [52] More women are telling their truths on the public stage, but on a personal level, a spiritual level, many truths still need to be told. You are the bard of your own epic poem. Your history is part of the world's history.

In the past, letters and diaries preserved personal history for future generations. I recently bought an old five-year diary at a junk sale and was so moved by the brief entries there, most of which were quite ordinary. The writer wasn't recording her musings and dreams, as we might in a journal—her diary was just a daily record of her activities, sometimes with commentary and sometimes not. It was fascinating to see her life day by day, from the vantage point of fifty-plus years later. What was trivial in the moment became a window into another time. Your own stories will be the same for others, whether in the form of letters, a diary, or a memoir.

To begin, try a simple exercise in remembrance. Take a single sheet of paper and a pen that is comfortable in your hand. Light a candle and ask Brigid to illuminate a single memory in your mind. Then start to write. Don't edit or censor yourself or worry about grammar. Brigid is guiding your hand. Write until the page is full, turning it over if you wish to continue, but don't use more than this one page for now. When you have finished, sit quietly with the candle and thank Brigid for blessing your words. You may want to read over what you wrote or you may prefer to tuck it away for future reading. Write the date on the paper and store it safely.

Listen for inner guidance on how to proceed from here. One idea is to continue just as you began—taking each memory as it comes, on a single sheet of paper, and putting them all away in a box—or you may be inspired to do something more structured. Here are some thought-starters:

- Write everything you remember about your earliest memory. It may be just a flash of a color or sensation, or it may be rich with detail. Don't be hard on yourself for not remembering more or

---

52. Rukeyser, "Käthe Kollwitz."

going back further. If your earliest clear memory is at age nine, that's just fine. More may come in time.

- Write a school memory. Take the first one that comes to mind, good or bad. Then write two more to make a school tales trilogy.

- Write about your childhood best friend, then your closest friend as a young adult, then your closest friend now. If this is the same person, write about how you have both changed.

- Write about a female cousin, a grandmother, or an aunt. Keep in mind that it's the simple details that keep her memory alive: the cousin whose bedroom was completely purple, the tiny stitches your grandmother put in her quilts, or the aunt who made hand-churned ice cream redolent with vanilla on a sultry summer day.

- Tell the tale of your first love. Then tell the tale of your worst enemy.

- Write about a national or world event from your perspective. As I'm writing this, it is the fiftieth anniversary of the death of President Kennedy, and everywhere people are sharing where they were at the time. Such memories don't always have to be about sad events. Record your joys as well as your sorrows.

- Write down your family's folklore. You may have to glean these stories from relatives and piece together the big picture. Or they may remain as fragments, which taken together make an embroidered crazy quilt of memory.

- Write about your spiritual awakening.

Brigid will inspire you onward as you preserve your own history and the history of your foremothers. You may find yourself remembering things that at first glance seem trivial, but follow that thread back and see where it leads. The labyrinthine paths of memory will become illuminated as you walk them. Future generations will be moved by your remembrances, whether it is of a special meal or the important events of the age. It doesn't matter if you have children to bequeath your history to. It will be kept by someone, and heard, and passed on to become part of the body of collective lore.

BRIGID THE HEALER

Healer is one of the three main roles of the goddess Brigid as recorded in antiquity: healer, poet, smith. Saint Brigid was renowned for her healing powers and miracles and for her compassion for the sick and injured. People still seek (and receive) healing at Brigid's holy wells and springs, where her waters have flowed for millennia. But you don't have to travel to Kildare—Brigid the healer is ever-present.

Always listen carefully to your inner guidance when it comes to matters of healing, for Brigid's voice will be heard in the quiet moments. (She often speaks to me of health matters when I wake in the middle of the night.) Remember, Brigid is very practical, so her healing help may come in the form of a sudden craving for citrus fruit if you need more vitamin C. She may guide you toward a particular path of wellness, such as changing your diet, adding nutritional supplements, starting a new practice of movement, and so on. You may also come to understand more clearly the causes of ill health—practical things on the physical plane, or something in your soul's journey that required a challenge, or a combination of several causes.

We often think that prayers for healing are answered by the ailment simply going away, and indeed, that happens all the time. Belief in the power of prayer and the blessings of Brigid truly can work miracles both great and small. But sometimes Brigid's help comes not through direct healing of your body, but through guiding you toward the right healers and medical practitioners. This happened to me a few years ago. I had been experiencing some health issues and knew intuitively what the core cause was. I was used to handling such things myself, without outside assistance, but I felt a strong push this time to seek out a doctor. Money was an issue, as a self-employed person with no medical insurance. Trusting that Brigid would guide me, I did a simple web search for "low-cost health care in Portland." The very first website that came up was called Salvia Medica ("sage medicine"), and there was a beautiful photograph of a healing bundle of sage. It was a holistic practice, affordable and caring, with a woman MD who was oriented toward the spirit as well as the body, and it was absolutely what I needed. Once I put myself in Brigid's hands, she wasted no time in taking me to the exact right place for healing help.

Affirming wellness is a vital part of becoming well and staying well. It can be challenging, because all around us are people who are only too happy to affirm ill health. The Celts had many prayers against "the evil eye," which was considered a cause of illness and bad luck. My feeling is that the evil eye is still active, though perhaps not intentionally! For example, the media has thoroughly convinced us there is such a thing as "flu season" and that we are going to get sick, no matter what. Our friends, family, and coworkers—with all the best intentions—will warn us that whatever ailment we have is likely to last for weeks, because that is what happened to them.

Brigid as healer offers help in so many ways, but she needs you to cooperate in your own healing—not just through good physical practices, but by changing your attitude about your own healthiness. The prayer "Brigid, restore me to health" assumes that health is your natural state. Hold the vision that your natural state of wellness is vital, strong, clear, and radiant. Be careful what language you use when speaking of your health. There is a saying: "Your body believes every word you say." When you say, "I'm getting a cold," your body will cooperate, because that's what you're asking for! (In the interest of full disclosure, I'm working on not saying, "I have a bad knee.") Instead, try this:

1. Center yourself and ask Brigid to bless you with her healing hands. Clearly envision those hands placed warmly and firmly on your body, and the power of the Goddess flowing throughout your being.

2. While you are in that state of conscious visualizing, say aloud, "The cold has left my system." (Use other words that state whatever the ailment is, but be sure to say it in the present tense as if it has already happened.) Visualize Brigid empowering these words and thoughts.

3. Listen for her guidance as to what you should do next. It might be what you would expect, such as wrapping up in a warm blanket, taking a nap, or making a cup of herbal tea. But be ready for surprises too—Brigid may suggest you put on some music, or go outside and breathe the fresh air, or call a friend and have a good long talk. All aspects of your wellness are under her care, and they are all connected.

The Healing Waters of the World
REBECCA REEDER

*Rebecca Reeder is a shamanic therapist trained
at the California Institute of Integral Studies.*

On the west coast of County Clare, near the town of Liscannor, there is a holy well dedicated to Brigid where her presence is especially palpable. Within the well-house is a small corridor leading up to the waters where offerings from locals as well as pilgrims from all over have been left. The space is adorned with images of the holy mother, Brigid's crosses, relics of saints, and handwritten prayers for the healing of beloveds or well wishes for those departed.

When I approached the waters and touched them to my face, an immediate gush of tears washed over and through me to my soul. The presence of love and grace filled me completely, healing my spirit with the strength and courage of faith. As I looked around at the prayers and offerings of so many others who were guided here seeking something of the holy, I was again doubled over with emotion as I felt connected to all those who have come before and those who will come after in an unbroken lineage to find comfort here.

Through a series of dreams, visions, and waking experiences, I've come to see wells and waters as inseparable from healing and spirituality as well as social and environmental justice. This was also the case for my Celtic ancestors, for it is said that all the rivers of Ireland—almost all of which are named after goddesses—have their source in an Otherworld well of wisdom. Within Celtic lore surrounding the mysticism of water are the consequences for the people and the land when the waters, which are all sacred, are desecrated.

The first Waters of the World ceremony I engaged in was many years ago at an Earth Activist Training led by Starhawk. Participants were invited to bring water from whatever source they felt connected to and during the ritual to place a few drops of the water into a bowl. When all the waters came together, a prayer for the healing of the water was shared and some of it was returned to the earth. I learned that this ceremony began at a Brigid ritual and continued from then on as people brought waters together from all over the earth, from holy wells, sacred rivers, oceans, streams, creeks, and lakes. I was very inspired by this ritual and began to carry around my own vessel of the waters of the world. I would pray for the healing of the waters and make offerings whenever I went to a new body of water.

When most people think of modern medicine or healing practices, they are not usually thinking about the powerful healing to be found at holy wells or in Brigid's presence. In fact, practices that touch the mysterious or mystical have often come to be viewed as superstitious nonsense with no power at all, or as the work of some evil being, powerful perhaps but demonic nonetheless. And yet, there is something within our folk memory—an older, deeper connection that understands and yearns for ancestral ways that are lost or forgotten, whether that be by choice or by force. Like water running underground, the memories of our ancestors are stored in our bodies and in the unconscious, for these ways will seek to bubble up and be reckoned with whether we consciously intend it or not. I think this is part of the resurgence we see now of Celtic spirituality, of the Brigidine tradition, and of timeless healing wisdom.

For me, Brigid's influence in the world today is connected to the power of her resilience, as well as that of those devoted to her who have kept her memory and teachings alive. She is a bridge builder between people of different lands and different faiths, for she has persisted in the hearts of people for centuries. Many people are longing to return to the wisdom inherent in their ancestral roots, and so many are seeking her. And her traditions are needed perhaps more now than ever, as a protector of people and the land and an inspiration to those who are committed to living her values of generosity, peace, and justice. Encoded in the many stories about her and in the ways we may come into our own unique relationship with her are teachings we need to embody, share, and pass on to the generations to come. In this way, Brigid is a guide for the healing of our planet.

For more about Rebecca, see the Contributors appendix.

Bathing in Brigid's Well

This ritual bath invokes the spirit of Brigid's healing wells in the comfort of your own bathtub. (If you're not a bath person, you can adapt it as a hand-bathing or anointing ritual.) There are two steps of preparation for your first bath, and after that you'll have supplies on hand for more baths.

The Water

The first step is to make some lustral water. The word *lustral* comes from roots meaning to purify and brighten. Lustral water is perfect for Brigid-blessed baths because it's made by combining fire and water with ceremonial intention. Some ways to do this include:

- Burning floating candles
- Burning camphor in water (see page 145)
- Standing a taper or pillar candle in a vessel of water and letting it burn down until it is naturally extinguished
- Manually extinguishing candles in water

Whichever technique you use, give it your full attention and intention. You are changing the essence of the water from mundane to magical. Invoke Brigid's fire to imbue the water with her blessing. If you like, add crystals for additional energy—clear quartz is always a good choice, but use your intuition. Save your lustral water in sealed jars to add to baths.

THE POTION

The next step is to make some bath bag potions. You will need:

- 3 cups dry oatmeal (any kind, but Irish is a nice touch)
- 1 cup dried or powdered Irish moss[53]
- 1 cup dried hawthorn leaves
- 10 cotton muslin bath bags

I kept this bath mixture simple, but you can add other herbs and flowers if you wish. Oatmeal is wonderful for the skin and generally soothing to the emotions. It brings Brigid's blessing of nourishment to both body and soul. Irish moss isn't really a moss, it's a seaweed (*Chondrus crispus*). It's also called carrageen, from the Irish *carraigín*, "little rock," perhaps for the tidepool rocks where it is found. Seaweed was a valued resource for the ancient Celts (and into modern times) as food and to fertilize crops. It was traditional to harvest seaweeds at Imbolc, the time of the highest tides of the year. Energetically, it brings the everrenewing life force of living waters. Hawthorn is a faery plant associated with Brigid's sacred wells and often grows near them. When you

---

53. Irish moss, hawthorn, and muslin bags are all available at herb stores. See the Resources appendix.

bathe in hawthorn-infused waters, the immortal beauty of the fae is yours.

With your hands, mix the oats, Irish moss, and hawthorn in a large bowl. Take your time with this. Sift the mixture through your fingers, interact with it, let your intention radiate from your hands as you repeat this triad:

Threefold the healing of Brigid:
Health of the body, restoring;
Health of the mind, refreshing;
Health of the spirit, renewing.

When you feel complete with this part of the preparation, divide the mixture among the bags and tie them shut, knotting the drawstrings three times. Trim off the excess string. Store the bags in a dry, cool place until you're ready to use them.

THE BATH

Having made your lustral water and your bags, run a very warm bath and light some candles nearby so their light ripples on the water. Pour some lustral water into the bath and drop in one of your potion bags. Get in the bathtub and rest in the quiet warmth. Squeeze the bag to release its virtues into the water and gently caress your skin with the bag itself—the potion is silky and will make your skin wonderfully soft. When you feel relaxed and open to receive all the gifts of your healing bath, bless yourself with the following charm. With each "wavelet," cup water in your hands and pour it over your head and body. Visualize Brigid's loving hands performing this blessing.

A wavelet for thy form,
A wavelet for thy voice,
A wavelet for thy health,
A wavelet for thy luck,
A wavelet for thy good,
A wavelet for thy vision,
A wavelet for thy strength,

A wavelet for thy pluck,
A wavelet for thy faith:
Nine waves for thy grace.[54]

Stay in the bath as long as it feels good, then dry yourself off and go straight to bed to complete the healing with a good long sleep.

BRIGID'S SOUL FORGE

What is Brigid working on at her forge? You. Taking the raw materials that make up the essence of your being, she forms your soul. Soul-shaping requires effort. Metal doesn't just go into the forge and come out all shiny and ready for use.

Brigid and Excellence

I've always felt that excellence is a quality Brigid holds in very high esteem. By "excellence," I don't mean perfection and I don't mean superiority. Excellence isn't about comparing yourself to anyone else. Excellence is the personal best you are capable of, while always aspiring to do better.

In one of Madeleine L'Engle's memoirs, she writes about the way her college classmates categorized writers and other artists. They were either "majah," "minah," or "mediocah." Somewhere else, I read a funny line from an artist showing his work: "Remember, I'd rather stay mediocre than accept criticism." Mediocrity is comfortable; it's an easy place to stay in for a long time. It's perhaps especially easy for women, because for so many centuries we were told we couldn't really do *anything* well—that we were, in terms of the world's achievements, "minah." It can seem unsisterly to offer helpful criticism or self-defeating to question your own efforts.

When we are being nice—to ourselves or to others—we say, "You did the best you could." Looking at it in one way, that's always true. For whatever reason, we weren't able to do better than that. Sometimes this is logistical—circumstances get in the way. Sometimes we're just

....

54. Adapted from *Carmina Gadelica*, 217. If you wish, you can write the blessing and dissolve the paper in the water.

flattened by grief, anger, depression, exhaustion. But let's be honest—
sometimes we just don't aspire to excellence. An internal monologue
might go something like:

> *I know I'm not doing the best I could do with the rituals I've been creat-*
> *ing for circle. No one else has said anything, though, and I think they*
> *all feel fine with the work we're doing, so … okay! I'm being too hard*
> *on myself. If they're happy, I'm happy. I'm probably being overly criti-*
> *cal. What I'm doing is good enough.*

(In other words, "I'd rather stay mediocre than accept criticism.")
Remember the old report card comment "Needs improvement"? Ask
Brigid to help you shine a light into the murky places of your soul and
show you where there is room for improvement. A compassionate way
of approaching this might go something like this internal monologue:

> *I know that I am not doing the best I could do with the rituals I've been*
> *creating for circle. No one has said anything, and I think they are all*
> *fine with the work we're doing, but I know I could do better. I know*
> *there is inspiration and creativity within me that is not being tapped. I*
> *also acknowledge my own exhaustion and lack of time to bring my full*
> *energy to this. But because I aspire to excellence, I will look at how I can*
> *restructure my priorities to make this happen. I do this for me, and for*
> *love of Brigid, who blesses me with the knowledge that I have more to*
> *give to the world.*

When you maintain compassion for yourself—and even more important sometimes, your sense of humor—it's an act of self-love to
push yourself to really do well at whatever it is that you offer to Brigid.
You are using the gifts she gave you to the very best of your ability.

The Druid organization Ár nDraíocht Féin has as its motto "Why not
excellence?" Their unofficial motto tells how this excellence is achieved:
"As fast as a speeding oak!" The pursuit of excellence is ongoing, day by
day, with steady and patient growth. It doesn't mean working yourself to
death, and it never means beating yourself up. For myself, I feel lately that

Brigid has been trying to give me a "time-out." Bit by bit, she has been guiding me to a quieter and more intuitive place in my spirit, her Sacred Sheepdog nipping at my heels to get me heading in the right direction. Brigid called in Cerridwen to help with these changes, and I have a feeling a third sister-goddess will join them along the way. It is challenging to both be gentle with myself and pursue excellence, to honor my lifelong vow of service to Brigid that I believe in with all my heart. There is rest and replenishment of the body and spirit, and then there is just slacking off.

Brigid offers a metaphor for this balance of acceptance and aspiration in her process of tempering a blade. The blade is put through fire, hammered and shaped, then cooled in water. It is the repeated process of stressing and blessing—pushing to the next level of refinement—that creates an excellent blade, strong and flexible, able to withstand resistance. If you just have water—the nice, safe, accepting place where whatever you're doing is just fine—you're as much out of balance as if you were always in a hot forge, always molten, raw, unfulfilled.

Aspiring to excellence has its dangers. It's all too easy to stay in a state of constant self-criticism where you think nothing you do is good enough. Part of pursuing excellence is welcoming the idea that you still have things to learn, still have room to grow and deepen. With some practice, this puts the inner critic in her proper place, as an honest and friendly helper. Challenge yourself to push through self-imposed barriers of mediocrity. See yourself as that blade in Brigid's forge, made stronger by challenges, blessed by compassion. Ask her to show you where you really shine—and where you could use a little polishing.

Sword and Shield

You and I are not ancient Celts. You may not even be a modern Celt by blood or inherited culture. But Brigid is a goddess of the Celts, and her symbology reflects the attributes and values of that people. When we say in prayer, "Brigid is my sword and my shield," we are speaking metaphorically, but it was not always so. The Celts were warriors. It does no good to sugarcoat it, and indeed, it's not respectful to those fierce people to revision them otherwise. According to the Greek writer Strabo around the turn of the first millennia, the Celts were "ready to face danger even if they have nothing on their side but their own strength and courage." As the sword and shield were of vital importance, surely this is where Brigid as goddess of metalcraft was often invoked. Asking her blessing on these implements ensured victory.

Celtic shields were made for use in battle, but also for display and ritual. They were human-sized, decorated with magical and symbolic patterns, often with creatures such as birds and boars. There were light wooden shields for battle use, and magnificent metal shields for ceremony and ritual. Both individual and mass conflicts were considered a test of personal valor, and there was no false modesty about proclaiming one's skills and bravery. Before the combat commenced, high praise of each combatant would be shouted out to the accompaniment of drums. This battle chant had religious significance, calling upon the deities to witness their victory. All enemies of the Celts wrote about the noise they made in battle, raising power with howls and the blasting of ritual war trumpets. These horns were sculpted in the form of animal heads, as if summoning the wild spirit of the beast to strike terror in the heart of the enemy and inspire the Celtic warriors to glory.

Our lives are challenging, too, and we face troubling times and fearful situations. The fierce Celtic qualities we can retain and honor in ourselves are courage, determination, and commitment to a cause of action. What does it mean to have Brigid as a sword or shield?

Brigid's sword is the sword of righteous justice. As goddess and as saint, she is invoked for victory against the enemies of her causes, which always have the well-being of her people at heart. To hold Brigid's sword in your hand—or to invoke her presence, sword drawn—is a declaration to the universe that you have right on your side.

Brigid's shield is invoked more than her sword, naturally enough. Her protection is sought in every realm of life, on a daily basis, whereas swords should only be drawn in times of great need. Prayer after prayer call upon the shielding power of Brigid. Brigid's shield prevents undesirable energy from getting to you. The shield absorbs the blow; it is a psychic barrier against which harm falls away harmlessly. I don't believe in being defensive as such—what you defend against often grows stronger just because of the energy you put into fearing it. But invoking Brigid's shield as a regular part of your devotions places you in that state of protection all the time. The sword is for crisis; the shield is for every day.

> *I am under the shielding*
> *Of good Brigid each day;*
> *I am under the shielding*
> *Of good Brigid each night.*
> *On sea and on land,*
> *On the track and on the hill,*
> *Alone or in company.*[55]

The Celtic prayer known as a lorica (after the breastplate of armor) is a shield forged of words of power—which makes it truly a shield of Brigid. The best known of these is "The Deer's Cry," attributed to Saint Patrick, part of which is:

> *I arise today*
> *Through the strength of heaven,*
> *Light of sun,*
> *Radiance of moon,*
> *Splendor of fire,*
> *Speed of lightning,*
> *Swiftness of wind,*
> *Depth of sea,*
> *Stability of earth,*
> *Firmness of rock.*

Alas, Patrick went on (allegedly) to ask for protection against "incantations of false prophets, black laws of pagandom, false laws of heretics, craft of idolatry, spells of women and smiths and wizards." Ah, well. Before he went off on that little tirade, he offered this verse, which I have adapted as a lorica for Brigid devotees:

....
55. Adapted from *Carmina Gadelica*, 264.

I arise today
With Brigid's strength to uphold me,
Brigid's wisdom to guide me,
Brigid's eye to look before me,
Brigid's ear to hear me,
Brigid's word to speak for me,
Brigid's hand to guard me,
Brigid's way to lie before me,
Brigid's cloak to protect me,
Brigid's well to heal me.

Notice that there are nine invoking lines in both of these loricas. Remember that in Celtic spirituality, three is the number of ultimate empowerment. Forging a protective shield by the power of three-times-three intensifies its strength beyond any breaking.

Try your hand at creating your own lorica to use in your daily devotions or when you feel a special need for the shield of Brigid. Add to its potency by making a visual interpretation of it, such as a collage, to place on your altar.

Brigid's Ink: Celtic Tattoos

As with so much of Celtic lore, there is disagreement as to whether the ancient Celts practiced tattooing as we know it today. There are descriptions of people who painted their bodies with blue woad dye, which would have been temporary, perhaps for battle use only. Other contemporary accounts tell of "engraved" designs on the body, and coins show markings on faces that appear to be tattoos. The "painted people"—the Picts of the north and the Cruithne of Ireland—were said to have tattoos in the "forms of beasts, birds, and fishes" [56] and to go naked in order to show off their body art. Modern Celtic tattoos draw from this ancestral affinity.

Why include tattooing in a book about Brigid? Experiences such as tattooing, if undertaken in the right spirit, can be a rite of transformation. People who have tattoos are often asked by the un-inked, "Did it

....

56. MacCulloch, *The Religion of the Ancient Celts.*

hurt?" The answer depends on the person asked, but the question itself is interesting. When a new mother proudly shows off her infant, no one ever asks her if it hurt to give birth. The end product is what matters, and yet, the rite of passage the new mother has gone through has changed her forever. So it is with a spiritual tattoo.

Moving through a physical challenge is a transforming experience, a forge experience. Unlike pain from accident or illness, getting a tattoo is voluntary. You are making a commitment to seeing it through, no matter what, and you are making a commitment to the symbol you are adding to your body. From now until your death, that symbol will be part of you.

A tattoo in honor of Brigid can invoke her protection and shielding, declare yourself as her devotee, or be a secret affirmation of your faith known only to you (and whoever sees you without clothes). I have several tattoos, including three specifically for Brigid: oak leaves and a triskele badge on one shoulder, oak leaves and mistletoe on the other, and a triskele on the inside of my wrist that is part of a Celtic spiral wristband. (The other wrist has spirals and a raven.) My shoulder tattoos were to seal my dedication to Brigid as her priestess. The wristbands were a commitment to live that dedication openly in the world, for the rest of my life.

If you choose to get a sacred tattoo, remember that intention is everything. Take your time to find just the right art and just the right tattoo artist. Prepare yourself ceremonially before you go and after you return. During the process itself, let your artist know that you want to be quiet and go inward, not chat. Visualize yourself at Brigid's forge, where you are made and remade. Open yourself to her blessing as the Goddess marks you for her own.

Externalizing the Internal
PAT FISH

*Pat Fish is a tattoo artist who specializes
in bringing Celtic art to life in skin.*

———

I grew up an orphan raised by people with whom I had no genetic similarity, and I yearned to have heritage. When I was thirty, I decided to switch occupations and learn tattooing, and simultaneously paid a private eye to locate my birth parents. It turns out I am a Pict, of Clan Campbell from Scotland, and so I took the timing of that discovery as a sign that I ought to dedicate my tattoo career to bringing the intricate knotwork of the ancient Irish illuminated manuscripts and the patterns from the Pictish standing stones to life in skin. Most people take their ethnic heritage for granted—only someone who has lived without that connection can understand how much it meant to me to suddenly have it. Add to that the fact that the Picts were historically known for being heavily tattooed, and it felt meant to be.

I feel very strongly that everyone has atavistic ties to their bloodline, whatever it is, and for me I experience a lovely serenity when working with the knotwork. It is quite compelling to me, holds my attention like no other form of art, and the challenge is one I very much enjoy. It is unlikely that the tattoos the ancient Picts and Celts did were anywhere near as intricate as what I can accomplish now, but there is every reason to think that there would have been skilled artisans doing tattoos just as there were metalsmiths and stone carvers doing extremely complex work that survives to this day. It is those surviving pieces that I take as my inspiration as I design original tattoo designs for my clients.

I approach each tattoo as an opportunity to enhance that person's life, and I try not to be judgmental of their motivations or inspirations. But if I feel that the image or placement is likely to have a negative impact on their life, I feel it is my duty to refuse to do it. That's the responsibility you take on when doing a permanent alteration to someone's appearance. I need to be proud of what I do and to strive to do my best. If I light incense and play soothing music, it is for my own pleasure in my work environment, not to manifest sacred space for the client. Tattoo artists are like shamans for many people, because we are the agents of change. It is the client's responsibility to take this transformation with appropriate gravitas. Or not.

Women seem to live in constant fear of judgment about their bodies, and so the act of claiming their own skin as a canvas is a powerful one. For some, a symbol of their faith can give them the opportunity to witness to others about their beliefs. In all cases tattoos give people an externalization of their inner aesthetics. And being willing to express that in a form that can be seen and judged by others is a strengthening thing, causing the person to be willing to stand up for those enthusiasms.

For more about Pat, see the Contributors appendix.

Immrama

There is a world within each of us that is beyond the mundane world in which we walk every day. Whether we call it imagination or visualizations or daydreaming or journeying, it is an endlessly revealing realm of wisdom and wonder. In Celtic spirituality, explorations of this inner realm are sometimes called *immrama*. An *immram* is a voyage, a setting-forth upon the sea toward the unknown. In Celtic lore, tales of the great *immrama* tell of enchanted islands, each symbolic of a challenge that deepens the soul, whether the challenge is successfully met or not. The undertaking is always more important than the outcome. The same is true when you set forth on a visualized *immram*. Releasing expectations and the need to achieve something allows for pure and powerful messages to come through.

You can create your own *immram* by simply setting the scene and being in a receptive state of mind and spirit, and I provide a beginning for that here. Following that description, you can continue on your own or use the complete *immram* visualization I offer. Either way, what will happen on your voyage is between you and Brigid. Be ready for surprises.

PREPARING FOR YOUR IMMRAM

For any deep visualization, you need uninterrupted time and a quiet space. Only you know how much time such an inward journey will take, but my suggestion is to allow at least an hour for your first such journey. Some *immrama* take many hours. Dress yourself comfortably, or if you choose to not wear anything, be sure you are warm enough. Remember that you will be lying or sitting still for a while, so anticipate that you will cool down some. Cold feet can be especially distracting.

A silent space is best for inner journeying, or you might put on a quiet recording of ocean sounds. I don't recommend using music, even meditation music, for this purpose, as music influences the emotions and you want to be open and receptive to whatever comes.

Sit or lie down in a comfortable position. Lying down is more likely to lead to falling asleep, of course, and I for one would always fall asleep instantly. Have the room as dark as possible. If necessary, tie a soft scarf over your eyes to further block out any light. And so begin…

SETTING SAIL

> *Brigid of the green sea,*
> *Brigid of the swift wind,*
> *Brigid of the bright star,*
> *Guide my vessel.*

You are seated in a small wooden boat, large enough for one person. The boat is on a misty shore, just touching the edge of the sea, with small wavelets lapping at the bow. A mast rises at the center of the boat, with a furled sail wrapped at the top of the crossbar. There are no oars, no rudder or tiller, no way to steer. Take a moment to orient yourself in the boat. Run your hands along the smooth wood of the sides, and feel the firmness of the floorboards under your feet. Notice if there is anything else with you in the boat, anything you are taking with you.

Now give attention to your surroundings. Note the mood of the ocean, the sky, the weather. These will vary from *immram* to *immram*. Take a deep breath of the sea air. Feel the wind upon your face.

A wave comes in now, not an ordinary wave, but one sent from the depths of the ocean's magic to lift your boat and set it afloat beyond the turnings of the tides.

Once you are on the open sea, you unloose the ropes that tie your sail and it unfurls. Note the color of the sail and if there are any symbols on it. You make the sail secure, and the wind fills it. Your boat turns outward on its journeying…

———

From this point, you can create your own immram,
or you can continue with the one that follows.

———

After a time of sailing, your boat approaches a small island made entirely of grey stone. The shoreline seems unapproachable, piled high with boulders wet with sea spray and draped with seaweed. Your boat bumps gently against these boulders, and your eyes wander over the stone. There seems no way to land or enter this island, but with patience you can now make out a footfall, a place of damp sand just big enough to stand on. Tying your boat to a bronze ring set into one of the stones, you disembark and stand upon the land. Again, you observe with patience and full attention and see a narrow path that winds around and through and upward among the boulders.

Following this path up the gentle incline, you emerge at the top of the island, a wide expanse of bare stone, worn smooth over thousands of years of wind and water. Notice how the emptiness of the place affects you. Observe your thoughts, your emotions, your perceptions. You turn in place, to each of the directions in turn: west, north, east, south, and back to west, the direction from whence you came. There, where before there was only emptiness, you see a domed structure made of the same grey stone, open on one side but sheltered from the wind. You walk toward this structure.

As you draw near, you see that within this shelter is a great blazing forge. The stones glow red, and the dancing flames illuminate the enclosure. A black iron anvil, decorated with spirals and other mystical symbols, sits at the center of the shelter. There is something on the anvil, a gift for you. Pick it up, examine it, take your time with it. Give thanks in the way that feels right to you. When you are ready, return to your boat with the gift.

As soon as you are seated in your boat, the wind picks up your sail again and turns the little vessel away from the stone island and out to sea. You sail for a time, watching the horizon, observing the weather, the wind, any creatures of sea or sky. You see now that you are approaching a second island. Stairs are cut into the rock face, stairs that come right down into the sea and continue underwater, as they continue upward and curve around a white cliff face. You tie your boat to a silver ring set into a stair and disembark, standing on the white stone of the staircase, water swirling around your ankles. You gaze downward, seeing the stairs disappear in the deep clear water below, and then turn your gaze upward and begin to climb.

The stairs wind around and around the small island, not an arduous climb, but one that requires care and attention as you place your feet on the stone steps. The stairs end at an opening to a cave, high above the waves and your tethered boat. Light reflecting off water touches the walls of the cave, and you see they are made of mother-of-pearl, luminous with delicate colors. As you stand at the center of the cave, you become aware of a musical resonance within its walls, an echo of the sea combined with an enchanting otherworldly vibration. You feel this sound permeate your being. Notice how it makes you feel, what emotions you experience. You lift your hands in a gesture of receiving, and a gift is placed in your open hands. Give thanks in the way that feels right to you. When you are ready, return to your boat with the gift.

Place the second gift beside the first in your boat and observe as before as the wind lifts your sail and takes you out to the open sea. Notice any changes in the ocean, the weather, your mood, your awareness. In time, your boat approaches a third island, this one covered with a dense forest. Your boat comes to rest on a little beach and you disembark. This time the way seems clear, a path leading directly into the forest. But after going only a little way, the path forks, and you must choose a direction. A little distance longer, and it forks again. You move through the wood, choosing at each turning. Notice how you feel, what it feels like to choose, whether fearsome or exhilarating or something else entirely.

In time, you come to a clearing, and you can see that many paths have led to this place, from all directions, each ending at the same sacred grove. The tall trees move in the wind, sighing and singing with the voices of oak and rowan and willow. At the center of the grove is an ancient stone well. You look into its depths and see what you are meant to see. There is a bucket on a rope, and you lower it into the well and pull forth a gift. Give thanks in the way that feels right to you. When you are ready, return to your boat with the gift.

Now, with the three gifts beside you in the little boat, you feel the wind lift the sail one last time and guide your vessel toward the place from which you departed. But now you see three women awaiting you, cloaked and hooded, a stone altar table before them. Your boat is borne to shore by the tide and you move to stand before the altar. Place your three gifts there. The three women come forward and each touches a gift, and with the touch, it transforms into living flame, burning without apparent source or fuel upon the stone. The flames merge into one, and it seems that the three women also merge into one, and then she too becomes part of the flame. Gaze into its depths. Feel it warming your being, becoming part of you. Receive any message or knowledge that is meant for you. Take your time.

When you are ready, return to your waking awareness, giving thanks for the journey and its gifts. Stay quiet and absorb the experience, and then finish grounding yourself by eating something light and drinking a glass of cool water.

Fire in the Head

The ancient Celts recognized divine madness, "fire in the head," as the creative genius of poets and seers. Today we aren't taught how to manage this mind-fire when it overtakes us, as it may well do when you ask Brigid to enflame your soul. Too many ideas, too many thoughts, too much input, too many roles to play—in the forge of transformation, this is the stage at which you are molten. Very few of us have the luxury of running off to the woods to be a mad hermit. Here are a couple of things to try when the fire in your head is making steam come out of your ears.

RAVENS AND SWANS TOGETHER

Tactile meditations using stones are grounding when you are feeling confused or overloaded and on sleepless nights when your mind won't stop yammering. This calming meditation draws on imagery from two poems by W. B. Yeats, an Irish poet whose works are filled with the mystical Celtic spirit.

You will need:

3 candles

12 (or more) white stones

12 (or more) black stones

1. Sit at a table in a darkened, quiet room.

2. Light the three candles, invoking earth, sea, and sky.

3. Set the white stones to one side, and gather the black stones in front of you on the table. Hold your hands over them and feel the energetic connection flowing between you and the stones. Think about your worries, your confusion, your fears—all the mental cacophony that is disturbing you. Now begin to move the black stones around on the table while repeating these lines:
   There, through the broken branches, go
   The ravens of unresting thought...[57]

4. The black stones are the ravens, and they are trying to get their messages through to you, but something in you is disturbing

....
57. Yeats, "The Two Trees."

them so that they can't rest and speak their truth. Visualize this and keep reciting the lines as you stir and swirl and mix the black stones with your hands. Let yourself fall into a trance if it happens.

5. When you feel ready, lift your hands from the black stones and hold them over the white stones. Again, feel the energetic connection flowing between you. The white stones are the swans. They bring strength and quiet calm so you can hear the ravens' messages. The raven and the swan are not in opposition—they work together as Brigid's allies. One by one, bring the white stones in among the black stones while repeating these lines:
   They drift upon the still water, mysterious, beautiful …[58]

6. Keep reciting the lines as you move the stones around in any way that pleases you. You may want to swirl a line of swan stones through the raven stones, or make an arrangement of ravens above, swans below. Perhaps they form a circle, alternating black and white, or half black and half white, like night and day. Don't overthink it; let your hands move instinctively while your mind receives the insights and wisdom that have been trying to come through.

7. At some point, you will feel complete with this meditation. Take several deep breaths and give thanks to Brigid and her allies. Extinguish your candles or let them burn out on their own. Cleanse the stones and store them respectfully until you need them again.

CRIOS BRÍDE: THE GIRDLE OF BRIGID

Symbolic ropes called *crios Bríde*, "Brigid's girdle," are traditionally woven of straw and used in Imbolc ceremonies as a sort of gateway through which people and animals are passed and blessed. Like many folk customs, the origins of the *crios Bríde* are long forgotten, but one tale tells of how Saint Brigid gave her belt to a woman in need of income, saying that if she dipped the belt in water, that water could heal any ill (and hence, the woman could earn her living as a miraculous healer). Being encircled by Brigid's girdle, not just at Imbolc but every day, is a tangible affirmation of her healing power—and of your own participation in that healing.

....
58. Yeats, "The Wild Swans at Coole."

You can make a *crios Bríde* for any purpose. This one is for spiritual fragmentation.

Maybe you've been working too hard. Maybe you are being pulled in many directions because of the roles you serve—mother, partner, worker, artist, friend. For me, it was a matter of having so many different plates to keep spinning in the air that I couldn't find the time or strength to really sense what was going on with *me*. It wasn't until I started weaving the pieces together again that I realized how frayed and fragmented my spirit had become. The ritual act of creating a single braided strand from three separate strands symbolizes being made whole by the healing blessings of Brigid.

You will need:
Three lengths of satin cord (sometimes called rattail), at least twice as long as your waist measurement. Choose three colors to symbolize the integration of your being—cool colors for peace, fiery colors for strength, a blend of both, etc. Cord can be found at fabric and craft stores, and www.satincord.com has a wide selection of beautiful cords in many colors.

Before you begin, bless your workspace in the way you prefer and make sure you won't be disturbed as you work. Light a candle to invoke Brigid's presence. You may want to put on some deepening Celtic instrumental music.

1. Gather the three strands in your hands and set your clear intention that this will be a ritual object, imbued with the power of Brigid's healing:

    The girdle of Brigid is my girdle,
    The girdle of three strands.
    Brigid who is three in one,
    Guide this work of my hands.[59]

<hr>

59. Adapted from a traditional Imbolc verse.

2. Knot the three strands together about 8 inches from the end. As you begin braiding, you'll need a way to keep the braid from slipping away from you. I like to use a clipboard to hold the ends for the first few inches, and then when the braid is long enough, switch to tying it to the back of a chair or a doorknob.

3. Without rushing, begin the simple and repetitive rhythm of braiding the strands. Each time you cross one strand over the other and tighten the woven strands, envision the parts of your spirit that have become scattered coming back together in a stronger pattern of empowerment.

4. As you work, you may want to say a line of a triad with each movement. See page 172 for some suggestions on creating your own triad for this purpose.

5. When the braid is long enough to tie comfortably around your waist, you are done. Tie a knot at the end as you did at the beginning, and trim the dangling ends. You can add beads to these ends if you wish, but if you're going to wear the *crios Bríde* under your clothes on a regular basis, skip the beads.

Wear your *crios Bríde* for at least one moon cycle to keep your intention strong and keep Brigid's blessings close. (You don't need to leave it on 24/7.) After that, Brigid will tell you when to wear it.

BRIGID THE MIDWIFE

One of Brigid's most important aspects is that of midwife. She supports and protects birthing mothers—both human and animal—and blesses the new life that is welcomed into the world. But her midwife role isn't just about literal birth. The final stage of labor, called transition, is the most intense. The laboring woman may feel like it's all too much and want to stop, forgetting how far she's come already. Just as the earthly midwife reassures and encourages, Brigid eases our way through all significant life passages. Sometimes a long period of work or struggle can seem in vain. A project or goal can take more effort or time than you imagined, and you want to just give up. Put yourself in Brigid's hands and ask her to guide you through this stage of transition. Attune yourself to her messages and trust them when they appear. She'll tell you when it's time to push—you may feel a renewed sense of determination and urgency, a stronger commitment to your dreams, or a firm resolution to get out of a bad situation. Remember to breathe. You are birthing yourself, and Brigid the midwife is right there beside you.

Brigid at the Threshold of Death

"He cried out from his bed that he saw Brigit of the Gael, and that it was she herself was bringing him to his death." [60]

Brigid as midwife stands at the threshold of death as well as the threshold of life. Of all our transitions, this is the most profound, whether we are one who is dying or the one who is left behind. Until very recently, death happened in the home and the dying one was attended by people who had seen death many times before and who accepted it as natural. It's a much more complicated process now, and it can be difficult to connect to the deeper mystery and the beauty of life's end under modern circumstances. There is a profession now called death-midwife: healers and priestesses and others who support the dying and their loved ones. This is the kind of help Brigid gives. There is a time to heal the body and a time to help the soul release its connection with the earthly form, and Brigid is there for both.

The Celts believed in a glorious afterlife. Their vision of the eternal joys varied, but their surety of faith never wavered. To reach the shining land, the dying one must cross the "black river of the abyss," the between-place that is neither this world nor the next. As in birth, the death transition can be a time of fear, frustration, despair. When my mother was dying (at home, thank Goddess), the house full of people experienced just about every emotion you could name as she traversed that between-place for a day and a night. Brigid the death-midwife offered me reassurance that all was going well and all would be well in the end.

....

60. Lady Gregory, *A Book of Saints and Wonders*.

Her Hands on Mine

SUSAN SMITH

Susan is a nurse, a Reiki master, and a Celtic shamanic practitioner guided in her work by Brigid.

———

I use Reiki for my hospice patients, both as they are declining and during their death. Brigid is always present, with her hands on mine and on the patient. I see their breathing ease and feel their energy change—they seem less fearful. It is a very holy experience for Brigid to be present during their crossing over. I frequently see her flame while I'm working.

During the death process, a person may experience several stages that can affect them physically, emotionally, or mentally that can result in suffering. Hospice offers relief from that suffering by helping to control various crises that may develop. For example, a person may be admitted to an inpatient hospice unit for dramatically increased intractable pain, and during their stay their dose of pain medication can be carefully titrated to higher doses than would be allowed for healthy patients in order to control that pain. Then depending on their condition, they may be able to spend more conscious time with their loved ones. In another type of crisis, a person may become very agitated and irrational, and do things they would normally never do, like pulling out medication lines or trying to walk home in the middle of the night.

I have been present for many of these crises. It can be so easy to reach for a higher dose of medication in these cases, but in working with Brigid I've been guided to change my energy to match theirs—by squatting to a lower level than they are, by mirroring their chakra level or energy, and then asking questions about something I know they love, like their children, or something they are proud of. When they are absorbed in speaking about something they love, then with my energy matching their own, Brigid helps me to change my energy and theirs follows. This helps the patient to trust and helps keep them safe, and many times these difficult situations can be handled without medication, allowing the person to maintain their dignity.

Healing work in hospice is obviously not a physical healing of a dying person, but a spiritual and emotional healing that happens as a person comes to terms with their death and during the transition across the death threshold, which is considered an in-between time in many spiritual traditions. A person is open during the death experience and great change is possible. When Brigid is present in the room, her presence eases the dying person and helps to sustain me (the work is not easy) and also the friends and family of the patient. The energy in the room changes when she is there. It is very difficult to describe, but overwhelming compassion and tenderness, enfolding of a beautiful soul in her arms during the crossing, helping one to bear it all, comes close. Whether the experience leads to enlightenment, the Otherworld, heaven, or another life is not important. What matters is the reintegration of soul parts, the easing of emotional distress, and the end of suffering in this life.

My devotions make my work sacred, and my work makes my devotions sacred, if that makes sense. The two go hand in hand. My healing work *is* a devotion to Brigid.

For more about Susan, see the Contributors appendix.

SITTING WITH THE SORROW

There is no right way or wrong way to react to death. Grief comes as it comes. I grieved in a much sharper and immediate way for the loss of my cat than for either of my parents, for whom I felt a softer sense of mourning. Don't judge yourself for not feeling as bad as people expect you to feel, and on the other hand, don't feel that you need to "move on" on anyone else's timetable. Whatever you believe or intuit about the afterlife, here in the world you inhabit with your earthly body the dear one is gone, and the space that was theirs echoes in its emptiness. We grieve for ourselves, and for others who are left behind, and for what might have been. This is as it should be. Good grief is part of Brigid's healing, and she will share it with you. You will pick up the pieces and push onward, but it must come in its proper time.

In the Celtic tradition, time is made for sitting with the sorrow and giving grief its due. The Celts' faith in the soul's fulfillment doesn't mean they didn't grieve for the human life. Celtic lore and poetry are full of laments that ache with sorrow and strive to capture emotions that are beyond words.

> *Too sad is the grief in my heart! down my cheeks run salt streams. I have lost my Ellen of the hue of fair weather, my bright-braided merry daughter....Orphaned is her father, with a crushing wound in his pierced and broken heart.*[61]

In our modern world, we take a more restrained approach to eulogizing the dead—and I do mean restrained, held back, like a torrent of emotion slamming against a dam of propriety. Writing a heartfelt lament as an expression of your grief can release some of these waters.

You may not consider yourself a writer, but if you will pick up the pen, Brigid will guide your hand. I've found that this kind of soul-writing is best done at night, when the world is sleeping and the mysteries of the Otherworld seem especially close. Sit at a table in a darkened room, with one candle illuminating your writing space. Have paper and pen ready; don't use your journal for this, though you may want to copy your words into it later.

The circle of candlelight is your sacred space. Before you begin to write, press the palms of your hands over your eyes. In that deeper

---

61. Goronwy Owen, "Elegy for His Daughter Ellen," 1755, in Jackson, *A Celtic Miscellany*.

darkness, pull your emotions to the surface, in all their myriad colors. Feel Brigid's presence, close and warm. When you're ready, start writing. Here are some thought-starter phrases from Celtic elegies: [62]

I am bitterly sad, for I have lost too much...
Great longing, cruel longing is breaking my heart...
The night is dark and a heavy grief comes over me...
I am lonely, I am cold, I am bent with sorrow...

Write from the deepest place of your longing heart, with no censorship or worry about language. Use as many sheets of paper as it takes. Write until you are exhausted or weeping—or exalted, or at peace. In other words, don't anticipate or strive to achieve anything. Just let it all come. Brigid is with you, she from whom poetry flows and eloquence emerges. She is there to midwife your passage through the dark tunnel of grief. She won't let you fall into the void of despair.

When you feel complete—for now—stack your papers and roll them into a scroll. Tie them with a ribbon, knotting it three times. Put the scroll away in a private place. You may be tempted to destroy it, but please don't. When the pain is less sharp, as Brigid's healing soothes your heart, you may want to read those words again.

Another expression of deep heartache and loss is the ancient Celtic practice of keening (*caoin*, cry). It is a full-throated wailing, long and achingly sad, sometimes with words and sometimes just an intonation of mournful sounds. Keening is said to have originated with Brigid, who let forth with her grieving cry upon finding the body of her son on the battlefield. Ever afterward, the *bean-sidhe*[63] keened over the dead to set them on their path out of this world.

Expressing yourself in this way may seem too raw, especially when compared to the way our modern culture prefers us to deal with pain— pushing it down, snapping out of it, or taking medication to suppress it. Instead, sit with the sorrow in the company of Brigid, her arm around

....
62. Adapted from Jackson, *A Celtic Miscellany*. Lines date from the twelfth to the nineteenth century or earlier.
63. Faery women, pronounced "banshee."

your shoulders, her cloak sheltering your body, and let the emotions pour forth. You can help this process along by playing music; there are many recordings of Celtic music, in particular, that have an air of longing and even anguish, which can help tap the stuck places of grief within you.

Once the floodgates are opened, let the sounds of keening rise up from the depths and emerge to pierce the stillness. Rock back and forth, swaying your body, your hands covering your face (or veil yourself completely, to withdraw more deeply into the feelings). When you feel complete or exhausted, be still again, feeling the vibration of the silence, feeling Brigid's warm, steady presence. Wrap yourself in a soft shawl or blanket. Light a candle, breathe deeply, and let the peace enter in.

In times past, significant loss such as the death of a loved one was marked by a year or more of respectful mourning. Other types of loss (ending a relationship, losing a job, the disappointment of a long-held hope) also need to be mourned and released. As always, listen to your intuition and to the voice of Brigid guiding you toward comfort and consolation. You will know when it is time to move on.[64]

Brigid as Maman Brigitte
Ellen Lorenzi-Prince

Ellen Lorenzi-Prince's devotion finds expression through tarot. Her Tarot of the Crone, Dark Goddess Tarot, and Minoan Tarot are offerings she's made to the ancient ones.

––––

Brought to the New World by Irish and Scottish immigrants, Brigid found a home in the hearts of the African slaves and within their syncretic Vodou religion. She became their Maman Brigitte, their Queen of the Cemetery and Mistress of the

64. Read more about the custom of keening and traditional Irish mourning at Library Ireland, www.libraryireland.com/articles/IrishFuneralCry DPJ1-31.

Ghede, the spirits of the underworld, the ancestors, the beloved dead.

Alone among the lwa—the mighty spirits of Vodou—Maman Brigitte is said to have come from the British Isles. Though she dresses in purple and black, the colors sacred to the Ghede, she retains her pale skin and red hair. Brigid's skill in words and poetry transforms into tough talk in Maman Brigitte, whose speech is often obscene and confrontational, though never mean nor cruel. This is an avenue of power that Maman provided to her new children, who were often unable to express themselves in any way other than silence and subservience lest they be punished or killed. Brigid's capacity for healing has been conveyed to Maman Brigitte as well. Prayers are offered to the Mistress of the Ghede in cases of illness that appear to be lost causes, that have responded to no other treatments, for she alone has the power to rekindle the fire of life that is flickering and near to dying out.

Yet as her titles state, Maman Brigitte's consummate power lies within the realm of the dead. She reclaims the souls of those who have died, drawing them out from the mystical waters of that other world in which they swim without awareness or individuality. She draws them out by speaking to them, by naming them, by recalling to them their identity. She initiates souls into their new lives as lwa, as spirits reborn into power, cognizance, and memory. She is therefore the mother of all the ancestors. She creates their kinship. They become one family through her. They may become family to the reverential petitioner too, through the intercession of the goddess. As Maman Brigitte holds both life and death in her hands, the ancestors represent both the past and the future for the living, knowing as they do where the living have come from and where they will go in the end.

The ancestral spirits are accorded great respect by the followers of Vodou, as they are also by the Celtic tribes. Both have a holy day at the onset of the month of November, as the sun withdraws from the Northern Hemisphere and the people's world enters into its darkest time. Candles are lit for the spirits.

The candles are offerings of the light and the warmth of fire that the ancestors particularly miss in their new life. Specific foods are offered to them, for the spirits must be fed what they like if one would ask for their blessing, their guidance, and their protection. The Ghede of Maman Brigitte, the ancestors in the New World, enjoy the specialties found in this domain: rum and tobacco, peanuts and plantains, coffee and cornmeal.

Offerings and rituals for the dead and for their Mother are performed in graveyards. The grave of the first woman buried in any cemetery is sacred to Maman Brigitte. It is there her ceremonial cross is erected, there the offerings are given. The act of establishing her cross and recognizing her power consecrates the grave to the goddess. The grave then becomes a gateway for the lwa to reach out to their descendants, to touch them, to live in them, to speak to and through them, and to hear their songs of praise. It becomes a pathway for spiritual power and knowledge to cross from one realm into another.

Maman Brigitte opens the door between the worlds. She is a loving mother to both the living and the dead. She is wise and bawdy, she is sacred and profane. An alchemical mix of energies burn and flow within her being, and she offers these powers to her children with a fierce but tender heart.

For more about Ellen, see the Contributors appendix.

BRIGID THE FOSTER MOTHER

Among the praise-names for Saint Brigid is "foster mother of Christ." This may seem strange to us today, as modern foster mothers take in children whose own mothers can't care for them, and this doesn't sound like something Mary would need. But the Celtic custom of fosterage is ancient, going back many centuries before Brigid was known as saint. The Celts sent their children to live with other families as a way of strengthening bonds among clans, both symbolically and practically. Respect and trust were the foundation of these exchanges, with the implied affirmation that you honored your clan-kin as worthy of raising your child. When Christian devotees called Saint Brigid the foster mother of Christ, it was the highest compliment they could bestow. Mary herself had handed over the upbringing of the savior of the world to her friend Brigid.

Does it matter that this fostering took place about five hundred years before Brigid was born? Not really. After all, this is a woman who could turn nettles into butter and hang her damp cloak on a sunbeam to dry. What's a little time travel to her? On a less literal plane, the idea of Brigid as holy foster mother implies that she embodied the qualities needed for such a role: wisdom, courage, dedication, knowledge, and love.

We can see Brigid the goddess as our foster mother, too. It's a different flavor of mothering than when we speak of a mother goddess—not better or worse, just different. A mother belongs to you from your birth; you are part of her in an inextricable way. A foster mother belongs to you by choice; she has welcomed you into her home, promised to protect and nurture you. Celtic fosterage relationships were considered to be five times stronger than blood connections, and the children of the fostering family became true siblings for life with the fosterlings. To say that Brigid is your foster mother proclaims a clan connection, an interweaving of her lineage with yours. You have a connection to her as well as to your own mother and your own clan. And all her other foster daughters are your sisters.

BRIGID *ANAM CARA*

Anam cara…soul friend. A lovely name for a lovely idea. We need to reclaim the sacred name of "friend" in its deepest sense. Many of those we might have called acquaintances in earlier times are now called friends, and when you factor in social media, the term is diminished even more. An *anam cara* rejoices with your joys, celebrates your triumphs, encourages your talents. In times of trouble, she never wavers. She knows you, through and through, warts and all. You may be fortunate enough to have such a soul friend in your life—if so, stop right now and send her your thanks.

But you have another *anam cara*, one who has been with you always. Brigid is the soul friend you can always turn to for good advice, solace, and perspective. She can always be trusted to tell you the truth you need to hear. When you need cheering up, she helps you find the laughter again. She doesn't judge you harshly, but she doesn't let you get away with self-deception. She listens.

Friendship isn't a river, flowing in one direction only. It is a deep well from which both friends may draw freely, ever freshened by wellsprings of love. Brigid loves to connect with you as much as you love to connect with her. This kind of friendship with the Goddess may seem strange if you were raised in a religion with patriarchal limits on familiarity. Intimacy requires approachability. A heavenly deity can seem very far away sometimes. Brigid is down-to-earth, in every way.

Good for the Soul

In his book *How the Irish Saved Civilization*, Thomas Cahill describes how the Catholic practice of confession was a revolutionary concept when it was introduced. It was a strangely compassionate and peaceful idea that by telling your transgressions to someone else and receiving absolution and a penance, you could be restored to innocence again. The sinful act itself, if it affected other people, would still need to be atoned for, but it was a wise observation by the early Church that the real damage was done to the soul of the transgressor. Finding a way to be forgiven was empowering in a way that hadn't been experienced in that faith before. It offered a clean emotional slate from which to "go forth and sin no more."

Pagans don't observe the practice of confession, but sometimes we do need to tell our story to a trusted counselor and embrace self-forgiveness. We are so hard on ourselves, much harder than we are on others. It can be challenging to come around to seeing mistakes and errors as necessary lessons on the soul's path to wisdom—and to release the guilt or shame that may have come along for the ride. When people confessed to Saint Brigid, she "sained" (blessed) their eyes so they could see the truth clearly and find resolution. A wise counselor can help you find the courage to look at your life's lessons, accept them, bless them, and release them. When you do this healing soul-work, envision Brigid placing her hands over your eyes and saining your inner vision.

In Brigid's name:
Let blame be forgotten,
Let cause be forgiven,
Let fault be abandoned.

SONG AND SILENCE: BRIGID'S SOUL RESTORERS

As goddess of poetry, Brigid is also goddess of music, for ancient Celtic poetry was sung or chanted. The Celts named three types (or "strains") of music:

The Suantraighé, which no one could hear without falling into a delightful slumber; the Goltraighé, which no one could hear without bursting into tears and lamentation; and the Geantraighé, which no one could hear without bursting out into loud and irrepressible laughter. [65]

Brigid is present in each of these strains. Your body and spirit find healing rest with her *Suantraighé*. Her *Goltraighé* pulls at your heartstrings to bring a needed release of emotions. And when it's time to put things back in perspective or lift a sullen mood, Brigid brings out her *Geantraighé* to set your toes tapping. You can hear these themes in Celtic music, but they are present in all music. Think about the songs and melodies you love most and see where they fall in the three categories:

Suantraighé, the sleep-strain

Goltraighé, the sorrow-strain

Geantraighé, the joy-strain

These are not meant to be taken literally—you don't have to be conked out by the *Suantraighé* to find soothing serenity. The *Goltraighé* can be music of deep spiritual yearning, the longing of the soul toward

....
65. O'Curry, *Lectures on the Manuscript Materials of Ancient Irish History.*

its beloved. And the *Geantraighé* might offer heart-healing through a happy memory—taking you back to that summer day when you were riding in the front seat of your cousins' old truck, the three of you singing a Laura Nyro song together at top volume.

Speaking of singing, be sure to embody Brigid's healing music by making it yourself as well as listening to recordings or live music. We all sing when we are young; it's a natural part of human expression. Learn to play a musical instrument if you feel called to it—and no, you're not too old. Here's a tale of one of Saint Brigid's miracles: A feast was given in her honor at a great house, where she saw beautiful carved harps hanging on the wall. After the meal she suggested some music would add to the evening's pleasure. "Alas," said the lord of the hall, "there are no harpers present." Brigid's nuns teased their abbess that she should just bless the serving men's hands so they could play. And of course, she did, and of course, they did, beautifully. Forever after, they were master harpists. With Brigid's blessing on your hands, take up the harp (or piano, or drum, or trombone!) and make some music to add to her pleasure—and yours.

Sacred Sound Current
Lisa Thiel

Lisa Thiel is a visionary artist, ceremonial singer, and songwriter. She is a priestess of Brighid and Kuan Yin in the Fellowship of Isis. Her songs of the Goddess are sung in circles around the world.

———

As a musician, I draw upon the fire and water aspects of Brighid, the energies of inspiration and intuitive feeling. I feel my music has a spiritual healing aspect to it that I attribute to Brighid's blessing.

My favorite Brighid song is my Imbolc song from *Circle of the Seasons*, about the tradition of her being "invited into her bed" on Imbolc Eve. I believe this is inviting the spark of inspiration into the bed of our unconscious for the new year.

Blessed Bridget, comest thou in
Bless this house and all of our kin
Bless this house and all of our kin
Protect this house and all within
Blessed Bridget, come into thy bed
With a gem at thy heart and a crown on thy head
Awaken the fire within our souls
Awaken the fire that makes us whole
Blessed Bridget, queen of the fire
Help us to manifest our desire
May we bring forth all that's good and fine
May we give birth to our dreams in time
Blessed Bridget, comest thou in
Bless this house and all of our kin
From the source of Infinite Light
Kindle the flame of our spirits tonight [66]

Brighid came to me once in a dream. She was in a great shrine room with a sacred flame burning, and she held a staff of amber (symbol of the sacred fire of the sun and blood of ancient trees) and was sitting on an amber throne. There were crimson velvet curtains in the back of the room, and I was to bless and purify myself with the fire, ask for her blessing, and go into the velvet (womb) to give birth to my dream. Her crown was very strange— three thin circlets of gold at odd angles. I feel this unusual quality of her crown represented (in my personal symbology) the energy of Uranus, the planet associated with unconventional paths and also lightning inspiration that breaks up existing paradigms to create a new state.

As Brighid is the essence of inspiration and the creative life force itself, she is the true spirit of all music. When I begin to

....
66. "Imbolc," ©2004 Lisa Thiel (used by permission).

sing, my entire being is as open to that spirit as it can possibly be, especially my heart. Through the intensity of feeling and passion for the music, I experience that spirit energy flowing through me, down my crown, into my heart, and out of my throat as sound—and it is ecstatic.

Each individual must connect with the deity in their own way according to their needs, but I feel that every time a candle is lit, a fire is lit, we can think of her, remembering her Holy Flame. Throughout the Wheel of the Year we can remember her light, meditating on the fire that never dies, that is within us all.

Chanting, singing spiritual songs and prayers, creates a sacred sound current that transforms the consciousness. It invokes the sacred fire within, feeds it, sustains it, and clears all that blocks its way. This is the essence of my path and it is an integral part of my music, which is my offering as a priestess to the Goddess.

For more about Lisa, see the Contributors and Resources appendices.

Soulful Silence

We live in a loud age. It's not just the sounds of machines and traffic and other invasive noises that fill the air. There is also a constant barrage of mind-noise. Compare our time with, say, Jane Austen's era. It took time to write a letter, time for it to travel to its recipient, and time to read and absorb it at the reader's leisure. Today, the speed at which information moves seems to require that we keep up with it. Interruptions happen frequently. Most people carry a phone with them everywhere they go, and social media distractions tug and poke and nibble. I feel guilty if a couple of days go by without replying to an email, because I know my correspondent knows that I got it instantly. Jane would be astonished.

This information overload makes it hard to find the silence you need to hear Brigid's guidance and the wisdom of your own soul. It doesn't seem to matter much whether you live alone or with others, in the city or the country—real, nurturing silence is still hard to come by. I live in a quiet place and have plenty of outward solitude that would seem to foster a deep communion with all that is Goddess. Yet, because my mind is stuffed full of info-clutter, I need to consciously remind myself to shut it all down sometimes and seek the silent place. I find stillness most easily outside, in nature. With just a few moments under the open sky, a veil parts and I'm able to more clearly see where I am in my life and on my path. I ask my questions, and the answers come so lovingly and readily. My heart fills with gratitude for the presence of Brigid.

The real goal is to find that inner silence no matter where you are—in nature, in your kitchen, or sitting at your desk. While being mindful of exterior noise, also pay attention to how much you fill the corners of your mind with interior noise. You're not crazy—there really *are* voices in your head! Way too many, for most of us. Do some honest evaluation about the quantity of mind-noise that flows to you every day. Seriously consider how much you *really* need to be "plugged in" and how much it would change your life to unplug some of the time. For example, if you normally carry a phone with you, how much would it bother you to not carry it for a day? If you are old enough to know such a time, think back to the days when you didn't have a cell phone, didn't have email, didn't have instant communication available to you at all hours of the day and night. How was life different for you then? How was your inner life different? Was it more your own?

Sometimes we create noise because we are afraid of the silence. We've all known people who keep the TV or other external sounds going all the time because the silence bothers them so much. Do you have some of this fear in you? There are many ways to avoid inner silence too—even something positive like reading can be a way of avoiding what wants to come through in the silence of a truly open mind. Be aware of this and work on coming to balance with it as needed. Brigid encourages the acquisition of knowledge, but she wants you to have depth as well as breadth. Your curious mind is a gift from her, so don't waste it. Let there be times of taking in information and times of just letting the information you already have do its work. This is how we deepen, through thoughtful exploration of what is known—and what is unknown, the great Mystery.

Here is a simple way to feel the power of silence:

1. Sit comfortably in a place and at a time when you feel free to make some noise.

2. Close your eyes. Focus your awareness in the center of your chest. Envision a flame glowing there.

3. Begin to intone a low single-syllable sound, such as *Aum* (*Om*), *Ma*, or *Ah*. Start softly and gradually increase the volume. Take deep breaths so you can hold the note as long as possible. Keep intoning until you feel surrounded and submerged in the sound, to the point where you aren't consciously making the sound—it's just emerging from you, louder and louder.

4. And then stop.

5. Keep your eyes closed and feel the shimmering energy of the silence that follows sound. Don't direct your thoughts; just let the silence wash over you. When you feel complete, open your eyes.

A lengthy hermitage or retreat is at one end of the silence spectrum, but silence can be attained in much simpler ways, moment to moment. In some religious traditions, silence is observed when tending to sacred objects, even while washing them and putting them away. The silence keeps the action from becoming trivial, and it brings the full focus of attention to everything about the objects and their symbolic meaning. You can practice this when you are washing the dishes, taking the trash out, or walking the dog. Silence opens you to beauty and understanding, which you will then find all around you, every day.

BRIGID OF THE AUGURY

The ancient Celts used divination and seership to see the future, find the right timing for an endeavor, or learn about events happening at a distance. "Classical writers speak of the Celts as of all nations the most devoted to, and the most experienced in, the science of divination." [67] Priestesses, "divineresses," [68] and the *ban-drui* (woman-Druids) were all

67. MacCulloch, *The Religion of the Ancient Celts*.
68. Ibid.

known for their powers of in-seeing and far-seeing. Celtic methods of divination were often intense, and seers might go into ecstatic convulsions as part of the trance-utterance. Decisions were made with the help of auguries, often involving birds. This seership was part of the gift of the *fili*, Brigid's poets and keepers of lore. But divination wasn't left to the professionals alone—deeper meaning was accessible to all who cared to look for it. And it still is.

> *Brigid of the mantles,*
> *Brigid of the peat-heap,*
> *Brigid of the twining hair,*
> *Brigid of the augury.*[69]

As I stood at my kitchen window on a grey Oregon morning, filling my kettle for tea, a flash of black and white caught my eye—a white seagull and a black crow, both quite large, swooping among the bare February trees. "Balance," I thought. "The light and the shadow." I had been stuck in shadow for the past few days, and the birds reminded me to seek balance and come back into a more expansive (those great wings!) place in my soul. Now that I was aware of birds, my gaze was immediately caught by two tiny wrens darting around one of my apple trees. This tree was also winter-bare, but covered in vivid green moss. The old tree has knotholes where birds nest, and I'd seen these two flirting and courting the day before. Now they were pecking at the moss, perhaps readying a nest somewhere nearby. "Settle and get busy," came the message. "The time of creative awakening is near."

Once your mind is open to the acquisition of messages, they are everywhere and, as with my birds, often lead from one to the next. With my gaze drawn outward by gull and crow, I could then have gone on to read signs in the clouds and the wind that blew them, the sounds the wind carried to me, and so on. But as it happened, the next sound after watching the wrens was the tea kettle—a sign to come back to my indoor life of work and discipline. That too is a message.

....
69. *Carmina Gadelica*, 263.

As you learn to see the everyday world in terms of symbol and metaphor, it becomes easier and more commonplace to connect to the Otherworld of auguries and portents. The more you listen, the more you will hear. The more you look, the more you will see. It sounds ridiculously simplistic, I know, but divination is a learned skill. The root words *divinatio* and *divinare* mean "inspiration" and "guess." Open to Brigid's inspiration and learn to wisely guess at the meanings of signs you perceive. Celtic spirituality is always in tune with the mystical, so don't be surprised if you find yourself receiving divinatory messages at unexpected times. When you take out your tarot cards, you hope and expect to be in tune with the oracle, but if you suddenly see your dripping tea bag as a pendulum, heed its message!

Scrying

How many times have you gazed vacantly at something and suddenly seen a face or received an image in your mind, a flash of inspiration? Water, fire, natural patterns such as leaves or trees, clouds, smoke, even patterns like wallpaper—all offer opportunities in which to see *through* the obvious to the symbolic. This divination practice is called scrying.

Romantic media interpretations of scrying may have led the hopeful scryer to expect a sort of movie to form suddenly in the gazing bowl, mirror, or crystal ball. While this may happen for a lucky few, for most of us, scrying is a much more subtle art, involving trust and the willingness to go with our first intuitive impressions. The secret is to "soften" your gaze. Remember those pictures that were popular for a while that looked like a jumble of points until suddenly they swam together to form a 3-D image? This is what softening your gaze is about. It is a gently fixed stare in the middle-distance or in the direction of your gazing object. You are not watching, as you would watch television, but rather, you are allowing your eye to see through the obvious—and allowing your mind's eye to interpret freely.

For instance, when I lived near the ocean, I would go there on moonlit nights to watch the silver-white light on the moving water. One night as I sat alone on the cliff, the shimmering patterns came together to form a dancing sea-goddess. She was so clear and her presence so strong, all I could do was continue to gaze in rapture and gratitude for this vision. And after a while—suddenly or gradually, I don't know—it was just light on water again, quiet and steady and mysterious. I had not been trying to see anything, or scry for a shape or a message, but I had allowed my sight to soften so that the otherworldly impression could come through.

The ancient Celts had several ways of scrying, including observing the smoke and flames of sacred fires. This practice is perfect for devotees of Brigid, whether you do a formal flamekeeping practice or not. Fire-scrying at the hearth comes naturally—who hasn't fallen into a dreamy state while watching the flames? But it can be just as powerful to scry with a single candle, an oil lamp, or a group of floating candles in a bowl. Center yourself with an open intention to receive any messages, then soften your gaze and relax. The moment is precious no matter what happens. Release your expectations and let Brigid take over. For additional insights, before you extinguish your candle, drip some wax into a dish of water and interpret the shapes it forms. This is a variation on an old custom of melting lead or tin and dropping small molten bits into water.[70] Keep the melted shapes as talismans if they are fortuitous; melt them down again if they are ill-aspected.

A Poetry Oracle

As goddess of poetry and lore, Brigid may speak to you through divination that involves written or spoken words. This can be done in many ways, such as bibliomancy, where you open a book at random and place your finger on a page, then interpret what the indicated words might mean to you. Or even audiomancy: paying attention to the first few words you hear when you turn on your radio or television. I just kitchen-tested this one for you. The first words I heard were "flies through the air with the greatest of ease"—it was the sing-along on the bus in It Happened One Night. I then switched to PBS and heard "two things are given to you"—I had lucked upon an interview with one of my favorite spiritual

---

70. If this interests you, do a web search for "molybdomancy."

teachers, Brother David Steindl-Rast. I interpret these messages to mean that if I free myself from fear and just let my spirit fly, two things will be given to me. Time will tell what those will be!

Let's honor Brigid as goddess of wordsmithing and invoke her wise guidance by creating a poetry oracle. With this oracle, you will use fragments of poems as you might use runes, tarot cards, or other oracular tools.

You will need:
A basket, box, or jar that you can fit your hand inside
Printouts of two or more poems, with space between the lines
Scissors

1. Find at least two poems whose imagery and language appeal to you. Try to avoid assigning any divinatory meaning to the lines just yet—it helps to work quickly and not dwell on the words.

2. Print out your poems or write them out by hand, leaving space between the lines.

3. Cut the individual lines apart, so that you have many little slips of paper. If two lines insist on staying together, that's fine, but no more than that. Remember, the art of divination is in working with symbols, not having the message spelled out for you (literally).

4. Fold up the slips of paper, and toss them to mix the lines well. Place your papers in your chosen container.

5. Close your eyes and put yourself in a receptive and calm state of mind. Offer this triad to Brigid:
   Sense be in my thought,
   Understanding be in my heart,
   Wisdom be in my soul.

6. When you feel ready, draw out three slips of paper and open them.

7. Pay attention to your very first thoughts upon reading the lines— this is what you sense, what your intuition gives you without filtering or censoring.

8. Now explore the words for deeper understanding. What specific associations do they have for you? Does the order of the lines matter? Or do they seem to stand on their own, without connection? Take your time.

9. Finally, just sit quietly for a few moments, eyes closed, and ask Brigid if there is any wisdom she wants to add to your interpretation. Know that you may receive this at some time in the future, too. When you are done, fold up the lines and put them back into the jar.

I did this divination just now, using an ancient Irish poem, "King and Hermit," and my favorite Shakespeare sonnet, number 73, "That time of year thou mayst in me behold." The three fragments I chose were all from the Irish poem, as it happens:

> *The strains of the bright redbreasted little fellows*
> *in a great flock*
> *delightful music*

These lines don't fall together in the poem itself, but they work so well together here that it feels like a single message, rather than three. Because the last divination I did was the audiomancy I mentioned earlier, I see the two as being related—air energy, bird magic, a feeling of light and delight. A reminder to seek out those who encourage that in me—my great flock![71]

Add to your poetry oracle from time to time or make a completely new one. If you are part of a circle, this is a great oracle to make together. Have everyone bring a batch of lines, mix them all together, and then draw out enough to fill your individual containers. It's a poetry potluck! Or you might make a jar for a special friend and ask her to make one for you. When it's someone else's poetry choices, you are sure to be surprised, but you will be surprised in any case, I guarantee you. Brigid of the augury will send you the right words at the right time, exactly what you need to hear.

....

71. From "King and Hermit," in Meyer, *Selections from Ancient Irish Poetry.*

Emerging from the Forge: Your Name Poem

Celtic bards created name poems that could be used as prayer, meditation, affirmation, or spell. Such a poem could enlighten or confound those to whom it was spoken. Writing a name poem for yourself is a powerful way to honor what you are now, what you have been, what you hope to become. It's especially meaningful to create a name poem when you have been through a forge experience and emerged transformed.

There are many forms such a ceremonial name can take. A bard might sing a poem of naming as both introduction and riddle, playing with double meanings, revealing secrets only to those who understand the metaphors used. A famous example is the name poem attributed to the Welsh bard Taliesin, a fragment of which is:

I have been a narrow sword,
A drop in the air,
A shining bright star,
A letter among words
In the book of origins.
I have been lanternlight
For a year and a day,
I have been a bridge
Spanning threescore rivers.

Or this name poem, sung by the poet Amairgin upon first setting foot on Ireland's shore:

I am a dewdrop in the sun.
I am the fairest of flowers.
I am a boar for boldness.
I am a salmon in a pool.
I am a lake in a plain.
I am a word of skill.
I am the point of a weapon.

To begin your own name poem, create sacred space in the way that feels right to you, whether at your altar or in a spot where you feel creatively inspired. Light a candle and invoke Brigid's presence to illuminate your insight and inspire your word weaving. Start to write down attributes you would share if you wanted someone to know you very well, know your deepest soul. Proclaim your most powerful self, whisper of your most vulnerable self, delve into the mysteries of your psyche and give them a name. Incorporate symbols that speak to you, astrological lore, alphabetical plays on the letters of your name, or poetic metaphors for your life experiences. For example, if you have three daughters, you could express this in many ways, such as:

I am the birthgiver of women, three times have I delivered ...

or

From my womb have spilled forth three sweet fruits ...

Other things you may wish to include in your name poem are spiritual turning points, events that shaped you (for good or ill), challenges you have faced, or ways you have survived. Look back over your life's journey and see where you have deepened and grown. You may wish to give name to your shadow self, your anger, your fears, your temper, your failings and faults as well as your skills and strengths. These are all part of you and may need naming as part of healing.

Let the words pour from you. Don't edit yourself too much, and remember there is no way to do this wrong. Your name poem may change and grow over time, but the poem you create now marks who you are today, at this point in your life path. This isn't a place for modesty and humility (except perhaps to proclaim them as virtues you possess). For example, in my name poem, written when I was in my late thirties, I included the line *A luminous mind, knowing much*. My mind is perhaps not quite so luminous post-menopause, but what I know is deeper. When I write my crone poem, it will reflect that. Here is an excerpt from my friend Callista Lee's name poem:

She who finds comfort when her belly is upon the warm Earth, as a snake
She who shares the awareness and grace of a deer
She who is a mother to cats and shares with them a cougar's soul

She who is guarded by the Great Bear and beloved by the heavens ...
Our Lady of the Clipboard, She who understands and plans
She who breathes in wisdom and speaks so that others may hear
Teacher, student, mentor, facilitator, friend ...
I am a bit of moonlight.
I am a piece of the web.
I am a part of the world soul ...

When you have finished your name poem, be sure to read it aloud to yourself. In the bardic tradition, no poem was complete until it was declaimed by voice. Stand and speak it freely, sing it, offer it to Brigid. This is a powerful exercise to do in a trust-filled group.

I wrote my name poem in 1992. Some of it doesn't fit me quite as well as it did at the time, and some of it fits me more now than when I wrote it (your name poem may be prophetic!). This is my name poem:

Storm caller,
I hear the song of the misty hills,
I hear the song of the cold black seas,
I feel longing that never ceases.
Water of the ninth wave shall quench my thirst.
I am a hermit's anchorage, secret,
A luminous mind, knowing much,
A seeker of deep wisdom,
A harp string, vibrating.
Mine is the eloquence of the bard.
Beware of sorceresses, for they are quick to anger,
Quick of wit and quick of judgment.
I am she of the six opinions,
I am she who stirs the cauldron,
She who holds the Stone of Truth.
Oak and mistletoe wear I, the druid's sign,
The triple moon of the priestess.
I know the lore of tree and stone,
I know the power of words,

And the silence in which magic is born.
I am the opener of the gate,
I am the badger in its sett,
I am the owl, ever watchful,
First into battle, the raven's cry,
And at Brigid's forge I temper my blade.

Chapter Five

Tending Your Flame

I put songs and music on the wind before ever the bells of the chapels were rung in the West or heard in the East ... And I have been a breath in your heart, and the day has its feet to it that will see me coming into the hearts of men and women like a flame upon dry grass, like a flame of wind in a great wood. For the time of change is at hand.[72]

Different goddesses come to the forefront of our consciousness at different times, not just personally but culturally and globally. Brigid has stepped forward now for so many reasons. She offers us protection and healing, comfort and courage, nourishment of body and soul. As a practical goddess, she is a role model for change. Her planet is in trouble, her people are suffering, and Brigid is setting things to rights. When you are called to her in devotion, you may find that you are also called into her service. Is there any role that women undertake that isn't blessed in some way by Brigid? Whatever you do to give back to the world, where is she present in that work? I can promise you, she is there—or she wants to be there. She gives us her multifaceted strength to take on the complex ills of this complex world. Your contribution doesn't have to be big to be world-changing. Your small flame adds to the sum of light.

....

72. The words of Brigid, in Macleod, *The Winged Destiny*, 1911.

BRIGID'S CHARITY

Whether my house be dark or bright,
my door shall close on none tonight.[73]

I was at an interfaith thanksgiving service a couple of years ago where the featured speaker (let's call him Daniel) was the director of a Portland organization whose mission is to feed, clothe, and offer shelter and aid to those in need. Daniel offered us a real-life parable. As he was leaving the shelter late one night, a stranger knocked on the window of his van. Now, Daniel worked every day with people who were poor and homeless, many of whom were rough in appearance, and that never fazed him. Yet this stranger's sudden approach startled him, and he hesitated, feeling tired, vulnerable, and a bit resentful of more being asked of him after a long day. Gritting his teeth, he rolled down the window to see what was needed. "Hey, man, I just wanted to tell you that your door's open," said the stranger, pointing to the back of the van.

This encounter made Daniel question how open his door really was. He had given his life to opening the door of charity, but was it enough? If his heart wasn't open too, was he really welcoming? He was willing to listen to what the stranger needed and to help, but was he doing it in coldness or in warmth? Cold charity throws coins in a basket and hurries away without looking into the face of suffering. Cold charity judges and fears.

Brigid's charity is warm charity. Warm charity blesses and loves. Even if you only give a dollar, give it as Brigid herself would give. She has always welcomed society's castoffs. She feeds them, shelters them, wraps them in her own cloak against the storms—and she does this through her representatives on Earth. Brigid challenges us to ask: How open is our door? Who are the lepers in our society? How close are you willing to get to the real needs of the world? There's no right or wrong here—we all give in our own way. But ask the questions.

In the Benedictine monastic tradition, the portress lives right by the front door in case anyone knocks. The job description says this should be

---

73. Medieval Irish, from O'Faoláin, *The Silver Branch.*

a wise old woman who has the experience to deal with whoever comes to the door and the stability to commit to the task. When a knock is heard, the portress calls out, "Thanks be to God! A blessing!"—and this reply must come from the heart, every time. Whatever is needed by the visitor, the portress gives it with warm charity and true thankfulness. You are the portress of your own life. If Brigid sends someone to your door, call out, "Thanks be to Brigid! A blessing!"

In Brigid's Sacred Service
Selena Fox

Selena Fox is a psychotherapist, teacher, ritualist, and Pagan priest-ess. She is the founder of Circle Sanctuary, a Nature spirituality center headquartered on a 200-acre nature preserve in Wisconsin.

Circle Sanctuary is a Pagan resource center and legally recognized church serving Nature religion practitioners worldwide. I founded Circle Sanctuary in 1974 and serve as its senior minister and high priestess. Attuning to and working with the goddess Brigid is an important part of my priestess work, and facilitating Brigid rituals and meditations is part of my services for the Circle Sanctuary community, for the larger Pagan realm we serve, and beyond, including in interfaith settings. In addition, at Circle Sanctuary land, I tend Brigid's Spring, a year-round freshwater spring, which is a sacred healing place. Circle Sanctuary Nature Preserve, founded in 1983, is located near Barneveld, Wisconsin, and is the headquarters of Circle Sanctuary. At Brigid's Spring we do a form of the old clootie well custom—visitors hang prayer ribbons as part of healing ceremonies. We also have a place where healing ribbons are left above the Brigid healing altar inside our main temple.

I honor Brigid not only as a Celtic goddess, but also as an international, multicultural, and interreligious form of the Divine

Feminine. I've found that people of many paths and places are interested in her. When I did my "Brigid: Celtic Goddess, Celtic Saint" presentation in Cape Town, South Africa, at the 1999 Parliament of the World's Religions, the room was packed to overflowing with people from many countries and religious traditions.

Brigid is a goddess with many aspects, including a warrior form. When I work with Brigid in her warrior aspect, I often call upon her by one of her ancient names, Brigantia. In this aspect, she usually holds a spear. I also invoke Brigantia when I do rituals to bless, protect, and honor those serving and who have served in the military and emergency support services, including police, firefighters, and other first responders. I call on Brigid as warrior and transformer to aid religious-freedom battles and in other social justice endeavors. As executive director of the Lady Liberty League, the national and global Pagan religious freedom and civil rights service of Circle Sanctuary, I often do specific workings with Brigid to help with Pagan civil rights cases that the League is aiding. Sometimes this takes the form of working with Brigid for healing, protection, and support of those struggling to combat religious persecution. Other times it takes the form of working with Brigid power to win legal battles and defeat prejudice, ignorance, and discrimination. I attuned to and called on Brigid many times for inspiration, strength, courage, and success in the long yet ultimately successful quest to get the US Department of Veterans Affairs to add the pentacle to its list of emblems of belief that can be included on the grave markers it issues for deceased veterans.

One of the reasons that Brigid is central to my priestess work is her versatility and many facets.

Another reason is ancestral, although I already had been aligned and working with Brigid as part of spiritual practice for many years before I discovered that. I learned through research into my Scottish and Pictish heritage that on my father's mother's maternal grandmother's line I am said to descend from the keepers of Brigid's sacred site in Abernethy, Scotland. This place was reportedly dedicated to Brigid in Pictish Pagan times and was later dedicated to Saint Brigid when it became a site of a Celtic Culdee monastery. This probably explains why I not only connect with Brigid as a Pagan goddess but also attune to her in her form as Christian saint, and why I tend several Brigid sites as part of my priestess service, including the oak forest where I make my home.

For more about Selena, see the Contributors appendix.

BRIGID THE ACTIVIST

Brigid is a peacemaker, but that doesn't imply passivity. She is also a goddess of justice who battles on behalf of the enslaved and the oppressed. She speaks truth to power. She wants you to find your own true voice and use it to make the world a better place. The sustained strength of women's voices together weaves powerful magic for change. This is literal as well as metaphorical. The wailing cry of grief called keening has been performed publicly for thousands of years as a protest against society's ills and domestic abuses.

Keening in protest brings Brigid to the barricades in a profoundly feminine way. Women have always been the ones who keen. Until very recently, professional *mná caointe* (keening women) performed at funerals and wakes, and after "praising the deceased, mourning his/her passing, and aggressively criticizing his/her enemies, *mná caointe* articulated their own concerns and assorted social tensions. *Mná caointe* grieved incidents of domestic violence and social slights and cursed those who offended them." [74] In modern times, keening has been used in civil disobedience actions against nuclear power, war, and oppressive foreign policies.[75] A group of grandmothers have keened at airports against useless security practices that do nothing but increase fear. The *mná caointe* stand with

....

74. Brophy, "Keening Community: Mná Caointe, Women, Death, and Power in Ireland."

75. Watch a video of keening as political protest at www.theguardian.com /yourgreenham/video/page/0,,2075892,00.html.

Brigid at the threshold of life and death, and woe unto those who ignore their cries. Group keening is eerie, otherworldly, unsettling—frankly, it's scary. It's the sound of all the women of all the ages crying out for justice. Brigid's women will not be silenced.

Brigid is the goddess behind keening, having originated it in her own grief, but she is also behind it in the sense that her voice comes through the throats of those who keen in righteousness. Now, you may or may not want to take part in keening demonstrations for the causes you hold dear. But you can keep the spirit of the *mná caointe* alive by making your voice heard in every way you can. Merely signing an online petition doesn't cut it. Consider whether your actions will have a real effect and if you can do more. You don't have to go as far as Saint Brigid, who gave away so much that her nuns protested they didn't have food to feed themselves. In our age, crowd-funding means that your small contribution can help add up to a significant amount of aid. Be as generous as you can be, with your resources, time, and energy. Do all good works with love.

Brigid needs you to stand up for yourself and stand up for others. Speak out for the downtrodden—and for Goddess's sake, that certainly includes you. Get help if you are being abused, organize at work if conditions are unfair, or gather with your neighbors to work locally for change. Put your vote where your mouth is. Support women's causes. Refuse to tolerate injustice. Protect Brigid's beautiful green earth.

For a bit of inspiration, here's the mission statement of the organization Afri (Action from Ireland):

Afri's goal is the promotion of global justice and peace, and the reduction of poverty; this includes, but is not limited to, the progressive reduction of global militarisation, and responding to the threat of climate change, corporate control of resources and water, and interference with food sovereignty.[76]

....
76. Afri, Action from Ireland, www.afri.ie.

Justice, peace, care for the poor, protecting the earth, sharing the wealth, feeding the people—these are all things that Brigid holds dear. And this is no happy coincidence every February, Afri holds the Féile Bríde (Festival of Brigid) in Kildare. At Féile Bríde 2014, the theme was "Life: Source or Resource, Enslavement versus Sovereignty." The event began with harp music as the Brigid flame was carried into the conference hall. The topics discussed included ending human trafficking, sustaining local food sources worldwide, and other campaigns that combine the visionary with the practical. Brigid the midwife, the lightbringer, is surely present in the program that provides solar lamps to midwives in Kenya so they can deliver babies safely at night in remote areas. Féile Bríde concluded with more music, poetry, and the planting of an oak tree.

In the early 1990s, I co-created a ritual for Long Beach Womanspirit with my sister priestesses Callista and MaryScarlett.[77] We called it "The Snakes Return to Ireland: A Ritual of Celtic Mysteries," and it was an alternative celebration for St. Patrick's Day. We reclaimed hallowed objects in the name of the Goddess, we revised the words to "Danny Boy" to make a yearning hymn to Danu ("Oh Danu, the pipes, the pipes are calling…"), and we invoked the presence of Brigid with a mighty whoosh of flame in an alcohol thurible. I lit this flame, and I still get shivers at the memory of calling Brigid's name as the fire leapt up. After we introduced her to the crowd, we had them divide into three groups based on their field of work:

- **Healers:** Those who did any kind of healing, peacemaking, parenting, and other caregiving work.
- **Poets:** Those who worked with words in any way, such as writing, editing, music, teaching, and so on.
- **Crafters:** Those who created a product in their work, laborers, artists, and anyone who worked with tools.

....
77. Thanks to Callista for refreshing my memory on the details of this magical night.

Each of the priestesses then worked with a group to make a gift for the other groups. The healers made small herbal charms for everyone, and the poets created a lilting song. The crafters made snakes and other symbolic amulets using paper and pipe-cleaners. As each group offered its gifts, the others thanked them for their contributions to the community and to the world, and invoked Brigid to bless their work now and in the days to come.

You can do this too, both the offering and the thanking. As you pursue your passions and offer your gifts to the world, gather with others for support and inspiration. Brigid blesses spiritual circles, but she also loves political affinity groups, storytelling gatherings, writers' groups, book clubs, art collaborations, and needlework circles. Seek your tribe. Claim your clan.

Nineteen Flames for Brigid

This book opened with a woman lighting a candle in devotion to Brigid. Let's close in the same way, with nineteen candles this time. This prayer litany can be done all at once or over nineteen nights. You can offer one prayer each night or do it "twelve days of Christmas" style: on the first night offer Flame 1's prayer, on the second night offer the prayers for Flames 1 and 2, and so on until on the last night you offer all nineteen. However you get there, when you've lit that final flame, remember that Brigid holds the twentieth flame, which is eternal.

Flame 1: Welcome

Brigid of brightness, I bid thee welcome,
Brigid of blessing, come thou in.
Brigid of strength, I bid thee welcome,
This night and every night, this day and every day.

Flame 2: Hearth and Household

Brigid of the threshold, come thou in,
Brigid of the hearthfire, take your ease,
Brigid of the cook-pot, sup with us,
Brigid of all comforts, live in our hearts.

Flame 3: Ancestors

Ancestors all, I embody your legacy,
Ancestors all, I ask for your blessing,
Ancestors all, I offer Brigid's flame
To light the needfires of deep memory.

Flame 4: Flamekeepers

Brigid of the timeless flame, bless your daughters:
Those who keep the circle bright,
Those whose faith has never failed,
Those who keep your name ablaze.

Flame 5: Healing

Brigid of the holy waters,
Brigid of the soothing hand,
Brigid of the miracles,
Touch me with healing.

Flame 6: Poetry

Brigid of lore, deepen my understanding,
Brigid of bards, increase my eloquence,
Brigid of poetry, lead me to beauty:
Beauty of word and beauty of thought.

Flame 7: Courage

Brigid of the golden shield,
Brigid of courage,
Brigid of the sunbeam,
Increase thou my trust.

Flame 8: Righteous Causes

Brigid, lend your righteous sword
To those who work for justice,
To those who speak the truth,
To those who seek a better world.

Flame 9: The Oppressed

In the name of Brigid, who empowers the oppressed,
In the name of Brigid, who releases the enslaved,
In the name of Brigid, who lifts up the downtrodden,
May all her people be honored and free.

Flame 10: Children

Brigid the midwife, bless every birth,
Brigid foster mother, protect every child,
Brigid of springtime, bestow on each childhood
The innocence of wonder and the magic of joy.

Flame 11: Women's Causes

Mighty Brigid, your keening women call to you:
Strengthen our voice,
Strengthen our resolve,
Strengthen our sisterhood.

Flame 12: The Earth

Brigid, preserve this planet,
The stones and the seas and the skies.
Brigid, spread your green mantle
For the greening of the earth.

Flame 13: Animals

Brigid, protect the earth's animals,
The fish and the beasts and the birds.
Brigid, shelter your creatures
As your sheep shelter lambs from the wind.

Flame 14: Water

Brigid of the clear dewdrop,
Brigid of the pure wellspring,
Brigid of the pool of knowledge,
Teach us to honor the gift of water.

Flame 15: Creativity

Bright Brigid, flame of creation,
Kindle my enthusiasm,
Fire up my passion,
Ignite my imagination.

Flame 16: Nourishment

Brigid of the overflowing milk,
Brigid of the good brown loaf,
Brigid of the endless butter,
May all beings be nourished.

Flame 17: Peace

Peace of the swan and peace of the kine,
Peace of the hearth and peace of the open door,
Peace between neighbors and peace between nations,
The deep peace of Brigid within.

Flame 18: Gratefulness

Brigid, I thank thee three-times-three:
For my birth, my body, my spirit,
For my kin, my clan, my tribe,
For my home, my work, my knowledge of thee.

Flame 19: The Three Flames of Brigid

May the hearthfire of welcome warm me,
May the temple fire of faith sustain me,
May the forge fire of change strengthen me,
And Brigid's love encompass me, now and evermore.

RESOURCES

Music

Lisa Thiel, *Invocation of the Graces*. I love all of Lisa's music, and this is my favorite. Drawing from traditional Celtic sources for many of the songs, she has created a perfect musical offering to Brigid. Great for singing along and using in ritual.

Nóirín Ní Riain, *Celtic Soul*. Nóirín's albums are all beautiful and soulful. This one includes a haunting version of the traditional song "Gabhaim Molta Bríghde" (called "Ode to Bridget" on this album, but it's sung in Irish, as most of her songs are).

Aine Minogue, *Celtic Lamentations* (http://aineminogue.com/album/230649/celtic-lamentations-healing-for-twelve-months-and-a-day). "Songs to let go of that which we've lost and to move toward the joys that lie ahead."

Books

The bibliography contains many fine books that are well worth your time. Here are two of my favorites.

J. A. MacCulloch, *The Religion of the Ancient Celts* (Edinburgh: T. & T. Clark, 1911). Endlessly fascinating, very readable, and respectful of the beliefs of the ancients.

Patricia Monaghan, *The Encyclopedia of Celtic Mythology and Folklore* (New York: Checkmark Books, 2008). If you only get one book on Celtic lore (and why would you do that?), I recommend this one. Patricia was a scholar as well as a devotee of the Goddess, and all of her books are wonderful and reliable additions to your library. This one delves into all things Celtic in an eminently readable and approachable way.

Candles, Jewelry Supplies, Herbs

I get tall jar candles for my perpetual flame from General Wax (www
.generalwax.com). I've tried many candles over the years, and these
have the most consistent quality. They are available with colored
glass and white wax or clear glass and colored wax. If you buy by
the case, they're about $3 each. General Wax also carries many
other types of candles and candlemaking supplies, including sheets
of beeswax for rolled candles.

The best tealights I've found are made by Richland. They are scent-
free, burn for at least five hours, and have metal cups. At this writing, they are about $15 for 125 tealights. Available on Amazon.

Camphor pellets and other ritual supplies (including the world's best incense) can be found at Mermade Magickal Arts (www.mermadearts
.com). They sell a small brass "Chalice of Light" that is perfect for oil,
camphor, or alcohol flames. There is an article about burning camphor and a link to a beautiful video showing the Hindu saint Amma
using it to bless holy water. Mermade is owned by my dear friend
Katlyn Breene.

Flameless candles have made some great strides in technology, and Lu-
minara makes the best I've seen. Created by Disney for the Haunted
Mansion, the realistic flame effect is quite lovely. Do a web search to
find purchasing options (QVC has videos as of this writing) or buy
directly from www.luminaracandles.com.

The incredibly friendly and helpful folks at Fire Mountain Gems (www
.firemountaingems.com) offer jewelry-making supplies, tutorial videos, and project ideas of all kinds. But remember, also support your
local bead store!

Mountain Rose Herbs (www.mountainroseherbs.com) is an excellent
source for herbs and supplies (such as muslin bath bags). They've
been in business since 1987 and sell only organic, free-trade, green
products. Good energy all the way round.

CONTRIBUTORS

Wendy Alford is an artist blacksmith, associate of the Worshipful Company of Blacksmiths, and owner of St. Mary's Forge in Norfolk, England, which lies on the mystical Mary Ley Line. This ancient craft's fascinating traditions and alchemic connections weave into Wendy's appreciation of the seasonal cycles and celebration of celestial and Celtic fire festivals. Visit her online at stmarysforge.com.

Jenny Beale is the founder and director of Brigit's Garden, a role that weaves together her passions for nature, education, and Celtic spirituality. She grew up on a farm in the south of England and has lived in the West of Ireland for many years. For more on Brigit's Garden, see www.brigitsgarden.ie.

Sharon Blackie was raised on an imaginatively rich diet of Irish myth, poetry, and history. Her first novel was the critically acclaimed *The Long Delirious Burning Blue*. With her husband, she launched *Earth-Lines* magazine for writing about nature, place, and the environment. She lives in County Donegal, Ireland, where she is completing a nonfiction book about women, Celtic mythology, and the environment. Visit her website at www.reenchantingtheearth.com.

Joanna Powell Colbert is an artist, author, retreat host, and creatrix of the Gaian Tarot. She teaches e-courses and workshops on earth-centered spirituality, seasonal contemplative practices, creativity as a devotional path, the Divine Feminine, and using tarot as a tool for inner guidance and self-exploration. She leads Gaian Soul Retreats for women twice a year. Joanna lives on a small, magical island in the Salish Sea near Bellingham, Washington. Visit her online at www.gaiansoul.com. To go directly to her "Brigid's Fire" painting, see www.gaiansoul.com/shop/art-prints/art-print-brigids-fire.

Jen Delyth creates original Celtic paintings and illustrations that explore the language of myth and symbol inspired by Celtic folklore and the spirit within nature. Drawing from ancient metaphors and integrating the visual motifs and language of Celtic patterning into original new designs, Jen finds the symmetry of form and symbol that expresses living archetypes. Her work reflects spiritual and philosophical roots which embody universal themes that reflect her love of nature and Celtic symbolism. Visit her online at www.celtic artstudio.com.

Pat Fish has specialized in Celtic tattooing during a three-decade career, and delights in bringing the intricate knot works of the ancient Irish illuminated manuscripts and the patterns from the Pictish standing stones to life in skin. She owns a street studio in downtown Santa Barbara, California, where she tattoos clients from all over the world who are attracted by her unique understanding of the Celtic patterns. Visit her online at www.luckyfish.com and www.luckyfish art.com.

Selena Fox has a MS in Counseling from the University of Wisconsin–Madison, and does spiritual counseling and psychotherapy in private practice. Selena has been senior minister of Circle Sanctuary since its founding in 1974, and in addition to serving Nature religion practitioners and groups, she is active in interfaith ministry, locally and globally. She is founder and executive director of the 200-acre Circle Sanctuary Nature Preserve and its Circle Cemetery, located near Barneveld in rural southwestern Wisconsin. Find her online at www.selenafox.com, www.circlesanctuary.org, and www.facebook.com/SelenaFoxUpdates.

Mara Freeman is the author of *Grail Alchemy: Initiation in the Celtic Mystery Tradition* (Destiny Books, 2014) and *Kindling the Celtic Spirit* (HarperSanFrancisco, 2001). She is the director of the Avalon Mystery School, a training program in the Arts of Sacred Magic. An astrologer, psychic, and psychologist, Mara has been teaching Celtic and Western sacred and magical traditions for over thirty years in the US and UK. She lives in Wales and can be found online at www .chalicecentre.net and www.celticspiritjourneys.com.

Erynn Rowan Laurie is a poet who has been a flamekeeper and a devotee of Brigid for over twenty years. She spent most of her life in the Pacific Northwest of the US and now resides in Trieste, Italy. Erynn writes on matters of poetry and Gaelic spirituality, and is one of the many people who contributed to the founding of the Celtic Reconstructionist polytheist movement. She is the author of *Ogam: Weaving Word Wisdom* and other books; see more at her blog, *Searching for Imbas*, searchingforimbas.blogspot.it/p/erynns-publications .html.

Ellen Lorenzi-Prince is an artist, poet, and priestess. She presents her inventive, experiential, and engaging approach to tarot in talks, workshops, and rituals throughout the United States, with venues that include the Omega Institute in Rhinebeck, New York, and the Q Center in Portland, Oregon, as well as conferences in San Francisco, Dallas, Philadelphia, and New York. Now living in the Pacific Northwest, Ellen's primary focus is the creation of oracles to speak with the soul, the ancestors, and the gods. Visit her at darkgoddesstarot.com.

Margie McArthur has been a student of metaphysics, mysteries, and magic for nearly fifty years and a priestess of the Old Religion for almost forty of those years. She is an Archdruidess of the Druid Clan of Dana of the Fellowship of Isis. She is the author of *WiccaCraft for Families* (1994), *The Wisdom of the Elements* (1998), *Faery Healing* (2003), and *Lady of the Sea* (2014). For more information, visit her websites: www.brigidshearth.org, www.faeryhealing.com, and www.ladyofthesea.org.

Mael Brigde has an abiding interest in Brigit of Ireland and Celtic Paganism. Her group, the Daughters of the Flame, began tending Brigit's fire on Imbolc 1993—the same day the Irish Brigidine Sisters rekindled her flame in Kildare—thus helping to initiate the modern Brigidine flame-tending movement. Mael Brigde maintains the blog *Brigit's Sparkling Flame*. Her 75-page review of Brigit-related books,

A Long Sip at the Well, is available as a free PDF at both website and blog. Visit her online at brigitssparklingflame.blogspot.com and www.obsidianmagazine.com/DaughtersoftheFlame.

Mickie Mueller is an artist, author, and Reiki Master who has worked with Brigid and other Celtic deities along her Pagan path of discovery. Mickie has honored Brigid in many forms, including ritual, artwork, jewelry design, and statuary design. She works, lives, and creates her magic at her enchanted home of Aelfheim in the rolling hills of the Missouri countryside with her husband Dan, teenage son, and two cats. Mickie's goddess and other artwork can be found on her websites www.mickiemuellerart.com and www.etsy.com /shop/mickiemuellerstudio.

Domi O'Brien has been a priestess since 1968. From 1989 to 1996, she served on the MotherGrove of Ár nDraíocht Féin (ADF) as Preceptor. Domi was ordained as a Third Circle Priestess of ADF and ran ADF Groves in Washington and New Hampshire. In 1996, her Grove elected to leave ADF and became Grove of the Golden Leaves of Druidic Association of North America. Domi teaches Irish for the Gaelic League of New England, and she guides and mentors students who want to learn the lore.

Rebecca Reeder has a master's degree in Counseling Psychology and Expressive Arts Therapy from the California Institute of Integral Studies and a certificate in Integrative Medicine from the Institute of Health and Healing. Her healing art incorporates dance, story, theater, song, and poetry. She is the co-founder of the Rooted Seeds Project and co-director of Celtic traditions at Saphichay, an organization dedicated to protecting and developing indigenous rights. Find her online at www.saphichay.org/celt.

Susan Smith is a nurse and a certified Reiki master/teacher in the Usui Shiki Ryoho tradition. She is a Celtic shamanic practitioner guided in her work by Brigid.

Ruth Temple has settled into sacred community with fiber artists and creative folk of all walks. A supportive member of local and international guilds, she has a deep appreciation for and delight in connect-

ing those who teach traditional ways with spinning, braiding, weaving, and wearing wool with those who seek to learn, and expects to be somewhere in the middle of that continuum all her life.
Her work and thoughts may be found at RTDStudio.com and at @RuTemple in various social media outlets.

Lisa Thiel is a visionary artist, ceremonial singer, and songwriter. She is a priestess of Brighid and Kuan Yin in the Fellowship of Isis and honors the old Celtic Wheel of the year. She is also an astrologer, tarot reader, and interpreter of dreams. Her songs of the goddess are being sung in circles around the world. Visit her online at www.sacreddream.com.

Marvelle Thompson is a retired teacher living in California. The beauty and magic found in nature's cycles are a major influence in her life, from art and gardening to her spiritual practices. The book she co-created with Susan Kullmann, *Blessed Are These Hands*, is the fulfillment of a vow to honor the feminine face of the Holy. Marvelle connects strongly with Brigid's voice. Visit her online at www.blessedarethesehands.com.

BIBLIOGRAPHY

Brophy, Christina, PhD. "Keening Community: Mná Caointe, Women, Death, and Power in Ireland." PhD diss., Boston College, 2010.

Caesar, Julius. *Caesar's Commentaries on the Gallic War*. Book 6.

Cahill, Thomas. *How the Irish Saved Civilization*. New York: Doubleday, 1995.

Campbell, Archibald, Lord. *Waifs and Strays of Celtic Tradition*. London: David Nutt, 1889.

Campbell, Joseph. *The Masks of God: Occidental Mythology*. New York: Viking Penguin, 1964.

Carmichael, Alexander, ed. *Carmina Gadelica*. Edinburgh: Constable, 1900.

Catholic Encyclopedia. Volumes 2 and 8, "School of Kildare." Encyclopedia Press, 1913.

Clancy, Padraigín, ed. *Celtic Threads: Exploring the Wisdom of Our Heritage*. Dublin: Veritas Publications, 1995.

Cogitosus. *Vita Sanctae Brigidae*. Circa 650.

Connolly, Seán. "Vita Prima Sanctae Brigitae: Background and Historical Value." *Journal of the Royal Society of Antiquaries of Ireland* (1989).

Cunliffe, Barry. *The Ancient Celts*. London: Penguin Books, 1997.

Delaney, Mary Murray. *Of Irish Ways*. Minneapolis: Dillon Press, 1973.

Dixon-Kennedy, Mike. *Celtic Myth and Legend*. London: Blandford, 1996.

Evans, E. Estyn. *Irish Folk Ways*. London: Routledge & Kegan, 1957.

Gregory, Lady. *A Book of Saints and Wonders Put Down Here by Lady Gregory According to the Old Writings and the Memory of the People of Ireland.* London: John Murray, 1908.

Green, Miranda. *Celtic Goddesses.* London: British Museum Press, 1995.

Hyde, Douglas, trans. *Abhráin Diadha Chúige Connacht; or, The Religious Songs of Connacht.* London: T. Fisher Unwin, 1906.

Jackson, Kenneth Hurlstone, ed. and trans. *A Celtic Miscellany.* London: Penguin Books, 1951.

Jacobsthal, Paul. *Early Celtic Art.* Oxford: Clarendon Press, 1944.

Lucas, A. T. National Museum of Ireland, Dublin, quoted in *The Furrow*, vol. 3, no. 2 (1952). J. G. McGarry, ed.

Macalister, R. A. Stewart. *Lebor Gabála Érenn: The Book of the Taking of Ireland.* Part IV. Dublin: Irish Texts Society / Education Company of Ireland, 1941.

Mac Cana, Proinsias. *Celtic Mythology.* London: Hamlyn Publishing Group, 1970.

Mac Coitir, Niall. *Ireland's Animals: Myths, Legends, and Folklore.* The Collins Press, 2010.

———. *Irish Trees: Myths, Legends, and Folklore.* The Collins Press, 2008.

———. *Irish Wild Plants: Myths, Legends, and Folklore.* Doughcloyne, Cork, Ireland: The Collins Press, 2006.

MacCulloch, J. A. *The Religion of the Ancient Celts.* Edinburgh: T. & T. Clark, 1911.

Mackenzie, Donald Alexander. *Wonder Tales from Scottish Myth and Legend.* New York: Frederick A. Stokes, 1917.

Macleod, Fiona (William Sharp). *The Winged Destiny: Studies in the Spiritual History of the Gael.* New York: Duffield & Company, 1911.

MacLeod, Sharon Paice. *Celtic Myth and Religion.* Jefferson, NC: McFarland & Company, 2012.

Matthews, Caitlín. *The Elements of the Celtic Tradition.* Longmead, Shaftesbury, Dorset: Element Books, 1989.

Meyer, Kuno, trans. "King and Hermit." In *Selections from Ancient Irish Poetry.* London: Constable & Company, 1911.

———, ed. and trans. *Miscellanea Hibernica.* Urbana: University of Illinois, 1917.

———, trans. *The Triads of Ireland.* Dublin: Hodges, Figgis, & Co., 1906.

Monaghan, Patricia. *The Book of Goddesses and Heroines.* St. Paul, MN: Llewellyn, 1990.

———. *The Encyclopedia of Celtic Mythology and Folklore.* New York: Checkmark Books, 2008.

Moore, Thomas. "Oh the Shamrock." In *The Poetical Works of Thomas Moore.* New York: D. Appleton & Co., 1868.

Murphy-Hiscock, Arin, ed. *Out of the Broom Closet.* Avon, MA: Provenance Press, 2009.

O'Curry, Eugene. *Lectures on the Manuscript Materials of Ancient Irish History.* Dublin: Hinch, Traynor, 1878.

O'Faoláin, Seán. *The Silver Branch: A Collection of the Best Old Irish Lyrics, Variously Translated.* New York: Viking Press, 1938.

O'Grady, Standish H., ed. *Silva Gadelica: A Collection of Tales in Irish with Extracts Illustrating Persons and Places.* London: Williams and Norgate, 1892.

Ó hAodha, Donncha, ed. *Bethu Brigte.* Dublin Institute for Advanced Studies, 1978.

Ó hÓgáin, Dáithí. *The Hero in Irish Folk History.* Dublin: Gill and Macmillan, 1985.

Ó Súilleabháin, Seán. *Irish Folk Custom and Belief.* Cultural Relations Committee of Ireland, 1967.

Pennick, Nigel. *Celtic Sacred Landscapes.* New York: Thames and Hudson, 1996.

Rees, Alwyn, and Brinley Rees. *Celtic Heritage: Ancient Tradition in Ireland and Wales.* London: Thames and Hudson, 1961.

Rukeyser, Muriel. "Käthe Kollwitz." In *The Speed of Darkness*. New York: Random House, 1968.

Stokes, Whitley, ed. and trans. "The Colloquy of the Two Sages." *Revue Celtique* 26 (1905).

———, ed. and trans. *Lives of Saints, from the Book of Lismore*. Oxford: Clarendon Press, 1890.

———, ed. *Three Irish Glossaries: Cormac's glossary codex A. O'Davoren's Glossary and a Glossary to the Calendar of Oingus the Culdee*. London: Williams and Norgate, 1862.

Thompson, Melissa. "Interview with Sr. Mary Minehan," Feb. 19, 1999, www.tallgirlshorts.net/marymary/sistermary.html.

Wilde, Lady. *Ancient Cures, Charms, and Usages of Ireland*. London: Ward & Downey, 1890.

———. *Ancient Legends, Mystic Charms, and Superstitions of Ireland*. London: Ward & Downey, 1887.

Yeats, W. B. *Fairy and Folk Tales of the Irish Peasantry*. London and Felling-on-Tyne: William Scott Publishing, 1888.

———. "The Two Trees." In *The Countess Kathleen and Various Legends and Lyrics*. London: T. F. Unwin, 1892.

———. "The Wild Swans at Coole." In *The Wild Swans at Coole*. New York: The Macmillan Company, 1919.

Young, Ella. *Celtic Wonder Tales*. Dublin: Maunsel & Company, 1910.

TO WRITE TO THE AUTHOR

If you wish to contact the author or would like more information about this book, please write to the author in care of Llewellyn Worldwide Ltd. and we will forward your request. Both the author and publisher appreciate hearing from you and learning of your enjoyment of this book and how it has helped you. Llewellyn Worldwide Ltd. cannot guarantee that every letter written to the author can be answered, but all will be forwarded. Please write to:

Lunaea Weatherstone
℅ Llewellyn Worldwide
2143 Wooddale Drive
Woodbury, MN 55125-2989
Please enclose a self-addressed stamped envelope for reply,
or $1.00 to cover costs. If outside the U.S.A., enclose
an international postal reply coupon.

Many of Llewellyn's authors have websites with additional
information and resources. For more information,
please visit our website at
http://www.llewellyn.com